Master th Massage Therapy Exams

1st Edition

PETERSON'S

Publishing

About Peterson's Publishing

To succeed on your lifelong educational journey, you will need accurate, dependable, and practical tools and resources. That is why Peterson's is everywhere education happens. Because whenever and however you need education content delivered, you can rely on Peterson's to provide the information, know-how, and guidance to help you reach your goals. Tools to match the right students with the right school. It's here. Personalized resources and expert guidance. It's here. Comprehensive and dependable education content—delivered whenever and however you need it. It's all here.

For more information, contact Peterson's Publishing, 2000 Lenox Drive, Lawrenceville, NJ 08648; 800-338-3282 Ext. 54229; or find us online at www.petersonspublishing.com.

Bernadette Webster, Director of Publishing; Mark D. Snider, Editor; Ray Golaszewski, Publishing Operations Manager; Linda M. Williams, Composition Manager

ISBN-13: 978-0-7689-3310-9
ISBN-10: 0-7689-3310-2

Printed in the United States of America

10 9 8 7 6 5 4 3 2 1   13 12 11

First Edition

By printing this book on recycled paper (40% post-consumer waste) 27 trees were saved.

Petersonspublishing.com/publishingupdates

Check out our Web site at www.petersonspublishing.com/publishingupdates to see if there is any new information regarding the test and any revisions or corrections to the content of this book. We've made sure the information in this book is accurate and up-to-date; however, the test format or content may have changed since the time of publication.

Contents

Before You Begin ix

   How This Book Is Organized ix

   Special Study Features x

   Special Advertising Section. xi

   You Are Well on Your Way to Success xi

   Find Us on Facebook®. xi

   Give Us Your Feedback xi

PART I: Massage Therapist Basics

Chapter 1: What Is a Massage Therapist? 3

   Therapeutic Modalities 4

   Work Flexibility. 5

   Licensing Requirements 6

   Federation of State Massage Therapy Boards (FSMTB) 7

   National Certification Board for Therapeutic Massage and Bodywork (NCBTMB) 9

   Job Responsibilities. 13

   Personal Traits. 14

   Work Environments. 15

   Tools of the Trade 16

   Education. 17

   Salary and Benefits 18

   Advancement Opportunities 19

   Related Occupations 19

   Summing It Up 21

Chapter 2: Becoming a Massage Therapist 23

   Select and Complete an Educational Program 24

   Apply for an Examination. 26

   Schedule Your Examination 26

   Prepare for the Examination 27

   Test-Taking Tips and Hints 27

   Apply for Your License 29

   Keep Current 29

   Consider Your Career Options. 30

Get the Job Hunt Underway 32

Summing It Up 44

PART II: Diagnosing Strengths and Weaknesses

Chapter 3: Practice Test 1: Diagnostic **49**

Answer Key and Explanations 60

PART III: Prepare and Practice: Massage Therapy Subject Areas

Chapter 4: Anatomy and Physiology **71**

Anatomy, Physiology, and Body Systems 71

Exercises: Anatomy, Physiology, and Body Systems 74

Anatomical Position and Directional Terms 74

Exercises: Anatomical Position and Directional Terms 76

Systems of Special Note for the Massage Therapist 76

Exercises: Systems of Special Note for the Massage Therapist 79

Tips for Answering Questions on Anatomy and Physiology 79

Practice Questions 81

Answer Key and Explanations 82

Summing It Up 83

Chapter 5: Kinesiology **85**

Characteristics of Muscles 86

Exercises: Characteristics of Muscles 87

Planes of Motion 87

Exercises: Planes of Motion 88

Range of Motion 88

Exercises: Range of Motion 90

Postural Alignment 90

Exercises: Postural Alignment 91

Tips for Answering Questions on Kinesiology 91

Practice Questions 93

Answer Key and Explanations 94

Summing It Up 95

Chapter 6: Pathology **97**

Causes and Transmission of Disease 98

Exercises: Causes and Transmission of Disease 99

Common Pathologies 99

Exercises: Common Pathologies 103

Drugs and Drug Interactions 103

Exercises: Drugs and Drug Interactions 105

Working with Particular Populations 105

Exercises: Working with Particular Populations 106
Tips for Answering Questions on Pathology 106
Practice Questions 107
Answer Key and Explanations 108
Summing It Up 109

Chapter 7: Therapeutic Massage and Bodywork Assessment **111**
Client Consultation and Intake Procedures 113
Exercises: Client Consultation and Intake Procedures 114
Assessment Techniques and Treatment Plans 114
Exercises: Assessment Techniques and Treatment Plans 116
Client Recordkeeping 117
Exercises: Client Recordkeeping 118
Tips for Answering Questions on Therapeutic Massage and Bodywork Assessment 118
Practice Questions 119
Answer Key and Explanations 120
Summing It Up 121

Chapter 8: Therapeutic Massage and Bodywork Application **123**
Holistic Principles and Mind-Body Practice 124
Exercises: Holistic Principles and Mind-Body Practice 126
Effects of Massage 126
Exercises: Effects of Massage 127
Soft Tissue Techniques 127
Exercises: Soft Tissue Techniques 128
Client Positioning and Draping 129
Exercises: Client Positioning and Draping 130
Massage and Bodywork Tools 130
Exercises: Massage and Bodywork Tools 131
Client Self-Care 131
Exercises: Client Self-Care 132
Standard Precautions 132
Exercises: Standard Precautions 135
Body Mechanics for Therapists 135
Exercises: Body Mechanics for Therapists 136
Tips for Answering Questions on Therapeutic Massage and Bodywork Application 137
Practice Questions 138
Answer Key and Explanations 139
Summing It Up 140

Chapter 9: Professional Standards and Legal and Business Practices **141**
Professional Standards 142
Exercises: Professional Standards 147
Legal Practices 147

Exercises: Legal Practices 149
Business Practices 149
Exercises: Business Practices 152
Tips for Answering Questions on Professional Standards and Legal and Business Practices 153
Practice Questions 154
Answer Key and Explanations 155
Summing It Up 156

PART IV: Two Practice Tests

Practice Test 2: Massage and Bodywork Licensing Examination (MBLEx) **161**
Answer Key and Explanations 172

Practice Test 3: National Certification Examination for Therapeutic Massage and Bodywork (NCETMB) **183**
Answer Key and Explanations 198

APPENDIXES

Appendix A: NCBTMB Code of Ethics and Standards of Practice **211**
NCBTMB Code of Ethics 211
NCBTMB Standards of Practice 212

Appendix B: NCBTMB National Examination for State Licensing (NESL) Option **219**
What is the NESL Option? 219
Who Should Take Advantage of the NESL Option? 219
How Does NESL Conversion Work? 219

Appendix C: Helpful Resources. **221**
American Massage Therapy Association (AMTA) 221
Associated Bodywork and Massage Professionals (ABMP) 221
Commission on Massage Therapy Accreditation (COMTA) 222
Federation of State Massage Therapy Boards (FSMTB) 222
National Center for Complementary and Alternative Medicine (NCAAM) 222
National Certification Board for Therapeutic Massage and Bodywork (NCBTMB) 223

Appendix D: Complementary/Alternative Medicine **225**

Special Advertising Section

f www.facebook.com/CareerResource

Before You Begin

OVERVIEW

- **How this book is organized**
- **Special study features**
- **Special advertising section**
- **You are well on your way to success**
- **Find us on Facebook®**
- **Give us your feedback**

HOW THIS BOOK IS ORGANIZED

Massage therapy is an excellent career choice for individuals who enjoy working closely with others and have the ability to affect positive change through touch. Massage therapists enjoy many benefits such as the choice of working environments, a flexible schedule, and the ability to make a competitive salary with part-time work. The U.S. Bureau of Labor Statistics reports that the number of available massage therapist jobs is expected to increase by 19 percent through 2018, faster than the average for all occupations.

If you are interested in becoming a massage therapist, you must meet all requirements set by your state regulatory board before you can practice. Although requirements vary, most states require massage therapists to complete a formal educational program as well as pass an examination before licensing will be granted. The examinations most frequently used for this purpose are the National Certification Examinations (NCEs) offered by the National Certification Board for Therapeutic Massage and Bodywork (NCBTMB) and the Massage and Bodywork Licensing Examination (MBLEx) offered by the Federation of State Massage Therapy Boards (FSMTB).

This book was carefully researched to help you prepare to successfully enter this career field. To get the most out of this book, take the time to read each section carefully and thoroughly.

- **Part I** provides an overview of personal traits that lend themselves to this career field, as well as general job responsibilities and the kinds of places you can expect to work. Part I covers educational requirements and the content areas covered on most licensing examinations. It also emphasizes the differences in licensing requirements from state to state and points you to resources that will help you determine the requirements which apply to you.

- **Part II** is a diagnostic examination designed to help you pinpoint your trouble areas with the content commonly found in the licensing exams. You will have the opportunity to answer questions in anatomy, physiology, kinesiology, pathology, and therapeutic massage assessment and application, as well as in the ethics, standards, and business practices you are expected to follow in your practice. A complete answer guide is provided, including explanations, so that you can check your knowledge.

- **Part III** is an overview of the different content areas covered on the NCE and MBLEx. Each chapter is devoted to a specific subject area and provides a brief review of the topic to refresh your memory of what you learned in school. At the end of each chapter you will find multiple-choice questions similar to those you can expect to answer on the examinations. You will also find answer explanations that you should read, even when you answer the questions correctly. The explanations may include additional information that may help you to answer other questions.

- **Part IV** provides two complete practice tests. One of these tests is a sample MBLEx and the other is a sample National Certification Examination for Therapeutic Massage and Bodywork (NCETMB). Although the questions are not those you will answer on either of the exams, they are designed to mimic the examination content closely. You will get the most from these exams if you time yourself and work through the exam in one sitting.

- The **Appendixes** section offers a variety of resources that will help you in your quest to become a licensed massage therapist. Take the time to review these references as you work your way through this book.

SPECIAL STUDY FEATURES

Peterson's Master the Massage Therapy Exams is designed to be user-friendly and complete. It includes several features to make your preparation more efficient.

Overview

Each chapter begins with a bulleted overview that lists the topics covered in the chapter. This feature allows you to see what is covered and quickly find those areas of greatest interest to you.

Summing It Up

Each chapter ends with a point-by-point summary of the most important items in the chapter. The summaries offer a convenient way to quickly review everything that was covered in the chapter.

Notes

Notes highlight need-to-know information.

Tips

Tips provide valuable strategies and insider information to help you maximize your score.

Sidebars

Sidebars provide additional information that you may find helpful.

SPECIAL ADVERTISING SECTION

At end of the book, don't miss the special section of ads placed by Peterson's preferred clients. Their financial support helps make it possible for Peterson's Publishing to continue to provide you with the highest-quality test-prep, educational exploration, and career-preparation resources you need to succeed on your educational journey.

YOU ARE WELL ON YOUR WAY TO SUCCESS

You have made the decision to become a massage therapist and have taken a very important step in that process. *Peterson's Master the Massage Therapy Exams* will help you score high on your licensing examination and prepare you for everything you need to know on the day of the exam and beyond. Good luck!

FIND US ON FACEBOOK®

Join the career conversation on Facebook® at www.facebook.com/CareerResource and receive additional test-prep tips and advice. Peterson's resources are available to help you do your best on these important exams—and others in your future.

GIVE US YOUR FEEDBACK

Peterson's publishes a full line of books—career preparation, test prep, education exploration, and financial aid. Peterson's publications can be found at high school guidance offices, college libraries and career centers, and your local bookstore and library. Peterson's books are now also available as eBooks.

We welcome any comments or suggestions you may have about this publication. Your feedback will help us make educational dreams possible for you—and others like you.

PART I

Massage Therapist Basics

CHAPTER 1
What Is a Massage Therapist? 3

CHAPTER 2
Becoming a Massage Therapist 23

What Is a Massage Therapist?

OVERVIEW

- **Therapeutic modalities**
- **Work flexibility**
- **Licensing requirements**
- **Federation of State Massage Therapy Boards (FSMTB)**
- **National Certification Board for Therapeutic Massage and Bodywork (NCBTMB)**
- **Job responsibilities**
- **Personal traits**
- **Work environments**
- **Tools of the trade**
- **Education**
- **Salary and benefits**
- **Advancement opportunities**
- **Related occupations**
- **Summing it up**

A massage therapist is a health practitioner who manipulates the muscles and soft tissues of a client's body to affect a positive physical outcome for the client. Massage is a popular means of relaxation that also improves body circulation, relieves anxiety and stress, reduces muscle soreness and pain, promotes a greater range of motion in the joints, and facilitates a variety of other health benefits.

If you are interested in massage therapy as a career, you will find this field to be an excellent way to provide the type of meaningful personal services that can genuinely improve quality of life for other people. You will learn how to use your personal qualities and strengths to directly affect how other people are feeling. You will use your hands and fingers to touch others with a high degree of care and consideration.

As you learn about this new career field, you will come across many new concepts and terms. For example, some people refer to their work as massage therapy while others call it bodywork. Although these terms are sometimes used interchangeably, massage therapy is generally a legally protected term that cannot be used by a practitioner unless he or she has been granted a massage therapy license from the state of residence. Bodywork is more of an umbrella term, encompassing a wider variety of alternative therapies and holistic practices. Massage therapy tends to focus on soft tissue work, relaxation, and the relief of physical symptoms, while bodywork might focus not only on physical relief but also on promoting emotional and spiritual wellness and helping clients achieve a greater mind-body connection.

THERAPEUTIC MODALITIES

When you think about the practice of massage, you probably picture a room in a day spa, dim lighting, soft music, aromatic oils, and a body skillfully kneaded and stroked into a state of great relaxation. The techniques pictured in this scenario are known as Swedish massage and are sometimes called traditional or Western massage therapy. Swedish massage is the most popular, well-known style of massage. Swedish massage techniques use long gliding movements along with kneading, compressing, and rocking of the body. Swedish massage is the practice you will learn in massage school, and you will find that it forms the basis of many other massage treatments as well.

What Is a Modality?

As you launch your career as a massage therapist, you will come across the term modality quite frequently. Modality is most often used to describe various broad categories of massage theory or technique, such as Swedish massage, myofascial therapy, connective tissue massage, and so on. The word modality is also used to refer to a narrower, more specifically defined therapeutic practice, such as Rolfing® or the Feldenkrais Method. To further confuse matters, modality can also describe a specific application of tools or materials in the healing process, such as thermal modalities (hot/cold therapy) or electromagnetic modalities (practices such as infrared or ultrasound). This latter treatment of the term is derived from the physical therapy and chiropractic fields, where its usage is more specifically defined.

The bodywork field is wide and quite varied. At least eighty individual techniques can be identified in current practices, and some of these are of quite ancient origin. Some therapists are generalists while others are trained and certified to offer more advanced techniques. Some therapists even combine different techniques to form their own unique style. However, at any time, the type of massage provided is driven by the therapist's education and experience and the needs of the client.

Some of the more commonly practiced techniques are outlined below. Most of these techniques are beyond the scope of an entry-level therapist and are unlikely to be part of your initial training, but they are practices with which you may want to become more familiar through advanced training opportunities.

- **Acupressure:** During an acupressure session, the fingers are used to press key healing points in the client's body. Acupressure reduces muscular tension, increases circulation, relieves pain, and enables the client to achieve states of deep relaxation. Acupressure is focused on balancing body energy and facilitating both spirituality and physical health.

- **Connective tissue massage (CTM):** CTM techniques are designed to release the connective tissue (commonly referred to as *myofascial tissue*) in the body and break up scar formations. CTM practitioners believe this therapy relieves chronic tension, facilitates greater range of motion, promotes the attainment of deep relaxation states, and even improves client posture.

- **Deep tissue massage:** During a deep tissue massage, slower strokes are applied with deeper pressure to access and realign underlying layers of muscles and connective tissue. Deep tissue massage is particularly helpful for areas afflicted with tension and chronic pain, such as a stiff neck, tight hamstrings, a tense lower back, sore shoulders, and so on.

- **Hot stone therapy:** Hot stone therapy involves the placement of flat heated stones at specific sites on the client's body. River stones are generally selected for this type of therapy due to their smooth surface. The stones retain heat because they are made of *basalt*, a type of rock that is rich in iron. (Useful fact: iron conducts heat.) Hot stone massage alleviates stress, promotes relaxation, and opens the body's *meridians*, or energy pathways, forging a stronger sense of wellness in the client.

- **Myofascial (trigger point) therapy:** Myofascial, or trigger point, therapy focuses on relieving chronic pain by working on the myofascial trigger points in the body. Myofascial literally refers to muscle tissue (*myo*) and the connective tissue that surrounds it (*fascia*).

- **Neuromuscular therapy (NMT):** NMT is a type of soft tissue manipulation that focuses on correcting imbalances among the nervous, immune, and musculoskeletal systems. NMT therapists use their fingers, knuckles, elbows, and tools such as pressure bars to stretch, lengthen, and strengthen muscles.

- **Reflexology:** During a reflexology session, the reflexologist applies varying degrees of pressure to the client's hands and feet using specialized techniques.

- **Prenatal massage:** Prenatal massage techniques are practices expressly designed to meet the special needs of pregnant women. Prenatal massage can help relieve back pain and other discomfort or soreness related to pregnancy.

- **Shiatsu massage:** Shiatsu massage is a popular technique in which specific pressure is applied to the client using the fingers, palms, and thumbs. Shiatsu massage practices can vary widely as they rely on a combined knowledge of physiology, traditional Japanese massage, and Chinese medicine.

- **Sports massage:** Sports or athletic massage is a specialized form of therapy that is utilized before, during, and/or after an athletic event. This type of massage is designed to prevent injuries by relieving swelling, reducing muscle tension, and promoting flexibility during or after an athletic event.

WORK FLEXIBILITY

One of the benefits of working as a massage therapist is the flexibility you have with where you work and who you work with. Therapeutic massage opens many career options because it is conducted in a number of different settings for a number of different purposes.

- Hospitals, medical centers, and clinics frequently offer massage therapy services to patients in order to minimize patient stress and discomfort during illness or while recovering from injury and surgery.

- Nursing homes and assisted living centers provide therapeutic massage to their elderly residents to relieve residents' chronic pain, decrease muscle stiffness caused by age and/or limited activity, and increase general mobility.

- Sports facilities and physical therapy centers focus on providing deep tissue massages for targeted areas of the body or on relieving general muscular tightness that occurs as a normal part of physical fitness training. Sports therapists also concentrate on injury rehabilitation, usually with the collaboration of other health-care providers such as physicians and physical therapists.

- Cruise ships, spas, resorts, and similar venues offer massage as a luxury treatment or service for their clientele.

Massage therapy is a burgeoning career field with many options available to suit all kinds of lifestyles, needs, and interests. Which option seems the most interesting to you?

LICENSING REQUIREMENTS

As with many other professional occupations, most massage therapists are required to be licensed by their state or local government before they are allowed to practice. Licensing is the means by which the industry is regulated and the public protected from predatory business practices. Licensing provides some assurance that parties offering particular services are actually qualified to render them. Operating without a license when one is required is considered a criminal act punishable by law.

Today, no single national standard or process is in place to manage the licensing and practice requirements for all members of the massage and bodywork professions. Rather, standards and requirements vary—sometimes quite dramatically—by geographic location. For an aspiring therapist, this means the minimal requirements you must meet in order to practice may differ depending on where you intend to practice.

> **NOTE**
>
> Throughout this discussion, we use the word *state* to describe the level of the government body that regulates the practice of massage therapy. This term is used for ease of reference; in actuality, local ordinances may also apply. Therefore, the term *state* is meant to be inclusive of any regulatory body at any level of government responsible for setting standards for practicing massage therapists.

Requirements may vary at the state, county, or even municipal level. Due to this variability, you will find the greatest opportunities for success by making sure you are aware of all requirements before you launch your massage career.

Although every state has its own rules and regulations regarding the practice of massage therapy, most state regulatory bodies require therapists to become licensed before opening for business. Licensing means the aspiring therapist is formally approved to practice by the regulatory board that oversees the profession in that location. As part of this process, you will apply for a license by providing personal and professional information such as number of education hours, work experience, character references, and so on. Most regulatory boards compel you to possess a minimal amount of education and/or experience in order to be licensed. You may also have to demonstrate entry-level skill by taking and passing a written examination. In addition, you will probably need to undergo both credit and criminal background checks.

Note that most regulatory boards also require you to renew your license at some regular interval (annually, for example).

Each state can select the examination it uses in the licensing process. This examination can be one that has been developed by the state in question, or it might be one of the examinations available through the National Certification Board for Therapeutic Massage and Bodywork (NCBTMB) or the Federation of State Massage Therapy Boards (FSMTB).

The most-used examinations for licensing purposes are the National Certification Examinations for Therapeutic Massage and Bodywork (NCETMB) offered by NCBTMB and the Massage and Bodywork Licensing Examination (MBLEx) offered by the FSMTB.

Because licensing requirements vary so much by location, it is important that you understand those that apply to you. Information meant to assist you in this research is provided at the end of this book in *Appendix C: Helpful Resources.*

FEDERATION OF STATE MASSAGE THERAPY BOARDS (FSMTB)

The Federation of State Massage Therapy Boards (FSMTB) was created in 2005 to "ensure that the practice of massage therapy is provided to the public in a safe and effective manner." The FSMTB is made up of state regulatory boards who manage the rules and regulations of the massage profession at the state level (the Pennsylvania State Board of Massage Therapy or the California Massage Therapy Council, for example) as well as other agencies that have a vested interest in the profession.

Besides its mission to protect the public from predatory or dangerous practices, FSMTB also exists to protect the needs of the regulatory community. By providing the means by which state boards can participate in the decisions that ultimately affect the way the profession is managed, FSMTB gives the individual boards a voice in the process even as standardization becomes the norm across the country.

The mission of FSMTB is to facilitate consistency in both the scope of practice and entry-level standards across the country; develop a valid, reliable licensing exam that will be accepted by all jurisdictions; and create a single database to store licensing and disciplinary information across all jurisdictions.

Massage and Bodywork Licensing Examination (MBLEx)

As part of its mission to serve the interests of its member boards, FSMTB developed the Massage and Bodywork Licensing Examination (MBLEx). The MBLEx has been carefully designed to reflect current standards of professional practice across the country. MBLEx content was developed from an extensive job task analysis survey conducted across the country and further validated by input from nearly 8,000 practicing professionals.

The MBLEx is currently accepted by 29 states, the District of Columbia, Puerto Rico, and the U.S. Virgin Islands. This wide acceptance gives the FSMTB and state member boards considerable control over the national entry-level standards for the profession as well as the ability to oversee and standardize the licensing process. For participants, the connection between the FSMTB and the state regulatory boards means a shorter process from application to examination to licensing. In addition, it is easier to move your practice from one location to another, since the examination is recognized by the regulatory boards of so many different locations. FSMTB also provides the means by which you can easily share your exam results with states other than the one in which you originally tested.

EXAMINATION CONTENT

The foundation for the MBLEx is actual practice, meaning that the core competencies, skills, and knowledge being tested have been identified by current practitioners as necessary for safe and effective entry-level practice. The MBLEx covers a variety of subject matter areas from assessment and treatment to ethical practices and the benefits of soft tissue work. The examination content breaks down as follows:

- **Overview of massage and bodywork history/culture/modalities:** 5 percent

- **Guidelines for professional practice:** 10 percent

- **Kinesiology:** 11 percent

- **Ethics, boundaries, laws, regulations:** 13 percent

- **Pathology, contraindications, areas of caution, special populations:** 13 percent

- **Anatomy and physiology:** 14 percent

- **Client assessment, reassessment, treatment planning:** 17 percent

- **Benefits and physiological effects of soft tissue techniques:** 17 percent

ELIGIBILITY REQUIREMENTS

You can request to take the MBLEx in two different ways:

1. Applying directly to the Federation of State Massage Therapy Boards (FSMTB). (Submitting an application directly to FSMTB does not guarantee your eligibility to take the examination. Your application will be reviewed by FSMTB personnel. You will then be notified by FSMTB as to your eligibility.)

2. Applying via your state regulatory board/agency.

Apply to FSMTB

To apply for the examination directly to FSMTB, complete the MBLEx application, either by filling out and mailing in a paper form or by completing the application online. Both options are available from the FSTMB Web site (www.fsmtb.org).

You will be required to do the following:

- Confirm your review and understanding of the content outline.

- Include information about your massage/bodywork education.

- Agree to abide by FSMTB's policies and procedures.

- Indicate the state in which you intend to practice, so your exam results can be sent to the correct regulatory board.

- Pay the required fee, by certified check/money order, Visa, or MasterCard.

Apply via Your State Regulatory Board

To apply for the examination via your state's regulatory board, first check the state's Web site to make sure the state allows you to apply through them. Unless your state board directs you to proceed otherwise, you will then do the following:

- Apply for your license. You will need to meet all of the requirements in your state/location. You will have to provide all necessary documentation, school transcripts, etc., before you will be allowed to schedule the MBLEx.

- Agree to abide by FSTMB's policies and procedures.

- Pay the required fee, by certified check/money order, Visa, or MasterCard.

EDUCATIONAL REQUIREMENTS

FSMTB does not set a minimum number of educational hours to be completed in order to be eligible for taking the MBLEx. Instead, FSMTB allows each individual state regulatory board to continue determining the number of educational hours appropriate for practice in that state.

NATIONAL CERTIFICATION BOARD FOR THERAPEUTIC MASSAGE AND BODYWORK (NCBTMB)

The written examinations offered by the National Certification Board for Therapeutic Massage and Bodywork (NCBTMB) are accepted for licensing in over 39 states, the District of Columbia, and various local licensing bodies. Along with being accepted as part of the licensure process, successful completion of either of NCBTMB's examinations confers national certification on the test-taker.

NCBTMB was founded in 1992 to "define and advance the highest standards in the massage therapy and bodywork profession."

As a private, independent organization, NCBTMB strives to

- establish national certification as a recognized credential of professional and ethical standards.

- promote the worth of national certification to health, therapeutic massage and bodywork professionals, public policymakers, and the general public.

- assure and maintain the integrity, stability, and quality of the national certification program.

- periodically update the program to reflect state-of-the-art practices in therapeutic massage and bodywork.

As part of its mission to promote national standards for the massage and bodywork professions, the NCBTMB offers massage therapists and bodyworkers two different national certification examinations.

1. National Certification Examination for Therapeutic Massage (NCETM)

2. National Certification Examination for Therapeutic Massage and Bodywork (NCETMB)

To take either of these examinations, you must meet certain eligibility requirements. In addition, the examination you opt to take depends upon your expertise and areas of interest as well as requirements set by your local regulatory body.

Which Exam Is Right for You—NCETMB or NCETM?

If you choose to become certified via NCBTMB, you will need to indicate if you wish to take the National Certification Examination for Therapeutic Massage and Bodywork (NCETMB) or the National Certification Examination for Therapeutic Massage (NCETM). Both examinations are sponsored by NCBTMB and successful completion of either results in the granting of national certification by NCBTMB. However, some important differences exist.

First, the content of the exams differ. While neither examination covers specific massage or bodywork techniques in depth, they both measure related knowledge and skills required to practice massage and/or bodywork competently at the entry level.

The questions on the NCETM focus exclusively on those subject areas related to the practice of massage therapy (i.e., soft tissue manipulation). The questions on the NCETMB, on the other hand, cover all of the subject areas from the NCETM plus additional questions about the assessment and application of other types of bodywork. This broader focus is meant to give you the opportunity to demonstrate a deeper level of therapeutic expertise. In addition, it simplifies the certification process since you only have to take one examination and maintain a single certification.

The content breakdown of the examinations also differs slightly. It looks like this:

NCETMB

- **General knowledge of body systems:** 16 percent

- **Anatomy, physiology, kinesiology:** 19 percent

- **Pathology:** 13 percent

- **Therapeutic massage & bodywork assessment:** 18 percent

- **Therapeutic massage & bodywork application:** 22 percent

- **Professional standards, ethics, business and legal practices:** 12 percent

NCETM

- **General knowledge of body systems:** 16 percent

- **Anatomy, physiology, kinesiology:** 19 percent

- **Pathology:** 13 percent

- **Therapeutic massage assessment:** 16 percent

- **Therapeutic massage application:** 24 percent

- **Professional standards, ethics, business and legal practices:** 12 percent

Second, and this is important, not all regulatory bodies recognize the NCETM. This means that even if you pass the NCETM, if your state's regulatory board does not accept it as part of its conditions for licensing, you will not qualify for a license in that state. This type of variability is one of the reasons you must make sure you understand the requirements of the location where you intend to practice before registering for or taking any examination.

ELIGIBILITY REQUIREMENTS

You must meet the following minimum requirements in order to take either of the national examinations:

- You must be at least 18 years of age at the time of testing.

- You must agree to a background check.

- You must agree to abide by NCBTMB's professional standards for behavior, as outlined in the NCBTMB Standards of Practice and Code of Ethics.

- You must possess the appropriate level of education and/or experience to demonstrate mastery of core skills, abilities, and knowledge at the entry level. This requirement can be met in one of three ways:

1. Education/Training

You must satisfactorily complete a minimum of 500 hours of formal instruction from an NCBTMB-assigned institution. *Satisfactory completion* generally means you have achieved a passing grade in all courses and have successfully graduated from the program. At a minimum, your instruction should include the following:

o Minimum 200 hours of assessment, theory, and application

o Minimum 125 hours of anatomy, physiology, and kinesiology

o Minimum 40 hours of pathology

o Minimum 10 hours of business/ethics, with 6 ethics hours required

o Minimum 125 hours of specialties and/or related disciplines

2. Portfolio Review Process

The portfolio review process is for individuals who have attended school outside of the United States or for those persons who have trained at institutions that are not designated as NCBTMB-assigned schools. The portfolio review process involves an individualized review of your education and experience. If you intend to pursue this option, you can find more information and complete instructions on this option on the NCBTMB Web site.

3. National Examination for State Licensing (NESL) Option

The National Examination for State Licensing (NESL) option is available for individuals who plan to practice in states that recognize the validity of NCBTMB exams but do not *require* applicants to become certified by NCBTMB in order to be licensed. The primary difference with the NESL option is that it allows the individual to take either of the national examinations at *any* time during the student's training. (In other words, you generally do not need to graduate from your training program before taking the exam.) Successfully passing the examination allows you to become immediately eligible for licensing in your location, as long as you have met all other requirements set by the regulatory body in question. If you pursue the NESL option, under certain circumstances, you can later convert this to full certification. For more information on this process, review *Appendix B: NCBTMB National Examination for State Licensing (NESL) Option* at the end of this book.

NCBTMB Code of Ethics and Standards of Practice

Massage therapy and bodywork present unique challenges to practitioners due to the close physical contact inherent in therapist-client relations. To ensure that all NCBTMB members understand and follow appropriate standards of professional conduct, the NCBTMB has developed both a formal code of ethics as well as standards for professional behavior.

A code of ethics outlines the ethical and moral standards and practices members of a sponsoring organization are expected to uphold. The NCBTMB Code of Ethics deals specifically with many of the challenges massage therapists and bodyworkers face on the job.

> **NOTE**
>
> NCBTMB-assigned schools are those institutions that meet the operational and educational standards developed by NCBTMB. These institutions have been carefully reviewed by NCBTMB and formally designated as NCBTMB-assigned. You can locate a list of NCBTMB-assigned schools on the NCBTMB Web site (www.ncbtmb.org).

Standards of practice provide a blueprint for expected professional conduct. According to the NCBTMB Standards of Practice, these are "the guiding principles by which certificants and applicants for certification conduct their day-to-day responsibilities within their scope of practice. These principles help to assure that all professional behaviors are conducted in the most ethical, compassionate, and responsible manner."

The NCBTMB Standards of Practice address the following key areas:

- Professionalism

- Legal and ethical requirements

- Confidentiality

- Business practices

- Roles and boundaries (including the forbidding of sexual contact)

As part of the certification process, certificants must pledge to uphold both the NCBTMB Code of Ethics and the NCBTMB Standards of Practice. For your convenience, these items are reprinted in full in *Appendix A: NCBTMB Code of Ethics and Standards of Practice.* You should familiarize yourself fully with the expectations and requirements to which you will be expected to conform in your practice.

If ethical violations are alleged against an individual certified by NCBTMB, a committee will carefully examine the charges and determine the appropriate action. Depending upon what comes out of this review, the committee might dismiss the case, issue letters of warning or reprimand, place the individual on probation, require retraining in particular areas of practice, suspend the certificant's membership in NCBTMB, or revoke certification altogether.

In the event of serious violations, NCBTMB is empowered to turn the case over to the appropriate law enforcement officials.

JOB RESPONSIBILITIES

Now that you know a little about the profession, understand the degree of variability that exists in regulatory requirements, and recognize the benefit of successfully completing one of the national examinations, you are probably wondering, what is it that a massage therapist actually does?

Massage therapy is a client-centered profession focused on general health and well-being. While the goals of individual clients differ, generally most clients are looking for relief from stress, pain, or general anxiety; they are hoping to find tools to help them relax or better manage a chronic physical condition; or they may simply want to indulge in an hour or two of personal pampering.

Some therapists, such as those who work for spas or resorts, work from a limited menu of services. Clients select the treatment they would like and this is administered by the therapist during the session. Typical services offered in such environments include Swedish massage, shiatsu massage, deep tissue massage, hot stone therapy, and others. The therapist will then customize the service as necessary so it is appropriate for the physical condition of the client.

Other therapists, such as those who are self-employed or those who work in institutional settings like hospitals and assisted living centers, are expected to first conduct a more formal assessment of the individual. In an institutional setting, this intake interview is often coordinated with other caregivers such as physicians and physical therapists. The therapy to be administered is then planned in an individualized manner as part of the holistic treatment plan for the particular client-patient.

To administer treatment, therapists use their fingers, hands, forearms, and elbows to work superficially or more deeply on a client's body. The therapist can and frequently does employ any number of massage techniques based on his or her education as well as what the client needs or wants. Therapists also employ other agents during these sessions, including lubricants such as oils or lotions; assistive devices such as vibrators and massage wheels; thermal agents including hot or cold therapy packs; and so on.

Some of the duties you can expect to complete once you are ready to practice include:

- Assessing and documenting the client's condition and needs by completing/reviewing client intake forms, observing the client's posture and movement patterns, palpitating the client's body, formally assessing the client's range of motion, and possibly consulting and coordinating with other care providers

- Using this information to determine if massage therapy/bodywork is indicated or if the client would be better served by referral to another type of health-care practitioner

- Developing an individualized treatment plan based on assessment findings

- Understanding and accurately performing standard soft tissue massage techniques:

    o Compression

    o Effleurage (gliding/stroking)

    o Friction

- o Holding

- o Joint movements such as range of motion, stretching, and traction

- o Petrissage (kneading)

- o Tapotement (percussion)

- Facilitating treatment by applying friction-reducing products such as oils, gels, lotions, creams, powders, rubbing alcohol, liniments, antiseptics, ointments, or other preparations

- Utilizing hot and cold applications such as heat lamps, compresses, ice or hot packs, or hot stones

- Applying other topical nonprescription treatments such as herbs, salts/sugars, poultices, and mudpacks

- Using assistive tools and/or electric massagers as needed

- Utilizing aromatherapy as appropriate

- Drawing on other techniques to enhance the client's overall wellness and facilitate the feeling of wholeness or the mind/body connection

- Following ethical business practices, such as fully explaining procedure risks and benefits to clients, allowing clients to stop treatment at any time, maintaining appropriate professional boundaries, acting in an ethical manner, complying with all current health legislation, securely storing patient records, and responding appropriately to insurance companies as required

PERSONAL TRAITS

One of the characteristics that makes massage therapy such a unique profession is the connection between the massage therapist and the client. This connection is called a therapeutic relationship. It is therapeutic in the sense that your goal is to effect a positive change in the client's health and well-being. It is a relationship in that it produces the most positive outcomes when both you and the client feel safe and comfortable in relation to each other.

Touch transmits feelings and intentions to and from the giver and recipient on both conscious and unconscious levels. If you are operating out of altruistic love and a real desire to help people, your clients will sense this. However, if you are operating from some other motivation, your clients will also sense that. Even if he or she does not consciously realize it, if the client has felt on some level that you do not have his or her best interests at heart, that person is less likely to become a regular in your practice or to recommend you to others.

People like you who are interested or involved in health-care–related careers tend to choose such paths not only because of interest in the well-being of others, but also because they (and you) have a strong sense of empathy and compassion. This is especially true in massage and bodywork fields, where success is almost entirely based on the ability to produce meaningful change in others through your sense of touch.

The most successful massage therapists and bodyworkers possess most or all of the traits described here.

- **Patience:** To perform bodywork effectively, you must be patient and comfortable taking the time to carry out the treatment successfully. Rushed bodywork has limited benefits and a rushed client is unlikely to return for repeat business.

- **Calm demeanor:** Because one of the key benefits of massage therapy is relaxation, clients need to be able to reach a comfortable, tranquil state. Your demeanor before and during treatment will either facilitate or impair the client's ability to relax. In addition, a calm demeanor is especially effective when dealing with clients who are nervous or agitated.

- **Effective communication skills:** Good communication skills are essential in any profession, but especially so in those that are other-centered like massage. It is critical to practice active and reflective listening skills so that you really hear and understand what clients are telling you verbally or otherwise as they share their issues with you. In addition, if you wish to be self-employed, it is important to develop an authentic rapport with your client base.

- **Good general health:** Bodywork is a wellness-oriented career; therefore, it is assumed that individuals interested in working in it have a good understanding of wellness that they apply to themselves. You will be most inspiring to others if they sense that you take as good care of yourself as you promise to take of them.

- **Physical strength and dexterity:** Bodywork is a physical profession. It requires you to stand on your feet for extended periods of time. It requires you to use your body as a tool to administer treatment to others. You must be able to utilize your hands, fingers, elbows, and forearms when working on clients; therefore, physical stamina and manual dexterity are very real requirements.

- **Flexibility:** Because massage therapists frequently deal with a cross-section of the public, you can expect to encounter many different types of people. A good massage therapist is skilled at making anyone comfortable no matter the client's personality type. In addition, clients may have specific needs that require you to adjust your approach. You need to be able to think on your feet and adapt to the needs of the person on your table.

- **Professionalism:** Last but certainly not least, therapists and bodyworkers should possess a high degree of professionalism. Clients will be mostly unclothed in your presence and they need to be confident that you are not judging them, gossiping about them with others, or looking at them in an inappropriate way. Making offensive remarks about the client's physical or emotional state or about other clients' physical or emotional states will teach people that you are not worthy of their trust. In addition, over-sharing personal information about yourself or acting in a belittling way will make it difficult for clients to relax in your presence. It is necessary to remain objective, personable, and approachable while avoiding the temptation to chat or become friends. Your office should be run as a business, not a social club.

WORK ENVIRONMENTS

Massage therapy is a burgeoning career field offering opportunities in a wide array of settings, both private and public. Factors that influence where you might work include your degree of education/training, your professional interests and goals, and your lifestyle choices.

- Independent practitioners provide services to the community at large. If you go into business for yourself, you may own or rent a dedicated facility and/or travel to your clients' homes or workplaces.

- Therapists in fitness centers or sports facilities work with amateur and professional athletes to improve athletic performance and prevent or rehabilitate injuries. If you work in a fitness center or sports facility, you will have many opportunities to work with people who are interested in athletics or general physical fitness.

- Therapists in hospitals or medical clinics provide palliative (soothing) care for patients with particular injuries or conditions, such as cancer patients in an oncology clinic. This career field requires a high degree of patience, empathy, and interest in others.

- Therapists in other types of clinics are generally geared toward injury rehabilitation. For example, if you work in a physical therapy clinic, your services will be used to help clients regain range of motion or otherwise rehabilitate from injury or illness.

- Therapists in multidisciplinary health centers might offer a holistic, integrated health-care experience in conjunction with acupuncturists, medical doctors, physical therapists, chiropractors, psychotherapists, or alternative health-care providers.

- Therapists in airports or shopping malls provide chair massage for travelers, with a focus on providing brief stress relief and relaxation. Clients remain fully clothed and receive massage on the back, neck, shoulders, arms, and/or hands.

- Therapists in spas generally offer an array of relaxation services designed to pamper, invigorate, and refresh clientele.

- Therapists in retreat centers work with participants on self-actualization activities and fostering a stronger mind-body connection.

TOOLS OF THE TRADE

Once you begin working in the field, you will use a variety of tools and equipment in your work. Many specialties include specialized tools specific to the discipline. What follows are some of the more common tools and pieces of equipment you will need to become familiar with as a massage therapist.

- **Massage tables:** A quality massage table is one of the most fundamental pieces of equipment for the massage therapist. Massage tables should be comfortable for the client and ergonomically correct for the therapist's body, which means they should be the correct height and width to give you access to the client without being overstretched. Tables should be able to support the client's weight even while you are exerting strength on it during various therapeutic techniques. If you are an independent practitioner and intend to travel to client locations, the table should also be easy to set up and break down and lightweight. Generally, the type of practice and volume of clients play a large role in determining the type of massage table required.

- **Massage chair:** Traveling therapists or those who work in airports or shopping malls sometimes utilize massage chairs to provide bodywork to clients. Some standard features include wheels, removable kneepads, and side-entry access for the elderly and women wearing dresses or skirts.

- **Linens and pillows:** Surprisingly, you'll find that appropriate linens are an important aspect of your practice as they provide the client with both warmth and modesty and contribute to the feeling of luxury. Part of your training involves learning to drape clients appropriately so the more personal aspects of their bodies remain covered and only the part you are working on is exposed. Pillows give support to the head and neck when the client is in a reclined position, either facedown or face-forward. Pillows come in a variety of shapes and sizes. Since you'll be working with many different body shapes and sizes, you may need to have several pillows on hand.

- **Lubricants and emollients:** Oils, creams, gels, and lotions allow easier movement of your hands over the client's body. Oils are frequently warmed prior to use, so you should be familiar with the operation of a warmer machine. Therapists select oils or lotions for their practice based on personal and professional preference. It is important to use products formulated specifically for bodywork as these are the least likely to irritate the client's skin or cause allergic reactions. In addition, the selected product(s) should not have an excessively strong odor as these may sicken either the client or you. Finally, you may also work with lubricants designed specifically for special conditions or particular body parts. For example, at some point in time, you might use foot/leg lotion, cuticle oil, sunburn creams, and others.

- **Aromatherapy oils:** Massage therapists with advanced training might incorporate aromatherapy into their sessions. Aromatherapy is the practice of inhaling the aroma of essential oils extracted from flowers and plants. Aromatherapy is widely believed to enhance psychological and physical well-being by stimulating brain function and promoting whole-body healing. Safety precautions must be followed and consent from the client is required.

- **Hot stones:** Hot stone massage is a therapeutic technique that involves placing smooth, heated flat stones on key points along the body. The heat warms and softens the tissues, allowing the therapist to work effectively while providing the client with a sense of deep relaxation. The warmth also improves circulation and calms the nervous system. Stone therapy requires the use of stones and an electric heating device, which assures they are within a safe temperature range.

- **Assistive tools:** A variety of electric and handheld tools is available to support any number of therapeutic approaches. These tools can facilitate the goals of the session while minimizing the therapist's risk of hand injury. Handheld tools are commonly used to apply concentrated pressure to trigger points in the body and act as percussion instruments to promote deep muscular relief.

- **Thermal agents:** Hot (*thermotherapy*) and cold (*cryotherapy*) agents are used to soothe inflammation, relieve pain, improve range of motion, reduce joint stiffness, and accelerate healing. Commonly used thermal agents include ice packs, cold gel packs, heat packs, heat lamps, and moist heat packs. The use of such items is dependent upon the therapeutic setting and the goals of the session as well as the therapist's level of education and training. It is important to understand how these agents work on the body so that the appropriate one is selected for the client's condition.

EDUCATION

As you already learned, educational requirements for massage therapists vary greatly by location. However, most states require aspiring massage therapists to complete some type of formal education program before they are licensed to practice. The actual number of educational hours varies by state and is usually a reflection of licensure requirements. This number can vary from 200 hours to over 1,000 hours. Topics covered include anatomy and physiology, kinesiology, ethics, general business management, and hands-on massage techniques. Practitioners are also required to complete a certain amount of continuing education (CE) courses each year (or every two to three years) to maintain standing.

As with any career training, it is important for potential students to select a school that is appropriately accredited. Accreditation indicates the school has met at least the minimal educational standards that qualify graduates to practice professionally or to continue their studies at a more specialized/advanced institution. Many schools are accredited by the states in which they are located. You should make sure any school you are considering is accredited by the state. In addition, many schools also choose to be accredited by a voluntary regulating body, such as the Commission on Massage Therapy Accreditation (COMTA) or the National Certification Board for Therapeutic Massage and Bodywork (NCBTMB). This level of accreditation indicates the school's program meets the rigorous standards set by the accrediting organization. These organizations seek to promote the standardization and professionalism of the massage and bodywork fields. This level of accreditation means the school and the program have undergone and passed a stringent review process.

As mentioned earlier in the text, many states require massage therapy practitioners to be licensed to practice. Licensure requirements vary by state, but most compel the candidate to possess a certain amount of education and experience as well as attain a passing score on a written examination. The examination is meant to demonstrate that the candidate possesses the appropriate professional knowledge to practice at the entry level. The examination may be one that has been developed by the state, or it may be one of the examinations offered by other bodies: the Massage and Bodywork Licensing Examination (MBLEx), the National Certification Examination for Therapeutic Massage and Bodywork (NCETMB), or the National Certification Examination for Therapeutic Massage (NCETM).

Check *Appendix C: Helpful Resources* for more information on finding specific requirements for your location.

SALARY AND BENEFITS

According to the U.S. Department of Labor, the job outlook for the bodywork field is excellent. It is likely you will be able to find work immediately after completing your training and becoming licensed in your state. In addition, the rate of growth for this occupation is expected to increase faster than the average for all occupations. In 2006, 118,000 massage therapists were in the workforce; by 2016, it is anticipated the workforce will consist of 142,000 massage therapists, which represents a growth rate of about 20 percent. Obviously, this is a promising field for aspiring therapists.

The salary outlook is quite positive, although pay can vary greatly based on

- geographic location.
- years of experience and knowledge of specialties.
- employment status (if you work for yourself or for someone else).
- type of facility (if you work for someone else).
- per-massage pricing/ability to collect tips.

Massage therapists generally work either by the hour in a facility or on a per-massage basis if they are self-employed or working for a spa or resort. According to the U.S. Department of Labor, the top 10 percent of massage therapists, who tend to be self-employed massage therapists with a large client base built over time, earn upward of $69,000. The bottom 10 percent of therapists earn an average of $16,000—these are generally entry-level workers fresh out of school.

On average, a massage therapist with a reasonable amount of experience and training can expect to earn about $35,000 annually.

If you are employed on the staff of a facility such as a spa, hospital, or sports clinic, you may be eligible for typical employment benefits:

- Sick leave
- Vacation pay
- Holiday pay
- Health benefits
- 401k plan

If you are self-employed and/or if you contract your services to other facilities, generally the only employment benefits you receive will be those you grant yourself. This lack of benefits, however, is offset by the ability to make a full-time wage working part-time hours and by the convenience of setting your own hours and working at those times that are most convenient for you.

ADVANCEMENT OPPORTUNITIES

Many massage therapists work only part-time because of the physical demands of the work; it would be physically exhausting to perform massages 40 hours a week! Because it is possible to pursue this work quite effectively on a part-time basis, some people choose to become massage therapists as a secondary career and source of income.

Advancement opportunities as we typically think of them are somewhat limited in this field due to the nature of the work; however, advancement is possible and can be achieved by gaining experience and pursuing advanced knowledge and skills. The most successful massage therapists work for themselves, pursue educational opportunities, and have acquired a significant number of clients over time.

RELATED OCCUPATIONS

Massage therapists provide services that focus on human movement patterns and the physical well-being of their clients. Some other occupations provide similar types of services.

- **Personal (sports) trainers:** Personal trainers provide individualized fitness instruction to clients looking for exercise programming tailored to their specific needs. Trainers assess the fitness level of clients and monitor their progress over time to ensure the programming is working as designed. Personal trainers usually work directly with clients to motivate them and make certain they are performing exercises safely and in the correct sequence. Sessions are typically conducted at health clubs or in the client's own home. Some trainers work with individuals who are physically challenged by medical conditions or those who are rehabilitating from specific kinds of injuries. Some personal trainers are even certified to provide nutritional counseling to clients, thus enabling those trainers to address all of the client's diet and exercise needs in a holistic fashion.

- **Physical therapy assistants and aides:** Physical therapy assistants and aides work under the supervision of physical therapists. They follow prescribed procedures to help patients improve mobility, relieve pain, and minimize physical disability caused by diseases or injury. Physical therapy assistants and aides generally work in hospitals, nursing homes, and clinics that provide physical therapy as a service on an in-patient or out-patient basis. They usually work closely with physicians, occupational therapists, social workers, and others. Physical therapist assistants generally work more closely with patients using massage, exercise, and thermal agents such as heat, cold, and light. Patients frequently rely on physical therapist assistants to educate them on the use of durable medical equipment such as wheelchairs, walkers, or braces.

SUMMING IT UP

- Massage therapists manipulate the muscles and soft tissues of a client's body to effect a positive change in that person's physical state. Massage has been shown to improve body circulation, relieve anxiety and stress, reduce muscle soreness and pain, promote a greater range of motion in the joints, and facilitate other health benefits.

- Massage therapy is a skilled profession requiring knowledge of anatomy, physiology, kinesiology, and pathology as well as specific therapeutic techniques. Many different massage techniques, some of which may require specialized training before they can be used, are available to practitioners.

- Massage therapists work in a variety of settings, such as hospitals, clinics, sports facilities, and spas. Many massage therapists are self-employed and contract their services to another facility or offer therapy to the community at large. Self-employed therapists may work in their own facility, out of their home, or they may travel to the client.

- Due to the unique nature of the work, most massage therapists are licensed by regulatory bodies at the state level. Licensing usually requires a minimum amount of education and training or work experience. Requirements vary greatly by location. You should understand requirements in the state in which you intend to practice *before* you start on your massage journey.

- To obtain a license, many regulatory bodies also require you to successfully complete an examination that proves you possess entry-level skills and knowledge. Regulatory bodies may develop their own examination or they may utilize examinations offered by the Federation of State Massage Therapy Boards (FSMTB) and/or the National Certification Board for Therapeutic Massage and Bodywork (NCBTMB).

- The salary outlook for the profession is good, with the average therapist earning about $35,000 a year, frequently working only part-time hours. The most successful practitioners tend to be those who are motivated, experienced, knowledgeable, self-employed, and capable of handling a large clientele.

CHAPTER 2

Becoming a Massage Therapist

OVERVIEW

- **Select and complete an educational program**
- **Apply for an examination**
- **Schedule your examination**
- **Prepare for the examination**
- **Test-taking tips and hints**
- **Apply for your license**
- **Keep current**
- **Consider your career options**
- **Get the job hunt underway**
- **Summing it up**

As you start down this exciting new career path, you will find that one of the biggest challenges in the profession is the lack of a single national standard or process for licensing and regulating the profession. What exists instead is a patchwork of varying requirements that can differ considerably depending on where you intend to practice. You will find that requirements can vary at the state, county, and even the municipal level. For this reason, you will be most successful in this new career if you take the time to research and understand requirements for your area *before* you get started.

Your first step is to determine exactly what is required to become a licensed massage therapy practitioner in your state. You can use the information provided in *Appendix C: Helpful Resources* to start your research. The organizations and Web sites listed direct aspiring therapists through the maze of information out there and help you to determine specifically what is required in your area. The massage regulatory board in most states maintains a Web site and updates it regularly; however, it is still important for you to confirm that the information is still correct. If you are concerned about the age of the information or cannot locate information for your state, call your local state board. You should be able to find its phone number online.

How Current Is Your Information?

The Internet is a terrific tool for conducting research, because it can lead you to a wealth of information with just a few clicks of the mouse. However, not all of the information you find online is equal; some sources may be outdated and others might be just plain wrong. Therefore, as you search for the specific regulatory requirements that apply in your state, take a few steps to make sure that the information you find is provided by a reputable source and current.

The links we provide for you in *Appendix C: Helpful Resources* lead to a variety of different Web sites maintained by reputable massage-related organizations. These organizations have a vested interest in the profession and provide access to essential information and resources that will help you jumpstart your massage career. However, the best source for regulatory information is almost always your state government's Web site.

Government Web sites can be identified by the ".gov" indicator in the domain name. For example, Pennsylvania's official government Web site is located at http://pa.gov, New York's official government Web site is located at www.ny.gov, and so on. Once on the Web site, search for "massage therapy," "regulatory board," "professional board," or some other logical search term. You should be able to find the pages you seek with relative ease.

You will also want to make sure the information is current. You can do this by checking the publication date on the pages in question. You can usually find this "last updated" date near the bottom of the page. If the information has not been updated in the last 6 months or so, you should probably follow up with a phone call directly to the board to make sure licensing requirements have not changed.

SELECT AND COMPLETE AN EDUCATIONAL PROGRAM

Once you know what requirements you need to meet to practice massage therapy in your state, the next step is figuring out how to meet these requirements.

As you begin searching for educational opportunities in this field, you will find that massage training is available from a variety of sources, from community colleges to vocational schools to private institutions. Choosing the right program is critical, so here are some factors to consider while making this decision.

- **Accreditation level:** Accreditation indicates that an educational institution or program has met a set of standards developed by an official accrediting body. Most educational institutions need to be accredited by the state in which they are offered, so state accreditation should be the first level you confirm. State accreditation means the state has reviewed the curriculum and determined that it is adequate to meet the stated educational objectives of the program. Depending upon state requirements and/or the licensing examination you plan to take, you should also ensure that the school or program is accredited by an industry organization with expertise and a vested interest in the profession. Voluntary accreditation is available from the Commission on Massage Therapy Accreditation (COMTA) as well as the National Certification Board for Therapeutic Massage and Bodywork (NCBTMB). Most institutions that have achieved either of these accreditations have undergone the process because they recognize the value of this independent accreditation, and they usually make it a point to prominently display this information in marketing materials or on their Web site. Therefore, look carefully for the accreditation level of any school or program that interests you. (Or ask questions! Staff and administrators from legitimate institutions will answer your questions openly and honestly.) Avoid schools or programs that are not accredited at any level, because they may be a waste of your time and money.

- **Business practices:** If you are considering a private institution or school, you will need to recognize that private institutions are essentially for-profit businesses, and its operational practices will matter to you. How long has the school been in operation? What are the school's operational policies (for example, what happens if you have to drop out? Will any of your tuition be refunded?) Does the school staff a business office and when is it open? Are administrative personnel available on a regular basis? You can also do a little detective work online. Check with the Better Business Bureau (www.bbb.org) to see if any complaints about shoddy business practices have been lodged or try to get a sense of the institution's reputation in the community. If possible, you can also talk to local massage therapists to see what they have to say about the program you are considering.

- **Program completion rates/school-to-work assistance:** How many students are currently in the program? How many students have actually graduated? What is the overall program completion rate? Does the school provide internship opportunities? Does it offer career assistance to its graduates? A high completion rate means students have found the program worthwhile. Schools that are plugged into the local community with internship and career assistance programs offer the best opportunity for you to find work after you graduate.

- **Admission requirements:** Do you meet the requirements for attending the institution? Most schools require a minimum high school diploma or equivalent. If you are not qualified to attend a particular institution, find out what you need to do to become qualified.

- **Course work:** If you select an accredited school, the course content will follow the standards published by the accrediting body. If you select a non-accredited school, you will need to carefully review the curriculum against the outlines published by one of the accrediting organizations to ensure that the program at a minimum prepares you for the examination you will need to take to become licensed. Use the materials on sites such as www.comta.org, www.ncbtmb.org, and www.fsmtb.org to determine the adequacy of the program. Most of these sites also include e-mail links for you to ask questions; take advantage of these resources.

- **Program length/course availability:** How many contact hours does the program require? Massage programs can run from a few months to as long as two years. Does the school offer full-time and part-time options? If you can only attend classes at certain times (i.e., in the day or in the evening), are all of the courses you need offered at those times?

- **Class size:** The best programs limit the number of students per class so that the student/teacher ratio is reasonable. A student/teacher ratio of 15:1, for example, indicates 15 students for every teacher, so you would expect an average of 15 students in most of your classes. Because massage is such a hands-on discipline, it is important that class size is not so large that you will not have adequate time to practice or work directly with your instructor if necessary.

- **Tuition/financial aid:** How much does the program cost and what kind of payment schedule is in place? (Make sure you consider all fees, such as lab fees, costs of books, etc., in addition to the tuition.) Is this tuition level comparable with other similar institutions? Is financial aid available if you need it? If you need to drop out of the program for any reason, is any portion of the tuition refundable?

- **Transferability of credits:** If you wish to transfer earned credits to other institutions, can you do so? For example, if you plan to switch to a different school at some point during your study, you will need to ensure that the institution has transferrable credits. Ask the administrators at both schools (if you know the school to which you will eventually switch). At a minimum, the administrator of your program should be able to tell you what, if any, institutions have accepted credits from the school in the past.

APPLY FOR AN EXAMINATION

After you have completed your formal education, you can apply to take the examination of your choice. Your state may mandate that you take one examination or another or it may allow you to choose which you will take. Check the state Web site for specifics.

Once you have applied to and been accepted for the examination, you will need to test within a set time frame. This time frame is essentially the same: 3 months for the two National Certification Examinations (NCEs) offered by the NCBTMB, which are the National Certification Examination for Therapeutic Massage (NCETM) and the National Certification Examination for Therapeutic Massage and Bodywork (NCETMB) or 90 days for the Massage and Bodywork Licensing Examination (MBLEx) offered by Federation of State Massage Therapy Boards (FSMTB).

> **NOTE**
>
> If you are testing under NCBTMB's National Examination for State Licensing (NESL) option, you can apply for the examination at any point in your studies. Review *Appendix B: NCBTMB National Examination for State Licensing (NESL) Option* for more information.

This means you should not apply for the examination until you feel reasonably certain that you are prepared to pass it. Examination preparation is covered in later chapters.

SCHEDULE YOUR EXAMINATION

MBLEx, NCETMB, and NCETM examinations are all administered via Pearson VUE computer-based testing centers. Once you are notified of eligibility to take the examination of your choice, you will be directed to locate a testing center in your area to schedule the examination. You can do this either on the Pearson VUE Web site (www.pearsonvue.com) or by calling Pearson VUE directly at 1-888-699-1808.

> **TIP**
>
> Candidate Handbooks are available for both the MBLEx and the NCETMB/NCETM. Candidate Handbooks contain complete instructions for applying for, scheduling, and taking each examination. You can find these handbooks on the FSMTB (www.fsmtb.org) and NCBTMB (www.ncbtmb.org) Web sites.

In order to maintain the integrity of its testing sites, Pearson VUE has strict requirements for testing. For example, you must arrive at the center 30 minutes prior to your scheduled test time; you must bring two forms of identification, including current valid photo ID; and you cannot bring anything into the testing room with you. These and other requirements will be provided to you with confirmation of your testing date. It is important to read and follow all instructions completely. If you do not conform to all testing guidelines, you may not be allowed to take your examination as scheduled.

PREPARE FOR THE EXAMINATION

Everything you need to know to maximize your examination score is included in this book. We have designed this material so that you can easily determine what you already know and where you need additional help. The material is self-paced so you can work through it at the speed that is right for you.

Once you finish the introductory material in *Part I: Massage Therapist Basics,* go to *Part II: Diagnosing Strengths and Weaknesses.* This section covers general testing guidelines and provides a diagnostic examination so you can determine your strengths and weaknesses. Although this test is not designed specifically as an NCE or MBLEx, it is designed to cover all of the content areas you will find on these tests. It is important to answer the questions honestly, using only the knowledge you already possess rather than consulting with textbooks or other resources. The point of this exercise is to figure out which content areas are your strengths and which you need to improve going forward. Analyze your results carefully to identify the topic areas that seem to give you the most trouble. Use this information to create an outline of study for yourself.

After completing the diagnostic test, go to *Part III: Prepare and Practice: Massage Therapy Subject Areas*. This section provides sample questions and practice exercises for all of the different subject areas that are tested on the examinations. The overview material covers the key points of the subject matter so you know what kind of knowledge you need to possess to do well on the examination. The questions are designed to mimic the kind of questions you can expect to see on the real examination. You will also find an answer key and answer explanations in each subject area.

To get the most out of Part III, answer each question and complete all exercises. Check your answers against the answer key provided. Analyze your results to identify the topic areas that continue to give you the most trouble and pay special attention when studying them. Try to determine the root causes of your issues. Take your time and make sure you really understand each content area before moving on.

Be sure to tackle each chapter individually, because you need knowledge across all of the content areas.

Some content is specific to one examination or another, and is marked as such. You need only worry about that material if you are taking the examination to which it applies.

Part IV: Two Practice Tests includes two full practice tests for your use. One of these tests is an MBLEx; the other is an NCETMB exam. These tests also include answer keys and explanations for your use. You can use these tests to gauge how much you have improved since you took the first test.

TEST-TAKING TIPS AND HINTS

Before you apply to take one of the massage therapy examinations, you should feel close to being ready to take and pass that examination. At a minimum, you should complete the diagnostic test before or near the time you apply. Because you will have only a 3-month (NCE) or 90-day (MBLEx) window to schedule your test once you are deemed eligible, it is important to feel confident in your knowledge so you do not feel rushed in your studies.

Once your eligibility has been confirmed, schedule your test. Even if you do not plan to test until nearly the end of the grace period, it is important to schedule your test date immediately to maximize the chance of getting the test day you want. Testing dates may be limited, depending on the location and the number of seats available. Pearson VUE centers provide testing services for many different examinations across a variety of professions, so other people will be scheduling their tests, too.

In the month before the test, pay special attention to the material you find most difficult. Follow the study strategies suggested in this book to overcome weak areas, but continue reviewing all information across all of the content.

About a week before the test, select random practice problems from each section to complete. By now you should feel comfortable with your comprehension of the information.

The night before the test, go to bed at a reasonable hour. You may be nervous but it is important to be as well-rested as possible. In the morning, get up early enough that you can eat something nutritious before the test. Try to relax and work on approaching the test with a positive attitude.

Most importantly, at all points in this process, *read and follow all confirmation instructions carefully.* You will receive instructions from the testing organization (FSMTB or NCBTMB) as well as instructions from the Pearson VUE test center. It is critical that you follow these.

Here are some tips for test day:

- Wear comfortable clothing. Layers are best, so you can remove a layer if you are too warm or add one if you are too cold.

- Arrive early— at least 30 minutes ahead of time. You will become stressed if you rush, and stress can negatively affect your performance. Make sure you locate the test center ahead of time, so you know how to get there on the day of the test. The testing monitor may reassign your slot if you are not signed into the testing center 30 minutes ahead of time.

- You will not be allowed to bring anything into the testing room with you, other than your ID and paper and pencil provided by the test monitor. Therefore, do not bring any unnecessary items with you to the test center. The testing monitor will provide a small locker for storage of essential items such as your car keys or purse, but this space is usually very limited so bring only what you absolutely need.

- Do not bring other people with you to the test center, particularly individuals who require supervision, such as children. Babysitting services are not available and no one else will be allowed to go into the testing room with you.

- Listen carefully to any and all instructions given to you by the test monitor. Read all written instructions carefully. Ask questions if you do not understand something.

- You will be escorted to the testing room and assigned a computer. The technology used for the testing is fairly simple so you need only be minimally knowledgeable with computer operations to successfully complete the examination. In addition, before your test begins, you will have the opportunity to complete a short tutorial walking you through the testing process. Even if you feel comfortable with the technology, it is in your best interest to take a few minutes to complete this tutorial. The time you take does not count as testing time. In addition, the tutorial includes some simulated questions so you will have the chance to practice before starting your exam for real.

- The MBLEx includes 125 random multiple-choice questions across the identified subject areas. You will have 2 hours and 30 minutes to complete this examination. The NCE tests include 160 random multiple-choice questions across the subject areas. You will have 2 hours and 40 minutes to complete this examination.

- No matter what test you take, answer every question that is presented! Incomplete questions are considered WRONG and count against your score.

- For all questions, read the question in its entirety before looking at the answer options. Try to mentally devise an answer before looking at the choices. This way, the way the answer options are worded will not confuse you.

- Read all answer options before choosing one.

- Usually, the first answer option you select is correct, so try not to spend a lot of time changing your answers once you have selected them.

- If you are having trouble with a particular question, you can flag that question and come back to it later. (The tutorial will show you how to do this.)

- If you are unsure of an answer, first try eliminating any answer option you believe is incorrect. Then make a guess from the remaining answer options.

- Double-check to make sure you are selecting the right answer before submitting it.

Because your test is computer-based, once you submit the examination, your score will be immediately calculated and you will be advised as to whether you have passed or failed. You can leave the testing room at that point. The testing center monitor will provide you with printouts of appropriate documentation based on how you score. You will be advised of any necessary next steps.

APPLY FOR YOUR LICENSE

Here is where your early research pays off. Because you knew the requirements for a license BEFORE you started your journey, when you apply for your license to practice, you will already know you have met the requirements. Thus, you can be reasonably confident that you will not have difficulty with this step.

Follow the application instructions posted on your state's Web site. Your school should also be able to assist you in starting this process.

KEEP CURRENT

Most states require a periodic licensing review. Your state may also require you to complete a certain number of continuing education hours to ensure that you are current on techniques and changes in the industry.

In addition, NCE certifications are valid for four years from the date of issue. To maintain your certification beyond that period, you will be required to recertify. A *Recertification Reference Guide* is available on the NCBTMB Web site (www.ncbtmb.org).

In any event, it is important to stay on top of current thinking and techniques in your field. Taking classes and pursuing advanced certifications are key ways to do this.

CONSIDER YOUR CAREER OPTIONS

Now that you are licensed and ready to practice, what is next?

Do you want to work for yourself?

The nature of the massage therapy profession makes it an ideal career choice for people who are looking to work for themselves. If you choose to go into business for yourself, you can set up your business in any number of ways. You can offer services to clients in their homes or workplaces. You can rent a room at a spa, health center, or gym, where you have the opportunity to meet people who are likely to be interested in your services. You can even set up a business area in your home and have clients come to you.

Obviously, plenty of options are available to aspiring entrepreneurs. If you think you may be interested in setting up your own business, a good first step is to do some research in your area to find out how other therapists practice, what they charge, and how they handle issues such as tips and commissions. Do they tend to work in public venues such as gyms or health centers? Do they work from stand-alone locations? Do they travel to clients or have clients come to them? It is important to understand the norms in your area; of course, you do not have to do what other people are doing, but you may find it helpful when you are getting started.

Professionalism is always critical for a massage therapist, but it will be of special importance for you as a business owner. For example, if you visit a client in his or her home, you should not act as if you are on a social visit. You should not accept snacks or beverages, nor should you sit down and chat with the client. Instead, remember you are there in a professional capacity. You should determine—politely and professionally—where the client would like you to set up your equipment and get to it.

If you plan to work out of your own home, you should first make sure your neighborhood or development does not have rules prohibiting you from running a business there. Once you are cleared to go ahead, it is best if you designate a specific area in your home for your work. In an ideal world, this area would be a room that is totally separate from your living quarters and might even have its own entrance. If that is not possible, at the very least, you should have a dedicated room that is used solely for business. It should be neat and inviting and set up in a way that is comfortable for the client. It should be roomy enough that you can easily access and move around the client as necessary. The room should be isolated from the rest of your home as much as possible, and should be off-limits to your family and pets, especially when clients are visiting. It should be kept free of clutter and of non-business items. In other words, it should look and operate like a professional work environment. In addition, you should have a dedicated restroom available for clients if at all possible. If not, make sure the restroom you use for your business is free of clutter and personal items/medications.

Keep records on each of your clients. Your records should include the client's intake forms, contact information, insurance information, preferences for particular techniques, and any notes you make regarding the client's physical condition or needs. You should update your records each time the client comes to you so that your information is always current. Keep these records confidential. If you work in a shared space, do not leave personal information about clients out in the open. Instead, maintain a file cabinet or box in a private area. If notes are kept electronically, password-protect them.

Your business should have a dedicated phone line and/or e-mail address so that clients and potential clients can easily reach you. Nothing is more frustrating than trying to set up an appointment and not being able to do so. Even though you are just starting out, it is important to operate as if you have been established for some time.

You will need to market and advertise your services to reach potential clients. For this reason, it is usually helpful to first rent a massage room from an operation such as a gym or a salon; these businesses cater to individuals who are likely to seek your services. If you act professionally and demonstrate a high level of skill, clients are more likely to become repeat customers and also recommend you to others. Word-of-mouth recommendation is often one of the best ways to build clientele. Other channels for reaching potential clients involve advertising, which you can do on the Internet, in the newspaper, on bulletin boards, etc. Focus on the channels you believe are targeted toward the clientele you wish to service. For ideas on making the most of your advertising and marketing efforts, contact the Small Business Administration (SBA) in your area. The SBA can provide you with resources and counseling as you start and grow your business.

In addition, the SBA can provide invaluable advice and assistance with financial recordkeeping, taxes, and general business licensing in your area.

Do you want to work for someone else?

If you are not ready for self-employment or if you want some real-world experience before striking out on your own, you can always seek work with someone else. As mentioned earlier, many therapeutic massage opportunities exist in a variety of environments. Before you begin your job search, consider the clientele you wish to work with and the type of environment you want to work in. Do you prefer a fast pace and relatively healthy client? Are you interested in rehabilitative work in a more therapeutic setting? Or is it your dream to work with the sick or disabled in a clinic or hospital?

Most massage therapists are employed part-time due to the physically demanding nature of the work, so you should make sure you understand the expectations of any employer before you start to work there. Consider if evening and/or weekend hours are required and whether or not you wish to work at those times. Depending on where you are employed, evening and weekend appointments may be the norm since you will need to be available when your clients are. In other settings, working hours may be a little more traditional.

Another consideration is how you will be paid. Is the position salaried? Is it paid hourly? Is it a per-massage fee? Will you receive commissions or tips? Will you be considered an employee or an independent contractor? Does the employer require you to be on-site when you do not have any sessions booked? If so, will the employer offer you an hourly wage? Do some research so you know what to expect in different environments. It is much better to know the norms beforehand than to be surprised later.

GET THE JOB HUNT UNDERWAY

If you wish to find outside employment, you will need to know how to prepare effective resumes and cover letters.

Create a Resume

Many avenues are available to you when you are searching for work. You can look for jobs using Internet job boards, industry trade magazines, local newspapers, job boards for specific employers, and so on. In addition, your school may have job placement assistance available; if so, take advantage of this service.

While conducting your job search, keep one thing in mind: the person responsible for finding you a job is *you*. The best approach is a proactive one. That means *you* take the initiative to look for openings in your area or take the steps necessary to get your business off the ground; do not wait for others to come to your aid.

If you intend to work for someone else, you will need to create a resume. A resume is a document that outlines your education, accomplishments, and skills. Resume styles can vary greatly, so choose one that is clear and easy to read. Your resume should showcase your professionalism and draw attention to your strengths. Your resume is the first thing a potential employer is likely to see, so it is critical to make a good impression. You should try to keep your resume to one page or two at the very most.

At a minimum, you should include the following information on your resume:

- **Contact information:** Your contact information includes your name, address, phone number, and e-mail address. If your e-mail address is silly and unprofessional, set up a new one specifically for your job search. It is best to use an e-mail address that is easy for potential employers to remember, such as a combination of your first and last names. For example, you might use your first initial and last name, such as jdoe@e-mailprovider.com, or you might write out your whole name, such as johndoe@e-mailprovider.com.

- **Certification:** If you have successfully achieved certification, you can use designated initials after your name. If you passed the NCETMB exam, you can use the initials NCTMB after your name: John Doe, NCTMB. This stands for Nationally Certified in Therapeutic Massage and Bodywork. Similarly, if you are NCETM-certified, you can use the initials NCTM: John Doe, NCTM. This stands for Nationally Certified in Therapeutic Massage. Most employers will be interested in your certification status, so it is important to include this information.

- **Objective:** The objective is your goal. Your objective may be simple, such as "To obtain a job as a massage therapist," or it may be more particular to the kind of job you are applying for, such as "To obtain a job as a massage therapist working with cancer patients in a clinical setting." It is best to be as specific as possible.

- **Education:** List your education, beginning with your most recent certificate or degree. If you are just starting out and your resume seems short, you may want to include a few bulleted points about your course of study. Be sure to include your school name and location, the dates you attended, and the degree or certificate you earned. (See the Sample Massage Therapist Resume in this section.) If your work experience is stronger than your education, you may want to list your work experience first. The goal is to make your resume look as impressive as possible so that others are interested in hiring you.

- **Work experience:** Beginning with your most recent job, and keeping in mind that it is not necessary to include every job that you have ever held, list your work experience. Include relevant experience that might apply to the job you are seeking, such as experience with a certain population (for example, the elderly), or experience in a particular environment (for example, a hospital setting). If you completed an internship, it may be best to begin with this, as it is likely the most relevant experience. If your job experience is not related to the career field, however, you should still include it, as it demonstrates that you are dependable and stable.

- **License/certification/professional memberships:** Indicate if you are licensed, certified, and/or if you are a member of any professional organizations.

In addition, you might also want to include one or more of the following optional sections:

- **References:** Most employers ask for references, so you may find it expedient simply to include these directly on your resume. Do not use friends or family members as references. Rather, it is best to list previous employers or instructors; your references should be able to speak objectively to your educational abilities or workplace skills. Be sure to ask each individual if it is okay to include him or her as a reference before doing so. Alternately, you can just write *References available upon request.* Just make sure you have the contact information available if you are called in for an interview.

- **Skills:** Some resumes include a list of sought-after skills or special qualifications. If you possess any noteworthy skills or if you are certified in particular techniques, you might want to include them here.

- **Distinctions and awards:** If you have achieved any special distinctions or awards, such as being a member of the National Honor Society in high school, or earning academic awards in your program of study, you might want to list them, also.

Sample Massage Therapist Resume

Christina J. Smith
1122 Waterfront Boulevard
Rochester, NY 14621
(585) 555-8877
christinasmith@yahoo.com

OBJECTIVE:
To obtain a position as a massage therapist in a health-care environment that will give me the opportunity to provide patients with superior and appropriate care.

SKILLS:
- Experienced with Swedish massage, deep tissue massage, sports massage, and range of motion/flexibility exercise techniques
- Excellent communication skills and high degree of empathy for the ill and injured

EDUCATION:
Massage Therapist Degree (May 20—)
ABC School of Massage Therapy
Over 600 hours of therapeutic massage and bodywork study; advanced course work in special populations, body awareness, and wellness support.

EXPERIENCE:
Therapeutic Massage Intern (January 20— to March 20—)
XYZ Hospital Oncology Unit
Rochester, NY
- Provided appropriate, effective treatment to cancer patients undergoing chemotherapy and radiation treatments.
- Worked with unit manager to assess patients and design individualized sessions based on physical condition/needs.
- Observed therapeutic approach of more experienced staff therapists as they worked with patients in more serious condition.
- Exhibited a professional and appropriate demeanor at all times.

Front Desk Clerk (September 20— to present)
Rockford Hospital
Rockford, NY
- Worked the hospital's information desk
- Provided excellent customer service to patients and visitors by answering questions, giving directions, and assisting with requests in locating particular hospital units, services, or personnel.

LICENSING/CERTIFICATION/PROFESSIONAL ORGANIZATIONS
New York State Licensed Massage Therapist (LMT) #000000
National Certification Board for Therapeutic Massage and Bodywork (NCBTMB) #00000-00
Fully insured member of Associated Bodywork & Massage Professionals (ABMP) #000000

REFERENCES:
Available upon request

Write a Cover Letter

You should include a cover letter when you send your resume to potential employers. In this letter, state your purpose, summarize your qualifications, mention any important or interesting facts about yourself you wish to showcase, and express your interest in working for the organization. Your cover letter gives prospective employers a glimpse of your personality, education, and experience. It also demonstrates your ability to communicate appropriately in writing, so you should make sure it is grammatically correct and does not include typos or misspellings.

It is not necessary to prepare a different cover letter for every place you apply; rather, it is standard practice to save the body of the letter and personalize it for each new position. However, it should not read like a form letter, so be sure to reference the specific employer and position to which you are applying. (See the following Sample Massage Therapist Cover Letter.)

Sample Massage Therapist Cover Letter

Christina J. Smith
1122 Waterfront Boulevard
Rochester, NY 14621
(585) 555-8877
christinasmith@yahoo.com

June 16, 20—

Ms. Nicole Jones
XYZ Hospital
123 Main Street
Rochester, NY 14621

Dear Ms. Jones:

As a recent graduate of ABC School of Massage Therapy with a certificate in massage therapy, I am very interested in joining the therapeutic massage team at XYZ Hospital. While I am primarily interested in working in the Joshua K. Frail Oncology Clinic, I would gladly work in any unit in the hospital. In addition, my schedule is completely flexible, so I am available to work evenings and weekends.

My education includes over 600 hours of course work in anatomy and physiology, kinesiology, pathology, therapeutic assessment and application, and ethics. My school's curriculum has a strong focus on Swedish and deep tissue massage; I also have experience with sports massage and range of motion/flexibility exercise. In addition, due to my personal interest in working with the ill and injured, I have completed elective course work in special populations, body awareness, and wellness support.

As part of my schoolwork, I completed a three-month internship in the hospital's oncology clinic. I worked under the supervision of Thomas Harmon. As an intern at the clinic, I participated in patient assessment and the development of individualized treatment plans for patients. I also provided excellent and appropriate therapeutic care to patients.

I do have other work experience, including working the front desk at Rockford Hospital, where I assisted in providing information to hospital patients and visitors. I also answered general questions about the hospital via e-mail and the phone.

Please contact me at any time for an interview, even if you do not currently have any available openings. I really enjoyed my work experience in the hospital and I would appreciate the opportunity to meet with you.

Sincerely,

Christina J. Smith

Christina J. Smith

Follow these guidelines when writing your cover letter:

- Include the date either on the left or right margin.

- Include your full contact information at the top of the page. This information includes your full name, home address, phone number, and e-mail address. You can center this information at the top of the page, or you can position it along the left margin.

- Include the name and address of the employer to whom you are applying. Use whatever information you have available or follow the instructions provided in the advertisement you are answering. If you do not have the hiring manager's name, use *Hiring Manager*, *Office Manager*, or *Human Resources Manager*.

- Your salutation should match the addressee indicated above. If you know the person's name, you can use it, but make sure your greeting is professional and not overly familiar. It is appropriate to use *Dear Ms. So-and-So* or *Dear Mr. So-and-So*. It is *not* appropriate to greet the person by his or her first name or to use *Mrs.* for a female addressee. The greeting should be followed by a colon, such as *Dear Hiring Manager:* or *Dear Ms. Jones:*

- Take your time when drafting the body of your cover letter. Remember, the employer will form a first impression of you based on this letter. The content of your message may vary, but in general you should:

  o state your name and express your interest in working as a massage therapist for the particular employer.

  o summarize your education and experience. If you just graduated and do not have relevant experience, include the duties you performed during your internship or skills you acquired at school.

  o request an interview and indicate when you are available. It is best to make a general statement about availability rather than indicate specific times you might be available. Say something like *available at your convenience*.

  o close the letter with the word *sincerely* or *regards* followed by a comma. Then, skip a few lines and type your name. After you have printed the letter out, you can sign your name in this blank space.

TIP

Always spell check and carefully proofread your cover letter and resume. Read each document word for word. Put your finger on each word and say it aloud. This will help you spot words that you inadvertently omitted. Have someone else proofread your cover letter and resume as well. Sometimes others will spot mistakes you have overlooked.

Browse Job Listings

With a click of a mouse, you can find dozens of massage therapy opportunities online. Many search engines allow you to search for jobs by city and state. For example, simply type "Massage Therapy in PA" into the search engine, and your search results should include all massage therapy positions in Pennsylvania. Look online for classified ads from your local newspaper; most newspapers now post job ads online as well as provide them in print.

Also, check the Web sites and job boards provided by professional organizations such as the American Massage Therapy Association (AMTA).

Contact Local Employers

While online listings are helpful in locating a job, some employers do not advertise jobs on job boards because they have their own Web sites or they have many resumes already on file. This is why it is important to be proactive in your job search. Access the employer's Web site online to see if jobs are posted; if so, follow the instructions to apply. If not, use the contact information provided to approach the employer directly. You can also drop off your resume and cover letter in person. If you do, make sure you are dressed professionally. (See sidebar Dress for Success in this chapter.) Also be prepared to fill out a job application, even if the employer does not have any current openings. You will learn what to bring with you to fill out a job application in the next section.

Applying for Jobs Online

Should you e-mail your resume to prospective employers? If you are responding to a job advertisement asking you to apply via e-mail, you should absolutely e-mail your cover letter and resume. If you are contacting employers who are not currently advertising open positions, or those whose ads indicate you should mail your resume, then the postal service is best. You want to demonstrate that you can follow instructions. You also want to make sure your resume receives the most attention possible.

Complete the Application

Most employers will ask you to complete a job application even after you have submitted a cover letter and resume. A job application requires you to provide specific details about yourself, your education, and your work history. You will need to include specifics about your education and past jobs, so you should have accurate dates, names, addresses, and phone numbers available when you are filling out the application. You may need to indicate if you have a criminal record (generally you only have to tell an employer about convicted felonies) and you may need to agree to a credit check. You will also have to list references and their contact information. Finally, by signing the application, you are attesting to the truthfulness of the information provided. If you lie on the application, you can later be dismissed.

You should gather the following items ahead of time to help you accurately complete a job application:

- Social Security card
- Driver's license
- Copy of your license and certification
- Name and addresses of the schools you attended, along with the dates of attendance
- Names, addresses, and phone numbers of past employers, as well as the dates you worked there
- Names, phone numbers, and e-mail addresses of three professional references

While job applications vary, most ask for the same types of information. Reviewing the following Sample Massage Therapist Job Application will give you an idea of what to expect.

Sample Massage Therapist Job Application

Application for Employment

Personal Employment

Last Name	First	Middle	Date
Street Address			**Home Phone** ( ) -
City, State, Zip			
Business Phone ( ) -			**E-mail Address:**
Are you over 18 years of age? ☐ Yes ☐ No If not, employment is subject to verification of minimum legal age.			
Have you ever applied for employment with us? ☐ Yes ☐ No If Yes: Month and Year _____ Location _____			**Social Security No.** - -
How did you learn of our organization?			
Are you legally eligible for employment in the United States? If no, when will you be able to work?			
Are you employed now? If so, may we inquire of your present employer?			
Have you ever been convicted of a crime in the past ten years, excluding misdemeanors and summary offenses, which has not been annulled, expunged or sealed by the court? ☐ Yes ☐ No If yes, describe in full.			
Are there any reasons for which you might not be able to perform the job duties (with a reasonable accommodation)? ☐ Yes ☐ No If yes, please explain.			
Massage License # **State**	**Certifications/Professional Memberships**		

Education

School	Name and location of school	Course of study	No. of years completed	Did you graduate?	Degree or diploma
College				☐ Yes ☐ No	
High School				☐ Yes ☐ No	
Massage/ Technical				☐ Yes ☐ No	

Licenses, certifications, areas of specialization, seminars, workshops, special training, volunteer work, and any additional information that you feel may be helpful to us in considering your application:

_____

_____

_____

_____

_____

_____

_____

_____

Have you had training in any of the following?

☐ Deep Tissue ☐ Hot Stone ☐ Prenatal Massage ☐ Spa

Employment History

Please give accurate, complete full-time and part-time employment record. Start with the present or most recent employer.

1.	Company Name	Telephone ( ) -
	Address	Employed (Start Mo. & Yr.) From To
	Name of Supervisor	Hourly Rate Start Last
	Starting Job Title and Describe Your Work	Reason for Leaving

- 2 -

2.	Company Name		Telephone ( ) -
	Address		Employed (Start Mo. & Yr.) From To
	Name of Supervisor		Hourly Rate Start Last
	Starting Job Title and Describe Your Work		Reason for Leaving
3.	Company Name		Telephone ( ) -
	Address		Employed (Start Mo. & Yr.) From To
	Name of Supervisor		Hourly Rate Start Last
	Starting Job Title and Describe Your Work		Reason for Leaving

We may contact the employers listed above unless you indicate those you do not want us to contact.	Do not contact Employer number(s)_____ Reason_____

References: Give below the names of three persons not related to you, whom you have known at least one year.

Name	Address	Business	Years Acquainted
1.			
2.			
3.			

The information provided in this Application for Employment is true, correct, and complete. If employed, any misstatements or omissions of fact on this application may result in my dismissal. I understand that acceptance of an offer of employment does not create a contractual obligation upon the employer to continue to employ me in the future.

_____   _____
                Date   Signature

- 3 -

Dress for Success

You should dress as professionally as possible for the environment. Some employers are more casual than others, and while it is okay to dress a little more casually in those environments, it is best if you wear dress clothing that is appropriate and fits you well. For example, casual slacks or a casual skirt is appropriate. A button-down shirt is a good option. If you are a woman, wear low-heeled shoes. Do not wear jeans, shorts, t-shirts, sneakers, sandals, or flip-flops. Make sure your hair is neat and away from your face. Remove any facial piercings. Men should shave all facial hair, although a neatly trimmed beard is often acceptable. Women should wear only light makeup.

Ace the Interview

You will be asked to participate in a job interview if an employer is interested in hiring you. A job interview is an opportunity for you and the prospective employer to get to know each other and determine if you are a mutually good fit.

When it comes to job interviews, preparation is the key to success. Always arrive about 10 minutes early. If necessary, scout out the area beforehand, so you know exactly where to go and where to park. Dress professionally; it is always better to be overdressed than to be too casually attired. (See the sidebar Dress for Success above.) Bring several copies of your resume as well as any documentation that you need to complete the job application.

When you arrive, be polite and friendly to anyone you meet. Introduce yourself, smile, and shake hands. Be patient if you are asked to wait. Respond politely to anyone who greets you while you wait. When you are introduced to the interviewer, greet him or her with a firm handshake. When you are escorted into the interviewer's office, refrain from taking a seat until you are instructed to do so.

Job interviews can be stressful. The best way to overcome that stress is to prepare beforehand. Think about the questions that you are likely to be asked and practice responding to them out loud. If a friend or family member is willing to assist you with this preparation, you can get another person's perspective on what you plan to say.

The following are some common interview questions. Practice your responses to these aloud, preferably with another person.

- **Tell me about yourself.** Respond with information about your education and work experience and any relevant skills you bring to the table. You can also make general remarks about personal traits that would be applicable to the workplace, such as the ability to learn quickly.

- **Tell me about the duties you performed during your internship/last job.** It is especially helpful to write out your answer to this question beforehand. While you cannot use these notes during your interview, composing the response beforehand will help you to think through a good summary of the tasks you completed.

- **Why do you want to work here?** Be honest. What interests you about the employment opportunity? It is fine to say that you are eager to begin a career as a massage therapist, but a response that considers the environment or work you will do is best.

- **How would you handle XYZ?** Most employers want to get a feel for how you behave in stressful or problematic situations. For a massage therapist, this might involve how to handle a client who is irate or behaving inappropriately, or what you might do if a client is late or does not show up for a scheduled appointment, etc. Consider what you learned during your educational program about how best to handle situations that may commonly occur in the particular environment.

- **Why should I hire you?** Why should they hire you? Consider your personal qualities, education, and work experience. How will the employer benefit from having you on staff? Remember, the interviewer is trying to determine what you can do for the organization, not what the organization can do for you. No matter how you choose to answer this question, be sure to back up your response with facts. For example, "Clients are able to relax fully in my care. During my internship, …"

TIP

While it is acceptable to ask questions during the job interview, you should plan to ask questions about the specific position, the clients, or the employing organization, as this shows interest. Refrain from asking about salary, benefits, or time off. Once you are offered the job, you can ask about salary and other perks.

When the interviewer is asking you questions, make sure you are listening. That means you will hear and respond to the entire question. The interviewer will notice that you are a good listener rather than one who is waiting for the other person to stop talking. Make sure you use appropriate grammar. Do not use profanity or slang in any of your responses (even if the interviewer does).

Answer all questions honestly and completely. Do not be afraid to say, "No, I don't have experience with that yet, but I would really like to learn." After the interview, thank the person for his or her time, and follow up with a thank-you note via e-mail or postal mail.

NOTE

When you interview for a job, some of the questions you will be asked are easy to answer. For example, you will likely be asked about your education and experience with clients or particular techniques. Other questions may be more difficult, such as "What is your greatest weakness?" These questions are not meant to trick you, but they are meant to show the employer how you view yourself. For this type of question, you should respond with an area where you are weak BUT you should also tell what you have done or what you plan to do to overcome this. For example, you might say that your greatest weakness is taking on too much at one time, and you are learning to ask for help when you need it.

SUMMING IT UP

- The first question to answer in this journey is: What are the requirements to practice massage therapy and/or bodywork in my location? Use the resources in the *Appendix C: Helpful Resources* to make sure the path you set for yourself will adequately prepare you to practice.

- Select your school carefully. Consider the school's accreditation status as well as factors such as business operation, reputation, tuition, class size, and class offerings. Make sure the program will work with your schedule and budget before you start.

- After you have completed your course of study, you can apply and prepare for the appropriate examination. Use all of the study materials in this book to make sure you can pass the exam of your choosing.

- Once you have successfully completed the exam, apply for a license in the location where you want to practice.

- You can decide if you want to work for yourself or if you would rather start out working for someone else. If you plan to work for yourself, contact the Small Business Administration (SBA) office in your area for assistance in setting up your business. If you plan to work for someone else, prepare your resume and cover letter and begin your job search.

- If you are selected as a potential candidate for a position, you will need to complete a job application and prepare for an interview. The job application asks for specific information that is usually not included on your resume, such as your Social Security number and references. You will also need to provide the particulars on former employers.

- Preparation is the key to easing your nerves during a job interview. Practice responding to common interview questions. You will find that the more you practice out loud, either by yourself or with another person, the more easily you will be able to answer questions during the interview.

PART II

Diagnosing Strengths and Weaknesses

CHAPTER 3
Practice Test 1: Diagnostic   49

ANSWER SHEET PRACTICE TEST 1: DIAGNOSTIC

1. Ⓐ Ⓑ Ⓒ Ⓓ	28. Ⓐ Ⓑ Ⓒ Ⓓ	55. Ⓐ Ⓑ Ⓒ Ⓓ	82. Ⓐ Ⓑ Ⓒ Ⓓ	109. Ⓐ Ⓑ Ⓒ Ⓓ
2. Ⓐ Ⓑ Ⓒ Ⓓ	29. Ⓐ Ⓑ Ⓒ Ⓓ	56. Ⓐ Ⓑ Ⓒ Ⓓ	83. Ⓐ Ⓑ Ⓒ Ⓓ	110. Ⓐ Ⓑ Ⓒ Ⓓ
3. Ⓐ Ⓑ Ⓒ Ⓓ	30. Ⓐ Ⓑ Ⓒ Ⓓ	57. Ⓐ Ⓑ Ⓒ Ⓓ	84. Ⓐ Ⓑ Ⓒ Ⓓ	111. Ⓐ Ⓑ Ⓒ Ⓓ
4. Ⓐ Ⓑ Ⓒ Ⓓ	31. Ⓐ Ⓑ Ⓒ Ⓓ	58. Ⓐ Ⓑ Ⓒ Ⓓ	85. Ⓐ Ⓑ Ⓒ Ⓓ	112. Ⓐ Ⓑ Ⓒ Ⓓ
5. Ⓐ Ⓑ Ⓒ Ⓓ	32. Ⓐ Ⓑ Ⓒ Ⓓ	59. Ⓐ Ⓑ Ⓒ Ⓓ	86. Ⓐ Ⓑ Ⓒ Ⓓ	113. Ⓐ Ⓑ Ⓒ Ⓓ
6. Ⓐ Ⓑ Ⓒ Ⓓ	33. Ⓐ Ⓑ Ⓒ Ⓓ	60. Ⓐ Ⓑ Ⓒ Ⓓ	87. Ⓐ Ⓑ Ⓒ Ⓓ	114. Ⓐ Ⓑ Ⓒ Ⓓ
7. Ⓐ Ⓑ Ⓒ Ⓓ	34. Ⓐ Ⓑ Ⓒ Ⓓ	61. Ⓐ Ⓑ Ⓒ Ⓓ	88. Ⓐ Ⓑ Ⓒ Ⓓ	115. Ⓐ Ⓑ Ⓒ Ⓓ
8. Ⓐ Ⓑ Ⓒ Ⓓ	35. Ⓐ Ⓑ Ⓒ Ⓓ	62. Ⓐ Ⓑ Ⓒ Ⓓ	89. Ⓐ Ⓑ Ⓒ Ⓓ	116. Ⓐ Ⓑ Ⓒ Ⓓ
9. Ⓐ Ⓑ Ⓒ Ⓓ	36. Ⓐ Ⓑ Ⓒ Ⓓ	63. Ⓐ Ⓑ Ⓒ Ⓓ	90. Ⓐ Ⓑ Ⓒ Ⓓ	117. Ⓐ Ⓑ Ⓒ Ⓓ
10. Ⓐ Ⓑ Ⓒ Ⓓ	37. Ⓐ Ⓑ Ⓒ Ⓓ	64. Ⓐ Ⓑ Ⓒ Ⓓ	91. Ⓐ Ⓑ Ⓒ Ⓓ	118. Ⓐ Ⓑ Ⓒ Ⓓ
11. Ⓐ Ⓑ Ⓒ Ⓓ	38. Ⓐ Ⓑ Ⓒ Ⓓ	65. Ⓐ Ⓑ Ⓒ Ⓓ	92. Ⓐ Ⓑ Ⓒ Ⓓ	119. Ⓐ Ⓑ Ⓒ Ⓓ
12. Ⓐ Ⓑ Ⓒ Ⓓ	39. Ⓐ Ⓑ Ⓒ Ⓓ	66. Ⓐ Ⓑ Ⓒ Ⓓ	93. Ⓐ Ⓑ Ⓒ Ⓓ	120. Ⓐ Ⓑ Ⓒ Ⓓ
13. Ⓐ Ⓑ Ⓒ Ⓓ	40. Ⓐ Ⓑ Ⓒ Ⓓ	67. Ⓐ Ⓑ Ⓒ Ⓓ	94. Ⓐ Ⓑ Ⓒ Ⓓ	121. Ⓐ Ⓑ Ⓒ Ⓓ
14. Ⓐ Ⓑ Ⓒ Ⓓ	41. Ⓐ Ⓑ Ⓒ Ⓓ	68. Ⓐ Ⓑ Ⓒ Ⓓ	95. Ⓐ Ⓑ Ⓒ Ⓓ	122. Ⓐ Ⓑ Ⓒ Ⓓ
15. Ⓐ Ⓑ Ⓒ Ⓓ	42. Ⓐ Ⓑ Ⓒ Ⓓ	69. Ⓐ Ⓑ Ⓒ Ⓓ	96. Ⓐ Ⓑ Ⓒ Ⓓ	123. Ⓐ Ⓑ Ⓒ Ⓓ
16. Ⓐ Ⓑ Ⓒ Ⓓ	43. Ⓐ Ⓑ Ⓒ Ⓓ	70. Ⓐ Ⓑ Ⓒ Ⓓ	97. Ⓐ Ⓑ Ⓒ Ⓓ	124. Ⓐ Ⓑ Ⓒ Ⓓ
17. Ⓐ Ⓑ Ⓒ Ⓓ	44. Ⓐ Ⓑ Ⓒ Ⓓ	71. Ⓐ Ⓑ Ⓒ Ⓓ	98. Ⓐ Ⓑ Ⓒ Ⓓ	125. Ⓐ Ⓑ Ⓒ Ⓓ
18. Ⓐ Ⓑ Ⓒ Ⓓ	45. Ⓐ Ⓑ Ⓒ Ⓓ	72. Ⓐ Ⓑ Ⓒ Ⓓ	99. Ⓐ Ⓑ Ⓒ Ⓓ	126. Ⓐ Ⓑ Ⓒ Ⓓ
19. Ⓐ Ⓑ Ⓒ Ⓓ	46. Ⓐ Ⓑ Ⓒ Ⓓ	73. Ⓐ Ⓑ Ⓒ Ⓓ	100. Ⓐ Ⓑ Ⓒ Ⓓ	127. Ⓐ Ⓑ Ⓒ Ⓓ
20. Ⓐ Ⓑ Ⓒ Ⓓ	47. Ⓐ Ⓑ Ⓒ Ⓓ	74. Ⓐ Ⓑ Ⓒ Ⓓ	101. Ⓐ Ⓑ Ⓒ Ⓓ	128. Ⓐ Ⓑ Ⓒ Ⓓ
21. Ⓐ Ⓑ Ⓒ Ⓓ	48. Ⓐ Ⓑ Ⓒ Ⓓ	75. Ⓐ Ⓑ Ⓒ Ⓓ	102. Ⓐ Ⓑ Ⓒ Ⓓ	129. Ⓐ Ⓑ Ⓒ Ⓓ
22. Ⓐ Ⓑ Ⓒ Ⓓ	49. Ⓐ Ⓑ Ⓒ Ⓓ	76. Ⓐ Ⓑ Ⓒ Ⓓ	103. Ⓐ Ⓑ Ⓒ Ⓓ	130. Ⓐ Ⓑ Ⓒ Ⓓ
23. Ⓐ Ⓑ Ⓒ Ⓓ	50. Ⓐ Ⓑ Ⓒ Ⓓ	77. Ⓐ Ⓑ Ⓒ Ⓓ	104. Ⓐ Ⓑ Ⓒ Ⓓ	131. Ⓐ Ⓑ Ⓒ Ⓓ
24. Ⓐ Ⓑ Ⓒ Ⓓ	51. Ⓐ Ⓑ Ⓒ Ⓓ	78. Ⓐ Ⓑ Ⓒ Ⓓ	105. Ⓐ Ⓑ Ⓒ Ⓓ	132. Ⓐ Ⓑ Ⓒ Ⓓ
25. Ⓐ Ⓑ Ⓒ Ⓓ	52. Ⓐ Ⓑ Ⓒ Ⓓ	79. Ⓐ Ⓑ Ⓒ Ⓓ	106. Ⓐ Ⓑ Ⓒ Ⓓ	133. Ⓐ Ⓑ Ⓒ Ⓓ
26. Ⓐ Ⓑ Ⓒ Ⓓ	53. Ⓐ Ⓑ Ⓒ Ⓓ	80. Ⓐ Ⓑ Ⓒ Ⓓ	107. Ⓐ Ⓑ Ⓒ Ⓓ	134. Ⓐ Ⓑ Ⓒ Ⓓ
27. Ⓐ Ⓑ Ⓒ Ⓓ	54. Ⓐ Ⓑ Ⓒ Ⓓ	81. Ⓐ Ⓑ Ⓒ Ⓓ	108. Ⓐ Ⓑ Ⓒ Ⓓ	135. Ⓐ Ⓑ Ⓒ Ⓓ

Practice Test 1: Diagnostic

Directions: Choose the option that best answers the questions.

1. The MOST important element of your practice is
   (A) working up your SOAP notes.
   (B) maintaining constant communication.
   (C) sharing detailed knowledge of techniques.
   (D) always being punctual.

2. One of your regular clients seems to be becoming more and more emotionally attached to you. During one session, she lets you know she's getting divorced. This situation might be an example of
   (A) the development of dual roles.
   (B) emotional transference.
   (C) a violation of the client's boundaries.
   (D) countertransference.

3. A business with only one owner is known as a
   (A) limited liability company.
   (B) corporation.
   (C) sole proprietorship.
   (D) partnership.

4. What reduces friction and absorbs shock in the joints at the end of the long bones?
   (A) Articular cartilage
   (B) Haversian canals
   (C) Canaliculi
   (D) Concentric lamallae

5. Muscular contractions that change the length of the muscle are called
   (A) resistant contractions.
   (B) concentric contractions.
   (C) isometric contractions.
   (D) isotonic contractions.

6. The sternocleidomastoid (SCM), hamstring, and biceps brachii muscles are all considered
   (A) adductors.
   (B) extensors.
   (C) flexors.
   (D) abductors.

7. The term *range of motion* can be best described as the
   (A) amount of movement at a joint.
   (B) volume of degeneration within a joint.
   (C) degree of hyperextension of the joint.
   (D) ability to stretch the joint fully.

8. In the skull, the frontal bone and the parietal bones are joined at the
   (A) lambdoidal suture.
   (B) squamosal suture.
   (C) coronal suture.
   (D) occipital crest.

9. The four concerns in a marketing plan include
   (A) product, place, price, promotion.
   (B) plan, product, price, promotion.
   (C) people, product, purpose, promotion.
   (D) product, people, purpose, promotion.

10. In states in which massage-related regulations define "massage" broadly, decisions as to whether a law or regulation applies to a certain form of bodywork are generally made by
    (A) county leadership.
    (B) state massage board.
    (C) municipal government.
    (D) chamber of commerce.

11. Which of these is true about static stretching?
    (A) It is always active and never passive.
    (B) It is always both passive and active.
    (C) It is neither passive nor active.
    (D) It is either passive or active.

12. All the following are physiological benefits of massage EXCEPT
    (A) increased nutrition to the muscles.
    (B) improved digestion process.
    (C) development of more blood cells.
    (D) enhanced healing process.

13. The muscle that adducts the arm, medially rotates the arm, and assists in arm extension is the
    (A) triceps brachii.
    (B) teres major.
    (C) teres minor.
    (D) infraspinatus.

14. The longest muscle in the body is known as the
    (A) sartorius.
    (B) rectus femoris.
    (C) rectus abdominis.
    (D) tensor fascia latae.

15. Heat treatments are contraindicated during massage for which of the following conditions?
    (A) Myopia
    (B) Muscular dystrophy
    (C) Myofibrositis
    (D) Multiple sclerosis

16. In the anatomical position, the radius is considered _____ to the forearm bone.
    (A) lateral
    (B) distal
    (C) proximal
    (D) superior

17. The _____ dermis is made up primarily of loose connective tissue.
    (A) reticular
    (B) papillary
    (C) merocrine
    (D) apocrine

18. Zoning laws serve to regulate the
    (A) interior design of massage establishments.
    (B) number of practices allowed in a certain region.
    (C) issuance of business licenses to massage therapy practitioners.
    (D) areas massage therapists can operate in a municipality.

19. During an anterior postural assessment, you notice the client's right shoulder seems to be elevated when compared with the left shoulder. This is considered a deviation off the
    (A) transverse plane.
    (B) sagittal plane.
    (C) medial plane.
    (D) bilateral plane.

20. During range-of-motion assessment, normal end feel is classified as
    (A) hard, soft, or firm.
    (B) soft, firm, or springy block.
    (C) firm, empty, or spasm.
    (D) hard, soft, or empty.

21. The triceps surae consists of these two other muscles.
    (A) Gastrocnemius and soleus.
    (B) Tibialis posterior and periosteum.
    (C) Tibialis anterior and plantaris.
    (D) Rectus femoris and tibialis posterior.

22. During visual assessment of a new client, you notice an area of skin that appears noticeably paler than others. You believe this might indicate a localized area of reduced blood supply. On your SOAP notes, the most appropriate description for this condition would be
    (A) "localized area of pale skin."
    (B) "possible localized ischemia."
    (C) "abnormal-looking patch of skin."
    (D) nothing; you would not include this information.

23. The soft connective tissue in the medullary cavity of a bone is called the
    (A) periosteum.
    (B) endosteum.
    (C) bone marrow.
    (D) spongy bone.

24. The chemical effects of hydrotherapy are felt when
    (A) water pressure is applied to the surface of the body.
    (B) the temperature of the water differs from body temperature.
    (C) water is taken orally or used for irrigation purposes.
    (D) the body surface comes in contact with moving water.

25. Which stroke technique involves the application of pressure intended to move superficial tissue across deep tissue?
    (A) Kneading
    (B) Percussion
    (C) Friction
    (D) Effleurage

26. The integumentary system does all of the following EXCEPT
    (A) protect against infectious microorganisms.
    (B) protect against dehydration.
    (C) store water, fat, and vitamin D.
    (D) promote the excretion of uric acid.

27. For which of the following conditions is massage absolutely contraindicated?
    (A) Irritable bowel syndrome
    (B) HIV
    (C) Deep vein thrombosis
    (D) Pancreatitis

28. Your client displays sagittal plane deviations of the knee joint demonstrated by an excessive degree of flexion. What assessment tool would you use to observe this phenomenon?
    (A) Gait assessment
    (B) Intuitive assessment
    (C) Muscular palpation
    (D) Stretching exercises

29. A massage therapist wants to find out more about a specific drug. Which of the following references would be the BEST one for the massage therapist to use?
    (A) A Web site such as Wikipedia
    (B) A drug reference book for physicians
    (C) A promotional pamphlet by the drug manufacturer
    (D) A personal conversation with a current user of the drug

30. To ensure the right amount of pressure is applied during a session, the therapist should begin by applying
    (A) varying pressure.
    (B) medium pressure.
    (C) light pressure.
    (D) firm pressure.

31. The basement membrane exists between which of the following?
    (A) Epidermis and dermis
    (B) Dermis and papillary layer
    (C) Epidermis and sweat ducts
    (D) Rete pegs and papillary layer

32. Which of the following is a function of a white blood cell?
    (A) Defending the body against viruses
    (B) Carrying oxygen to the body's cells
    (C) Helping the body digest food
    (D) Aiding body movements

33. While conducting a postural assessment, you note that the client's toes are deviated medially. This means the toes are
    (A) pointed inward.
    (B) pointed outward.
    (C) pointed downward.
    (D) in a normal state.

34. At what stage of mitosis do chromosomes form?
    (A) Prophase
    (B) Metaphase
    (C) Anaphase
    (D) Telophase

35. When it is no longer able to contract despite continued stimulation, a skeletal muscle fiber is said to be
    (A) refreshed.
    (B) fatigued.
    (C) resting.
    (D) immersed.

36. The joint with the greatest range of motion in the body is the
    (A) knee.
    (B) neck.
    (C) shoulder.
    (D) elbow.

37. In which of the following areas of the body is transitional epithelium found?
    (A) Lungs
    (B) Bladder
    (C) Taste buds
    (D) Skin

38. During a client assessment, you notice the appearance of several knots along the client's hamstring. When you palpate these areas, the client seems to experience discomfort. These knots most likely indicate the presence of
    (A) trigger points.
    (B) hypertonic joints.
    (C) tissue edema.
    (D) ischemia.

39. The left and right side of the human body have the same muscles. This is an example of body
    (A) duplicity.
    (B) stability.
    (C) symmetry.
    (D) originality.

40. Which of the following is the most effective way to assess a client's posture prior to massage treatment?
    (A) Postural analysis chart
    (B) Body scanner
    (C) Posture questionnaire
    (D) Floor mat

41. In which of the following would you find fibrous connective tissue?
    (A) Adipose
    (B) Bone
    (C) Tendons
    (D) Blood

42. Universal precautions are utilized by health-care professionals, including massage therapists, to stop the spread of infection. All of the following practices are useful in achieving this goal EXCEPT
    (A) using cloth rather than paper towels.
    (B) sanitizing the massage table cover.
    (C) washing linens after each use.
    (D) practicing regular hand washing.

43. Which of the following should be avoided when conducting massage treatment on a client with scleroderma?
    (A) Warming massage
    (B) Cold therapy
    (C) Massage while sitting up
    (D) ROM exercises

44. In the lungs, the structures responsible for exchanging oxygen from the air with carbon dioxide in the blood are called
    (A) alveoli.
    (B) trachea.
    (C) bronchi.
    (D) lobe.

45. Which of the following terms describes the relative position of the elbow to the wrist?
    (A) Anterior
    (B) Superior
    (C) Posterior
    (D) Inferior

46. If you could see the fascia of the body, it would MOST closely resemble a protective covering over the
    (A) muscles.
    (B) nerves.
    (C) entire body.
    (D) organs.

47. In scientific studies, researchers have learned that children who do not experience enough touch while they are young
    (A) tend to enter the health-care and medical fields.
    (B) develop emotional attachment and anger problems.
    (C) cannot bear to be touched as adults.
    (D) generally become more nurturing parents to their own children.

48. Which of the following techniques greatly stimulates nerve centers?
    (A) Kneading
    (B) Light stroking
    (C) Friction
    (D) Light percussion

49. Which structure in the heart delivers oxygen-rich blood to other parts of the body?
    (A) Aorta
    (B) Pericardium
    (C) Tricuspid valve
    (D) Right coronary artery

50. Metabolism is defined as the
    (A) breakdown of glucose to provide energy.
    (B) chemical reactions completed by the body.
    (C) conversion of pyruvic acid into ATP molecules.
    (D) total amount of energy produced by the body.

51. During a session, the massage therapist is concentrating on the anterior brachial region of the body. This means the therapist is mainly working on the client's
    (A) arms.
    (B) neck.
    (C) knees.
    (D) shoulders.

52. Which of the following parts of the body contains a hinge joint?
    (A) Hip
    (B) Elbow
    (C) Shoulder
    (D) Wrist

53. Which of the following statements about anabolism is true?
    (A) Anabolic reactions use energy.
    (B) Anabolic reactions produce monomers.
    (C) Anabolic reactions release energy.
    (D) Anabolic reactions consume adrenaline.

54. A massage therapist is treating a client with a mild case of hemophilia. Which of the following is the BEST approach to use with this client?
    (A) Inform the client that massage is contraindicated for individuals with hemophilia.
    (B) Focus on vigorous massage techniques during the therapy session.
    (C) Provide an intense massage but keep the session relatively short.
    (D) Use only gentle massage techniques while treating the client.

55. The levels of two body hormones are regulated by a negative feedback loop. Let's say hormone "F" is released in the brain. The release of this hormone stimulates the release of hormone "H." When this occurs, the release of hormone H will MOST likely
    (A) not affect the levels of hormone F.
    (B) inhibit the release of hormone F.
    (C) cause more of hormone H to be released.
    (D) stimulate the release of hormone F.

56. Which of the following is a characteristic associated with the anatomical position?
    (A) The feet are together.
    (B) The head is turned to the side.
    (C) The arms are held overhead.
    (D) The palms face forward.

57. What is the term for the plane that divides the body into left and right sections?
    (A) Coronal plane
    (B) Transverse plane
    (C) Frontal plane
    (D) Sagittal plane

58. Which of the following is a product of catabolism?
    (A) Nucleic acids
    (B) Proteins
    (C) Fatty acids
    (D) Lipids

59. The interphalangeal and metacarpophalangeal joints of the fingers are capable of different types of movement. Which of the following types of joint movement is possible for the metacarpophalangeal joints but impossible for the interphalangeal joints?
    (A) Flexion
    (B) Extension
    (C) Adduction
    (D) Opposition

60. Which of the following BEST describes the purpose of homeostatic mechanisms?
    (A) They help maintain balanced levels of nutrient concentrations and hormones within the body.
    (B) They help ensure that body systems are able to change in response to numerous factors.
    (C) They help maintain equilibrium or stability with respect to the internal functioning of the body.
    (D) They help ensure that body temperature remains the same regardless of the environment.

61. The transverse plane divides the body into what two regions?
    (A) Left and right
    (B) Anterior and posterior
    (C) Superior and inferior
    (D) Lateral and medial

62. The femur is adducted and medially rotated at the hip by the
    (A) gluteus medius.
    (B) quadratus femoris.
    (C) latissimus dorsi.
    (D) pectineus.

63. Which of the following hormones regulates blood calcium levels?
    (A) Parathyroid hormone
    (B) Oxytocin
    (C) Luteinizing hormone
    (D) ACTH

64. The largest body cavity in the human body is the
   (A) dorsal body cavity.
   (B) abdominopelvic cavity.
   (C) ventral body cavity.
   (D) thoracic cavity.

65. Which area of the body is associated with the posterior popliteal region?
   (A) Behind the ear
   (B) Below the stomach
   (C) Behind the knee
   (D) Under the lower back

66. Range-of-motion exercises in which the massage therapist moves the client's body part without assistance from the client are referred to as which of the following?
   (A) Active
   (B) Resistive
   (C) Resting
   (D) Passive

67. Which of the following is the etiology of Bell's palsy?
   (A) Low levels of glucose in bloodstream
   (B) Degeneration of the spinal cord
   (C) Compression of a cranial nerve
   (D) Weakening of bones around the skull

68. Which of the following is a posterior body region?
   (A) Occipital
   (B) Epigastric
   (C) Pectoral
   (D) Inguinal

69. While assessing a new client, you note that his calf muscles appear to be hypertonic. This means the client's calf muscles are likely
   (A) seriously injured.
   (B) in a normal state.
   (C) excessively loose.
   (D) excessively tight.

70. Which of the following represents the organism level of anatomic organization?
   (A) A heart
   (B) A person
   (C) A cell
   (D) A skeletal system

71. The part of the knee that would be classified as medial is the
   (A) back of the knee.
   (B) front of the knee.
   (C) inside of the knee.
   (D) outside of the knee.

72. A client is currently on her fourth day of a course of antibiotics. Based on this fact, how should the massage therapist alter treatment?
   (A) Make the treatment more conservative.
   (B) Ask the client for feedback less frequently.
   (C) Massage the tissues more aggressively.
   (D) Ask the client to sit up during treatment.

73. Which of the following structures supplies blood to the kidneys?
   (A) Renal pelvis
   (B) Renal arteries
   (C) Renal papilla
   (D) Renal corpuscles

74. In an embryo, one of the structures into which the mesoderm will develop is the
   (A) bladder.
   (B) intestines.
   (C) lungs.
   (D) heart.

75. Osteoarthritis is common among elderly individuals. All of the following are symptoms of the condition EXCEPT
   (A) joint tearing.
   (B) joint swelling.
   (C) joint stiffness.
   (D) joint pain.

76. Which of the following is a characteristic of superficial fascia?
   (A) It is somewhat flexible and allows organs to move.
   (B) It covers the muscles to divide and protect them.
   (C) It is a subcutaneous layer covering the entire body.
   (D) It can become knotted and cause extreme pain.

77. Which of the following is an example of an active stretch?
    (A) Performing a complete split
    (B) Holding a leg in the air
    (C) Bending your right wrist with your left hand
    (D) Placing your foot on a table and bending forward

78. At what stage during infancy do babies begin to develop control over head movements?
    (A) 1 month
    (B) 4 months
    (C) 8 months
    (D) 12 months

79. The human body includes how many major body systems?
    (A) 10
    (B) 11
    (C) 12
    (D) 13

80. The muscle located nearest the sciatic nerve is the
    (A) piriformis.
    (B) gracilis.
    (C) gluteus medius.
    (D) pectineus.

81. What musculoskeletal disorder is often caused by repetitive hand movements?
    (A) Degenerative joint disease
    (B) Scoliosis
    (C) Carpel tunnel syndrome
    (D) Sciatica

82. If you place your finger inside an infant's hand, the infant will grasp your finger tightly. This is known as the
    (A) galant grasp reflex.
    (B) plantar grasp reflex.
    (C) palmar grasp reflex.
    (D) babkin grasp reflex.

83. During what stage of wound healing do fibroblasts start to enter the site of injury?
    (A) Inflammatory
    (B) Clotting cascade
    (C) Proliferative
    (D) Remodeling

84. What is typically the first physical sign that a female is entering puberty?
    (A) Breast development
    (B) Hair growth
    (C) Onset of menstruation
    (D) Increase in height

85. During postural assessment, a lateral view of the client reveals a reduced lordotic curve; anterior head and pelvis positioning; and posterior, hyperextended knees. These symptoms most likely indicate
    (A) ideal posture.
    (B) flat-back posture.
    (C) possible scoliosis.
    (D) sway-back posture.

86. Reciprocal inhibition is a common occurrence between muscles in agonist/antagonist relationships. Reciprocal inhibition refers to the fact that when one muscle in the pair contracts, the other will
    (A) not be affected.
    (B) increase in size.
    (C) relax.
    (D) contract.

87. When autocrine action occurs, hormones act on
    (A) the cell producing the hormone.
    (B) cells near the cell producing the hormone.
    (C) the cell directly next to the cell producing the hormone.
    (D) cells far away from the cell producing the hormone.

88. Which of the following massage benefits can be assisted with cold therapy?
    (A) Increased blood flow
    (B) Anaesthetic effect on muscles
    (C) Increased joint mobility
    (D) Muscle tissue relaxation

89. All of the following are methods by which lymph travels through the body EXCEPT
    (A) the force of the heart's pumping.
    (B) massage and bodywork.
    (C) muscular contractions.
    (D) body movement.

90. A massage therapist is assessing a client using end feel. When the client's elbow is halfway extended, the client asks the massage therapist to stop because the client is experiencing pain. This is an example of what type of end feel?
    (A) Empty
    (B) Capsular
    (C) Springy block
    (D) Tissue approximation

91. Which of these BEST describes reflexology?
    (A) It is intended to return the body to a state of structural balance.
    (B) It is aimed at changing internal organs and tissues via the massage of specific body parts.
    (C) It is designed to help clients unlearn various restrictive movement habits.
    (D) It is a type of therapy in which the practitioner performs a series of rolling moves intended to stimulate the parasympathetic nervous system.

92. The posterior, superior iliac crest is an example of a(n)
    (A) endangerment site.
    (B) adhesion.
    (C) bony landmark.
    (D) soft tissue.

93. In which of the following techniques does the massage therapist provide enough resistance to prevent a joint from moving?
    (A) Muscle energy technique
    (B) Isometric contraction
    (C) Strain-counterstrain technique
    (D) Concentric contraction

94. All the following are physiological effects of massage EXCEPT
    (A) improved elasticity of the skin.
    (B) decreased joint mobilization.
    (C) increased blood circulation.
    (D) reduced stress.

95. When you perform any sort of work activity, according to the principles of ergonomics, you should exert muscular force using
    (A) your torso, primarily.
    (B) your legs and core muscles.
    (C) the largest suitable muscle groups available.
    (D) only the extremities.

96. Which type of stretching is NOT normally practiced by massage therapists?
    (A) Passive-assisted
    (B) Reciprocal inhibition
    (C) Active-assisted
    (D) Ballistic

97. A client comes in for an upper back massage, but is unable to get herself onto the table. How should you proceed?
    (A) Perform the massage with the client in a seated position.
    (B) Lift the client onto the table yourself.
    (C) Perform the massage with the client bent over the side of the table.
    (D) Break down the table and have the client lie on it on the floor.

98. During which type of contraction is the joint itself prevented from actually moving?
    (A) Isometric
    (B) Concentric
    (C) Isotonic
    (D) Eccentric

99. Which of these BEST describes the kneading technique?
    (A) It consists of rolling, lifting, and squeezing movements.
    (B) It is used to transition from one part of the body to another.
    (C) It is primarily intended to move superficial tissue across deep tissue.
    (D) It can loosen phlegm in the respiratory tract when performed on the back.

100. Which of the following soft tissue techniques is used primarily for working out adhesions and stretching and loosening the muscles and fascia?
    (A) Compression
    (B) Gliding
    (C) Vibration
    (D) Kneading

101. Heat therapy would be contraindicated for a client who presents with
    (A) poor circulation.
    (B) severe muscular tension.
    (C) inflammation.
    (D) muscle spasms.

102. When you introduce clients to the RICE technique, you are teaching them a method of self-care that focuses on
    (A) decreasing pain.
    (B) stretching.
    (C) increasing safety.
    (D) strengthening.

103. All of the following are commonly used to sanitize the various objects used in a massage therapy practice EXCEPT
    (A) wet sanitizers.
    (B) autoclaves.
    (C) moist heat.
    (D) dry sanitizers.

104. When working on a client, you can best avoid exaggerated wrist angles by
    (A) staying behind the massage movements.
    (B) using moderate force.
    (C) staying on top of the massage movements.
    (D) applying force with the fingers or thumbs.

105. Although massage involves both physical and psychological factors, your focus should always be on the client's physical well-being BECAUSE
    (A) psychological issues can be resolved physically.
    (B) client physical health supersedes mental health.
    (C) psychological treatment is outside your scope of practice.
    (D) physical needs can be treated more easily than mental ones.

106. A client you are treating for severe low back pain cannot comfortably lie face down on the massage table. To make him more comfortable, you should place some form of support under his
    (A) chest.
    (B) abdomen.
    (C) knees.
    (D) ankles.

107. During a massage session, the therapist may incorporate both static and dynamic stretching. What is the main difference between these types of stretches?
    (A) The degree to which the muscle is stretched
    (B) The application of assistance
    (C) The length of time the stretches are held
    (D) The application of resistance

108. After finishing a treatment session, you meet a colleague from another practice for dinner. During the meal, you reveal personal information about the client whose treatment you just completed. You did not have the client's consent to do so. As a result, you are in violation of
    (A) scope of practice.
    (B) client/therapist relationship.
    (C) HIPAA.
    (D) the client's boundaries.

109. A fire breaks out at your practice overnight and results in thousands of dollar's worth of damage. In order to be financially protected from a loss of this type, you would need to have
    (A) professional liability insurance.
    (B) workers compensation.
    (C) disability insurance.
    (D) business owner's insurance.

110. If you choose to make up an original name for your practice, you must first file a fictitious name statement with the
    (A) federal government.
    (B) state government.
    (C) county government.
    (D) municipal government.

111. Which of the following would fall outside your scope of practice?
    (A) Performing spinal manipulation on a client
    (B) Selling massage-related products at your practice
    (C) Asking a client how her sick child is feeling
    (D) Referring a client to a physician

112. In an effort to control pain, the human body releases which of the following?
    (A) Oxytocin
    (B) Aldosterone
    (C) Androgens
    (D) Endorphins

113. The primary source of energy in the human body is/are
    (A) oxygen.
    (B) ATP.
    (C) cofactor.
    (D) lysosomes.

114. The primary reason to form relationships with other local massage practitioners and medical professionals is to
    (A) become familiar with how others run their businesses.
    (B) build a network of professionals to refer clients to and from.
    (C) gain an edge over your competitors.
    (D) expand your technical and practical knowledge.

115. Instructing a client to take a specific medication for a physical problem she's experiencing would be an example of
    (A) breached scope of practice.
    (B) client transference.
    (C) dual roles.
    (D) HIPAA violation.

116. During the client interview, asking appropriate follow-up questions to the client's comments in order to avoid misunderstanding is an example of
    (A) intuitive listening.
    (B) active listening.
    (C) observational assessment.
    (D) visual assessment.

117. The nerves pass through the scapula via the
    (A) scapular notch.
    (B) greater tubercle.
    (C) glenoid fossa.
    (D) infraspinatus fossa.

118. Which of the following is a characteristic of healthy posture in a seated position?
    (A) The shoulders are rolled forward.
    (B) The back is slightly arched.
    (C) The feet are flat on the floor.
    (D) The knees are at a 45-degree angle.

119. An example of a chronic condition is
    (A) influenza.
    (B) bone fracture.
    (C) osteoporosis.
    (D) heart attack.

120. Which of the following statements about the effect of acute inflammation on tissue is NOT true?
    (A) Blood vessels in the area dilate.
    (B) Blood flow to the area increases.
    (C) Plasma flows into the tissues.
    (D) Tissues become less permeable.

121. Revealing personal information about yourself to a client during the course of an interview or a massage would be considered
    (A) transference.
    (B) self-disclosure.
    (C) a boundary violation.
    (D) countertransference.

122. Special instructions for the client should be included in which portion of the SOAP system?
    (A) Subjective
    (B) Objective
    (C) Assessment
    (D) Planning

123. Passive range of movement can be used to evaluate all of the following EXCEPT
    (A) joint capsules.
    (B) ligaments.
    (C) tendons.
    (D) joints.

124. Which of the following is a cause of macular degeneration?
    (A) Damage to the bone structure
    (B) Damage to the muscular tissue
    (C) Damage to the auditory hair cells
    (D) Damage to the retina

125. What is the region located at the end of the long bones called?
    (A) Endosteum
    (B) Diaphysis
    (C) Metaphysis
    (D) Epiphysis

Directions: The next ten questions are addressed on the MBLEx only. Questions of this type are not found on the NCETMB or NCETM. Choose the option that best answers the questions.

126. In 1894, the Society of Trained Masseuses was formed in
    (A) China.
    (B) the United States.
    (C) Canada.
    (D) the United Kingdom.

127. Which of the following famous medical professionals used massage as a treatment for hysteria?
    (A) Sigmund Freud
    (B) Carl Jung
    (C) Henry Heimlich
    (D) Leo Kanner

128. All of the following are countries in which massage was practiced thousands of years ago EXCEPT
    (A) Greece.
    (B) China.
    (C) Spain.
    (D) Rome.

129. Assessing a client from a holistic point of view means focusing on
    (A) traditional healing techniques.
    (B) the client's spirituality.
    (C) removing toxins from the body.
    (D) the mind-body connection.

130. Some common massage terminology, such as *effleurage* and *petrissage*, is derived from what language?
    (A) French
    (B) Indian
    (C) Japanese
    (D) Swedish

131. Which of the following is considered the first chakra?
    (A) Sacral chakra
    (B) Root chakra
    (C) Third-eye chakra
    (D) Heart chakra

132. Which of the following BEST describes the Vata dosha?
    (A) Combination of air and space
    (B) Combination of fire and water
    (C) Combination of water and earth
    (D) Combination of air and fire

133. All of the following are true about the triple warmer meridian EXCEPT
    (A) it can distribute energy throughout the entire body.
    (B) its meridian is yang.
    (C) its meridian is located on the lower half of the body.
    (D) it regulates energy.

134. Which of the following is the energy that coils at the root chakra and can be filtered through the body via yoga and meditation?
    (A) Kundalini
    (B) Muladhara
    (C) Swadhisthana
    (D) Vishuddha

135. Which of these is considered the natural energy of the universe?
    (A) Chi
    (B) Dosha
    (C) Chakra
    (D) Manipura

ANSWER KEY AND EXPLANATIONS

1. B	28. A	55. B	82. C	109. D
2. B	29. B	56. D	83. C	110. C
3. C	30. C	57. D	84. A	111. A
4. A	31. A	58. C	85. B	112. D
5. D	32. A	59. C	86. C	113. B
6. C	33. A	60. C	87. A	114. B
7. A	34. A	61. C	88. B	115. A
8. C	35. B	62. D	89. A	116. B
9. A	36. C	63. A	90. A	117. A
10. B	37. B	64. C	91. B	118. C
11. D	38. A	65. C	92. C	119. C
12. C	39. C	66. D	93. B	120. D
13. B	40. A	67. C	94. B	121. B
14. A	41. C	68. A	95. C	122. D
15. D	42. A	69. D	96. D	123. C
16. A	43. B	70. B	97. A	124. D
17. B	44. A	71. C	98. A	125. D
18. D	45. B	72. A	99. A	126. D
19. A	46. C	73. B	100. D	127. A
20. A	47. B	74. D	101. C	128. C
21. A	48. D	75. A	102. A	129. D
22. B	49. A	76. C	103. B	130. A
23. C	50. B	77. B	104. A	131. B
24. C	51. A	78. B	105. C	132. A
25. C	52. B	79. B	106. B	133. C
26. D	53. A	80. A	107. C	134. A
27. C	54. D	81. C	108. C	135. A

1. **The correct answer is (B).** Maintaining constant communication with the client is the most important element in your practice. Communication is the driving force behind any massage therapy practice. Nothing is more important than how you interact with your clients.

2. **The correct answer is (B).** In this situation, the client is becoming too dependent on the therapist to meet her emotional needs in relation to the issues she is having with her husband. As such, it exemplifies the concept of transference.

3. **The correct answer is (C).** A business owned by a single person is referred to as a *sole proprietorship*.

4. **The correct answer is (A).** Articular cartilage is the material that covers the ends of the bones of any joint. Haversian canals are any of the small canals through which the blood vessels ramify in bone. Canaliculi are tiny canals that connect adjacent cells in bone. Concentric lamellae are collagen fibers in bone.

5. **The correct answer is (D).** Contractions that permit muscles to shorten are called *concentric contractions*. Contractions that allow the muscle to remain the same are called *isometric contractions*. Contractions during which the muscle changes length are called *isotonic contractions*.

6. **The correct answer is (C).** The sternocleidomastoid (SCM), hamstring, and biceps brachii muscles are all *flexors*—which are muscles that flex joints. *Adductors* are muscles that draw body parts inward toward the median axis of the body or extremity. *Extensors* are muscles that extend joints. *Abductors* are muscles that draw body parts away from the midline of the body or extremity.

7. **The correct answer is (A).** *Range of motion* is defined as the range through which a joint can be moved, usually its range of flexion and extension.

8. **The correct answer is (C).** The lambdoidal suture joins the parietal and occipital bones. The squamosal suture joins the parietal to the temporal bone. The occipital crest is a ridge in the occipital bone.

9. **The correct answer is (A).** The four concerns of a marketing plan include product, place, price, and promotion.

10. **The correct answer is (B).** In states where laws or regulations broadly define the practice of massage, it is usually the state board of massage that decides questions regarding the application of the law/regulation to any particular kind of practice.

11. **The correct answer is (D).** Static stretching is a technique that can be either passive or active. In a passive static stretch, the therapist holds the stretch until resistance is felt. In an active static stretch, the client contracts the muscle until he or she feels the resistance.

12. **The correct answer is (C).** Massage can help the body in countless ways, including by increasing the healing process, improving digestion, and increasing nutrition to the muscles. It does not, however, stimulate the body to create new blood cells.

13. **The correct answer is (B).** The triceps brachii extends the forearm. The teres minor is part of the rotator cuff and laterally rotates the arm. The infraspinatus is also part of the rotator cuff and laterally rotates the arm.

14. **The correct answer is (A).** The sartorius is the body's longest muscle; it runs from the hip to the knee. The rectus femoris is a division of the quadriceps muscle lying in the anterior middle region of the thigh. The rectus abdominis is a long flat muscle extending along the length of the front of the abdomen. The tensor fascia latae is a muscle that arises from the anterior part of the iliac crest.

15. **The correct answer is (D).** For those who have multiple sclerosis, massage should focus on reducing stress and pain and maintaining mobility, but heat treatments should be avoided. Heat treatments are not contraindicated for those with myopia (a condition related to eyestrain), muscular dystrophy (muscle disorder), or myofibrositis (pain associated with myofascial trigger points).

16. **The correct answer is (A).** *Lateral* means toward the side. *Distal* means located away from the center of the body. *Proximal* means located toward the center of the body. *Superior* means situated toward the head and farther away from the feet.

17. **The correct answer is (B).** The reticular layer of the dermis consists of dense irregular connective tissue that differs from the papillary layer, which

is made up of mainly loose connective tissue. Merocrine and apocrine are types of sweat glands.

18. **The correct answer is (D).** Zoning laws are established to govern the types of businesses that are allowed to operate in various parts of a municipality.

19. **The correct answer is (A).** The transverse plane divides the body into upper and lower sections. The sagittal plane divides the body vertically into left and right sections that can be equal (median) or unequal (parasagittal) in size.

20. **The correct answer is (A).** Normal end feels are created by normal anatomical structures and are classified as hard, soft, or firm. Abnormal end feels are created by abnormal anatomical structures and are classified as hard, soft, firm, springy block, spasm, or empty.

21. **The correct answer is (A).** Collectively, the gastrocnemius and the soleus are known as the triceps surae.

22. **The correct answer is (B).** Your SOAP notes may be reviewed by other health-care providers; thus, it is important for you to use appropriate medical terminology wherever possible.

23. **The correct answer is (C).** Bone marrow is a soft connective tissue that occupies the cavities of most bones. Periosteum is the membrane of connective tissue that closely invests all bones except at the articular surfaces. Endosteum is the layer of vascular connective tissue lining the medullary cavities of bone.

24. **The correct answer is (C).** The chemical effects of hydrotherapy are felt when water is applied orally or used to irrigate one of the body cavities.

25. **The correct answer is (C).** Friction involves the application of pressure intended to move superficial tissue across deep tissue.

26. **The correct answer is (D).** As the body's covering, the integumentary system (the skin) functions in all the ways described, with the exception of promoting the excretion of uric acid; the urinary system supports this function.

27. **The correct answer is (C).** A person with deep vein thrombosis should not receive massage treatment since the associated increase in blood flow could possibly cause an embolism if a thrombus detaches from a vessel wall. Individuals with irritable bowel syndrome, HIV (as long as overall health is good), and pancreatitis (as long as it has been treated by a physician) are all candidates for massage treatment.

28. **The correct answer is (A).** Deviations of the knee joint as demonstrated by excessive flexion would be observed visually and most likely during assessment of the client's gait.

29. **The correct answer is (B).** When researching drugs, massage therapists should use authoritative sources that are accepted by the medical community, such as drug reference books designed for physicians, pharmacists, and other health-care providers. The other sources may not provide information that is sufficiently thorough or entirely accurate.

30. **The correct answer is (C).** The therapist should always begin with light pressure, which can be increased as necessary.

31. **The correct answer is (A).** The basement membrane exists between the epidermis and dermis. The papillary layer is part of the dermis. Rete pegs are elongated downward-projecting ridges of epidermis.

32. **The correct answer is (A).** White blood cells are a vital part of the body's immune system. Red blood cells carry oxygen, and muscle cells help with digestion and locomotion.

33. **The correct answer is (A).** *Medial deviation* indicates pointing inward.

34. **The correct answer is (A).** The chromatin in cells condenses into chromosomes that contain the cell's genetic information during prophase. Metaphase, anaphase, and telophase all occur after prophase.

35. **The correct answer is (B).** Muscle fatigue occurs when the muscle is taken past the point of exhaustion.

36. **The correct answer is (C).** The shoulder is a ball-and-socket joint. This type of joint has the greatest range of motion as it can move in each of the anatomical planes.

37. **The correct answer is (B).** Transitional epithelium is found in the bladder as well as the ureters and

the urethra. Squamous epithelium is found in the lungs, columnar epithelium is found in the taste buds, and keratinized epithelium is found in the skin.

38. **The correct answer is (A).** Trigger points are small knots within a muscle. During palpation, these knots feel uncomfortable or painful to the client.

39. **The correct answer is (C).** The body is symmetrical in many ways—the body of a person with good posture can be divided into two equal halves (left and right) if a line is drawn down the center.

40. **The correct answer is (A).** A postural analysis chart is a grid that assists the therapist in identifying problems that may need to be addressed during treatment.

41. **The correct answer is (C).** Fibrous connective tissue is made up of tightly packed collagen fibers. It is found in tendons, cartilage, and ligaments. Adipose, bone, and blood are all special types of connective tissue.

42. **The correct answer is (A).** Maintaining a hygienic environment should be a top goal for any massage therapist, and sanitizing equipment, washing linens after each use, and washing hands after each session can all help protect clients and the therapist from infection. Using disposable paper towels instead of cloth towels can also help prevent the spread of infection.

43. **The correct answer is (B).** Cold therapy and the application of extreme heat should both be avoided when treating an individual with scleroderma. Warming massage is indicated, ROM exercises can be beneficial even though ROM may be limited, and massage may need to be provided while the client is sitting up if he/she has breathing problems.

44. **The correct answer is (A).** Clusters of alveoli within larger alveolar sacs carry out gas exchange within the lungs. The trachea (or windpipe) and bronchi are organs that help carry air into the lungs, and the term *lobe* is used to refer to different areas of each lung (upper right, lower left, etc.).

45. **The correct answer is (B).** The elbow is superior to the wrist because it is located above it. The wrist is inferior to the elbow, and anterior and posterior are used to describe relative positions when one structure is in front of or behind another.

46. **The correct answer is (C).** Fascia creates a protective covering for all of the structures of the body, including the muscles, nerves, organs, bones, and blood vessels.

47. **The correct answer is (B).** Children who do not experience much bodily touch during their formative years can develop anger issues and have problems bonding with others. Findings like these help scientists prove that touch therapy like massage offers both psychological and physiological benefits.

48. **The correct answer is (D).** Light percussion stimulates the nerve centers; however, prolonged percussion can cause the nerves in the area to go numb.

49. **The correct answer is (A).** The aorta is the body's largest artery, extending all the way into the abdomen and delivering oxygenated blood throughout the body. The right coronary artery supplies blood to the heart, the tricuspid valve stops blood from flowing backward, and the pericardium is the protective sac that surrounds the heart.

50. **The correct answer is (B).** Metabolism is defined as all of the chemical reactions necessary to maintain life. Choices (A) and (C) describe two metabolic pathways (specific chemical reactions) that occur within cells; energy is the result of metabolic reactions.

51. **The correct answer is (A).** The term *brachial* is associated with the arm. Cervical, patellar, and deltoid refer to the body regions associated with the neck, knees, and shoulders, respectively.

52. **The correct answer is (B).** Hinge joints such as those in the elbows and knees only allow motion in a single plane. The hip and shoulder contain ball-and-socket joints, while the wrist contains gliding and other types of joints (but no hinge joints).

53. **The correct answer is (A).** Anabolic reactions combine simpler molecules (monomers) to create more complex ones (polymers), a process that requires energy. Catabolic reactions release energy, and adrenaline is an example of a hormone related to catabolism.

54. **The correct answer is (D).** Therapists can use gentle massage techniques on individuals with mild cases of hemophilia. More vigorous or intense techniques should not be used as they might cause injury.

55. **The correct answer is (B).** Hormone H will inhibit the release of hormone F, which will in turn inhibit the release of hormone H, thereby regulating the levels of both hormones. No feedback loop occurs if hormone H levels do not affect hormone F levels; choices (C) and (D) are outcomes associated with a positive feedback loop.

56. **The correct answer is (D).** In the anatomical position, the person is facing forward with palms forward, the feet slightly apart, and the arms held at the sides.

57. **The correct answer is (D).** A sagittal plane divides a body vertically into left and right sections that can be equal (median) or unequal (parasagittal) in size. The coronal (or frontal) plane divides the body into front and back sections, while the transverse plane divides the body into upper and lower sections.

58. **The correct answer is (C).** One example of a catabolic reaction is the breakdown of lipids into fatty acids. Nucleic acids and proteins are both products of anabolic reactions.

59. **The correct answer is (C).** Both joints are capable of flexion and extension, and the metacarpophalangeal joints are also capable of adduction and abduction. The carpometacarpal joint found in the thumb is capable of opposition.

60. **The correct answer is (C).** Homeostasis is the ability of an internal environment to remain at equilibrium, something that is accomplished through various homeostatic mechanisms. Choices (A) and (D) are examples of outcomes of homeostatic mechanisms but are too specific to be the best choices, and choice (B) is not consistent with the definition of homeostasis.

61. **The correct answer is (C).** The transverse plane divides the body horizontally into two regions: upper and lower (superior and inferior). The sagittal plane divides the body into left and right regions. The frontal plane divides the body into front and back (anterior and posterior) regions. Lateral and medial are not terms associated with body planes.

62. **The correct answer is (D).** The pectineus is the flat quadrangular muscle of the upper inner thigh. The gluteus medius is the middle muscle in the buttocks that rotates the thigh. The quadratus femoris is the small flat muscle in the gluteal region that rotates the thigh laterally. The latissimus dorsi is the broad, flat muscle of the lower back.

63. **The correct answer is (A).** The parathyroid gland secretes parathyroid hormone to control blood calcium levels—more is produced in response to low calcium levels and less is produced in response to elevated calcium levels. Oxytocin stimulates the contractions that occur during childbirth, luteinizing hormone stimulates ovulation (females) and testosterone production (males), and ACTH stimulates the production of steroid hormones.

64. **The correct answer is (C).** The ventral body cavity is larger than the dorsal body cavity and contains the heart, spleen, kidneys, and other organs. The abdominopelvic cavity and thoracic cavity are subdivisions of the ventral body cavity.

65. **The correct answer is (C).** The posterior popliteal region is the depression found on the back of the leg behind the knee joint. The area behind the ear is associated with the mastoid region, the area below the stomach is associated with the hypogastric region, and the area under the lower back (lumbar region) is associated with the sacral region.

66. **The correct answer is (D).** Moving the client's body parts through their range of motion without any assistance from the client is called *passive range of motion*. In this movement, the client's joints are completely relaxed. Active range of motion involves the client moving his or her body through the range of motion. In resistive range of motion, you move the client's body but the client resists the motions.

67. **The correct answer is (C).** Bell's palsy is caused by damage to the seventh cranial nerve. This nerve contains motor neurons responsible for facial expression, blinking, and other facial movements.

68. **The correct answer is (A).** The back of the head (posterior) is considered the occipital region.

The epigastric (abdominal), pectoral (chest), and inguinal (groin) regions are all anterior.

69. **The correct answer is (D).** *Hypertonic* means "excessively tight."

70. **The correct answer is (B).** The organism level of anatomic organization includes all of the systems, cells, and so on that are part of a living being. A cell is at the cellular level, a heart is at the organ level, and the skeletal system is at the organ system level.

71. **The correct answer is (C).** The inside of the knee is the portion closest to the center of the body, and is therefore considered medial. The outside of the knee is lateral. Neither the front nor the back of the knee would be classified as medial or lateral.

72. **The correct answer is (A).** It is usually acceptable to perform massage treatment after the third day of a course of antibiotics. However, the therapist should exercise caution to ensure that the treatment has no ill effects for the client.

73. **The correct answer is (B).** The renal arteries receive blood from the abdominal aorta and deliver it to the kidneys. The renal pelvis and renal papillae are involved in urine transport, while the main function of the renal corpuscles is filtration.

74. **The correct answer is (D).** The embryonic mesoderm develops into the heart, muscles, kidneys, and other structures. The bladder, intestines, and lungs are all formed from the endoderm.

75. **The correct answer is (A).** Osteoarthritis can affect the joints in almost all areas of the body, including those in the hips, knees, spine, and hands. Common symptoms are swelling, stiffness, and pain in the joints—but not joint tearing.

76. **The correct answer is (C).** Superficial fascia is the top layer of fascia lying under the skin. It covers the entire body. Choice (A) describes subserous fascia, while choices (B) and (D) describe deep fascia.

77. **The correct answer is (B).** An active stretch relies solely on the strength of the muscle. A passive stretch is completed with the aid of another object or body part. In choice (A), this assistance is provided by the floor; in choice (C), it is the left hand; and in choice (D), it is the table.

78. **The correct answer is (B).** Babies start developing head control at about 3 to 4 months. At 8 months most babies can sit up and at 12 months most can stand on their own.

79. **The correct answer is (B).** The human body has 11 major body systems: skeletal, muscular, cardiovascular, nervous, endocrine, lymphatic, respiratory, integumentary, digestive, urinary, and reproductive.

80. **The correct answer is (A).** The sciatic nerve starts at the back of the pelvis and runs under the buttock downward through the hip area into each leg. The piriformis muscle is located in the lower part of the spine and connects to the thighbone. The sciatic nerve runs beneath it.

81. **The correct answer is (C).** Carpel tunnel syndrome is often caused by repetitive hand motions. Symptoms include nerve pain and numbness in the median nerve. Degenerative joint disease can be caused by aging or injury, scoliosis is typically caused by a congenital defect or injury, and sciatica can be caused by poor posture, overexertion, and other factors.

82. **The correct answer is (C).** The palmar grasp reflex causes infants to grasp fingers or other objects placed across the palm. The galant reflex occurs when you stroke a baby's back; the plantar reflex occurs when the sole of a baby's foot is stimulated; the babkin reflex occurs when pressure is applied to both palms.

83. **The correct answer is (C).** The proliferative stage of wound healing occurs when fibroblasts enter the area, where they carry out important functions such as producing collagen. The inflammatory phase (which includes the clotting cascade) helps close over the wound and remove debris and bacteria from the area. The remodeling phase follows the proliferative phase.

84. **The correct answer is (A).** Although all of the choices are puberty related, breast development is typically the first change associated with puberty. Menstruation typically starts within two years of puberty onset. Hair growth and increases in height are generally observed during the time between breast development and menstruation.

85. **The correct answer is (B).** Ideal posture presents as symmetrical alignment along the plumb line. Scoliosis presents with non-level shoulders and ears as well as a deviation of the spine from the midsagittal line. Sway-back posture presents with excessive kyphosis, anterior head, shoulders, and pelvis, with the palms facing posterior.

86. **The correct answer is (C).** In reciprocal inhibition, muscles work in agonist/antagonist pairings. When one of the muscles contracts, the opposing muscle will relax.

87. **The correct answer is (A).** Autocrine action occurs when a cell produces hormones and the hormones act on that same cell. When endocrine action occurs, hormones travel through the blood and work on cells located far away from the hormone-producing cell. When paracrine action occurs, hormones act on a cell close to the hormone-producing cell.

88. **The correct answer is (B).** Cold treatments generally slow down the flow of blood to the outer parts of the body. They also work to numb, or anaesthetise, the muscles and other tissues.

89. **The correct answer is (A).** The force of the heart does not cause lymph to flow through the body. The cardiac circulatory system uses the heart as a pump to move blood through the body. The lymphatic system does not have a pump. Instead, it relies on muscle contractions, body movement, and massage to be moved through the system.

90. **The correct answer is (A).** An empty end feel occurs when a client will not allow the practitioner to push a joint to the end of its range of motion because of pain. A capsular end feel is when a joint capsule limits a joint's range of motion, a springy block is an end feel characterized by a rubbery sensation felt before the normal maximum range of motion is reached, and tissue approximation is an end feel in which motion is stopped by soft tissue.

91. **The correct answer is (B).** Reflexology is a type of bodywork centered on the belief that massaging certain parts of the hands, feet, and ears can effect positive changes in corresponding internal organs and tissues.

92. **The correct answer is (C).** A bony landmark is a groove or prominence on a bone that serves as a guide to the location of other body structures. An endangerment site is a part of the body not protected by connective skeletal tissue or muscle. An adhesion is a fibrous band or structure. Soft tissue is body tissue.

93. **The correct answer is (B).** During an isometric contraction, the therapist provides enough resistance to prevent joint movement. In a similar technique, the isotonic contraction, the massage therapist gives partial resistance.

94. **The correct answer is (B).** Massage helps increase, rather than decrease, joint mobilization. Massage and bodywork help loosen joints and improve their range of motion.

95. **The correct answer is (C).** The principles of ergonomics state that when you perform any work activity, you should exert muscular force using the largest suitable muscle groups available.

96. **The correct answer is (D).** The ballistic method of stretching is not usually performed by massage therapists, because it requires the practitioner to use a bouncing movement in an attempt to force the limb past the point of resistance.

97. **The correct answer is (A).** In the event that a client is unable to get on the table, you may be able to work on the client in a seated position, depending on the type of massage the client requires.

98. **The correct answer is (A).** In an isometric contraction, the client and the therapist each apply an equal amount of resistance so as to prevent the joint from moving.

99. **The correct answer is (A).** Kneading, which is also known as petrissage, consists of rolling, lifting, and squeezing movements meant to help loosen muscle tissue and fascia and improve muscle tone and circulation.

100. **The correct answer is (D).** Most often, kneading is used to work out adhesions and stretch and loosen the muscles and fascia.

101. **The correct answer is (C).** Heat therapy is not recommended for any client who presents with inflammation of any body part. In such cases, cold therapy would be a more appropriate alternative.

102. **The correct answer is (A).** The Rest-Ice-Compression-Elevation (RICE) technique is a self-care technique designed to help clients reduce the pain they experience due to an injury or other condition.

103. **The correct answer is (B).** Although the use of an autoclave is the preferred method of sterilizing objects in hospitals and other medical facilities, these devices are not commonly found in massage therapy practices.

104. **The correct answer is (A).** The best method of avoiding potentially dangerous exaggerated wrist angles is to stay behind the massage movements.

105. **The correct answer is (C).** Although massage treatment has both physical and psychological effects on clients, it is essential to remember that direct treatment of any psychological or emotional issues is outside your scope of practice.

106. **The correct answer is (B).** Many clients who suffer from severe low back pain experience discomfort when they attempt to lie face down. Providing these clients with some form of support under the abdomen can increase comfort level.

107. **The correct answer is (C).** The main difference between static and dynamic stretching is the length of time the stretch is held. Static stretching involves holding a stretch for a longer period of time, whereas dynamic stretching involves holding a stretch for a short period of time and performing that stretch a number of times.

108. **The correct answer is (C).** In this instance, you are in violation of HIPAA, which governs client confidentiality and privacy. According to the HIPAA law, you are required to obtain the client's consent before revealing her personal information to any third party.

109. **The correct answer is (D).** Financial protection from losses incurred as the result of fire, theft, and similar causes are generally covered by business owner's insurance.

110. **The correct answer is (C).** Business owners who devise an original name for their business are generally required to submit a fictitious name statement to the county government.

111. **The correct answer is (A).** Performing spinal manipulation on a client would fall outside the scope of practice of a massage therapist because this procedure is chiropractic in nature.

112. **The correct answer is (D).** Endorphins, produced by the pituitary gland, induce analgesia and a feeling of well-being. Oxytocin is a hormone that acts primarily as a neuromodulator in the brain. Androgens are natural or synthetic compounds that function as weak steroids or steroid precursors. Aldosterone is a hormone that increases the reabsorption of sodium ions and water and the release (secretion) of potassium ions in the collecting ducts of the kidneys.

113. **The correct answer is (B).** Adenosine triphosphate (ATP) is the primary source of energy in the human body. Lysosomes are saclike cellular organelles containing hydrolytic enzymes. Oxygen plays a vital role in breathing processes. Cofactors are non-protein chemical compounds that assist in biochemical transformations.

114. **The correct answer is (B).** The primary purpose of forming relationships with other massage practitioners and medical professionals is to build a network of professionals to refer clients to and from.

115. **The correct answer is (A).** Massage therapists do not prescribe medications under any circumstances.

116. **The correct answer is (B).** Active listening is a communication skill in which misunderstandings are avoided by actively involving both the sender and the receiver in the communication process. Active listening requires active participation on the part of the listener.

117. **The correct answer is (A).** The greater tubercle is the large projection located lateral to the head of the humerus. The glenoid fossa is the articular surface located at the junction of the superior and lateral borders of the scapula. The infraspinatus fossa is a broad depression located inferior to the spine of the scapula.

118. **The correct answer is (C).** When sitting, the shoulders should be back, the back should be straight, the feet should be flat on the floor, and the knees should be at a 90-degree angle.

119. The correct answer is (C). A chronic condition is one that persists over time, such as osteoporosis, diabetes, or epilepsy. In an acute condition, symptoms appear suddenly but persist only for a relatively short period of time.

120. The correct answer is (D). During acute inflammation, vasodilation occurs, more blood travels to the injured area, plasma flows into the tissues, and the tissues become more permeable.

121. The correct answer is (B). Revealing personal information about yourself to a client (whether consciously or unconsciously) during an interview or massage would be considered self-disclosure and should be avoided.

122. The correct answer is (D). Client instructions, suggestions for future treatments, and follow-up care information should all be included in the planning portion of the SOAP system.

123. The correct answer is (C). Passive range of movement is used to evaluate ligaments, joints, and joint capsules. Active range of movement would be used to evaluate tendons.

124. The correct answer is (D). Macular degeneration is the gradual deterioration of the macula, the center of the field of vision, which is caused by damage to the retina. This disease can result in progressive loss of vision.

125. The correct answer is (D). The endosteum is the layer of vascular connective tissue lining the medullary cavities of bone. The diaphysis is the shaft of a long bone. The metaphysis is the transitional zone where the diaphysis and epiphysis come together.

126. The correct answer is (D). In 1894, the Society of Trained Masseuses formed in the United Kingdom. This group helped popularize massage in Europe.

127. The correct answer is (A). Sigmund Freud used massage to treat hysteria. Freud believed hysteria was caused by repressed memories, and he thought massage would calm the anxiety some of these memories caused.

128. The correct answer is (C). Massage has been practiced for thousands of years in countries such as China, Japan, Greece, Rome, and India. There is no evidence it was practiced in Spain.

129. The correct answer is (D). When you approach a client from a holistic perspective, you take his or her whole being into consideration. This means a focus on the client's mind-body connection.

130. The correct answer is (A). Terms such as *effleurage* and *petrissage* are derived from the French language.

131. The correct answer is (B). The root chakra is the first chakra. The sacral chakra is the second chakra. The third-eye chakra is the sixth chakra, and heart chakra is the fourth chakra.

132. The correct answer is (A). The Vata dosha is a combination of air (essence of hearing) and space (essence of touch).

133. The correct answer is (C). The triple warmer meridian transverses the upper half of the body. The triple warmer meridian is a function rather than an organ, and it distributes and regulates energy throughout the body.

134. The correct answer is (A). The kundalini is thought to be an energy that is like a snake and coiled at the root chakra. Through proper yoga and meditative practices, the kundalini can be unleashed in the body.

135. The correct answer is (A). The *chi* is known as the natural energy of the universe. The literal translation of the word *chi* is "air" or "breath."

PART III
PREPARE AND PRACTICE: MASSAGE THERAPY SUBJECT AREAS

CHAPTER 4
Anatomy and Physiology
71

CHAPTER 5
Kinesiology
85

CHAPTER 6
Pathology
97

CHAPTER 7
Therapeutic Massage and Bodywork Assessment
111

CHAPTER 8
Therapeutic Massage and Bodywork Application
123

CHAPTER 9
Professional Standards and Legal and Business Practices
141

....

Anatomy and Physiology

OVERVIEW

- **Anatomy, physiology, and body systems**
- **Anatomical position and directional terms**
- **Systems of special note for the massage therapist**
- **Tips for answering questions on anatomy and physiology**
- **Practice questions**
- **Answer key and explanations**
- **Summing it up**

Knowledge of the body's configuration and functioning forms a critical foundation for the massage therapist. *Anatomy* is the study of the body's structure. *Physiology* is the study of the body's functioning. You should be able to identify the major structures and systems of the human body and understand what they do. You should also recognize how different structures and systems respond to the application of therapeutic modalities.

As part of your studies, you should be sure to utilize the standard medical terminology to describe the human body and its functioning. Not only will you need to know common terms for your exam, but using appropriate language will underscore your professionalism and facilitate communication with other health-care providers.

Although this chapter does not review every detail of these subjects, it highlights important information and gives you some practice questions in these areas. If you are having trouble understanding the information or answering the practice questions, take some time to review your textbooks and notes from school.

The number of questions you will need to answer on anatomy, physiology, and body systems varies by exam. If you are taking the MBLEx, you will be required to answer a total of 125 questions; of these, about 14 percent, or 18 questions, are on the topics of anatomy, physiology, and body systems. If you are taking the NCETMB, you will be required to answer a total of 160 questions; of these, about 35 percent, or 40 questions, touch on the subjects of anatomy, physiology, and body systems.

ANATOMY, PHYSIOLOGY, AND BODY SYSTEMS

Anatomy is the study of the body's structure. Accumulating and applying a deep knowledge of the way the body works will help you to provide the best treatment for your clients. You will be more likely to recognize when a client is suffering from a particular medical condition or injury. Also, you will understand how to adjust treatment so it is appropriate to a specific situation and how to refer the client to a more appropriate health-care practitioner if that is necessary.

The study of anatomy includes the major *body systems* as well as cellular structure and cellular chemistry. Cellular chemistry is not addressed on your examination, but it is necessary in order to understand how body systems operate. Other important areas of study include joints and muscles.

The human body is comprised of a variety of important systems. Each system has specific functions, but none of the systems is independent of the others; they work together to allow the body to function.

For your examination, you should be able to identify the location and function of the primary body systems, as follows:

- **Cardiovascular/circulatory system:** The cardiovascular or circulatory system controls the circulation of blood through the body and includes the heart as well as blood vessels such as capillaries, arteries, and veins.

- **Endocrine system:** The endocrine system manufactures hormones that affect things such as health, growth, and reproduction. The endocrine system includes endocrine glands such as the pituitary and thyroid glands.

- **Gastrointestinal/digestive system:** The gastrointestinal or digestive system breaks down food substances so they can be absorbed and used by the body. The gastrointestinal system includes the mouth, stomach, intestines, and salivary and gastric glands. Along with understanding how the digestive system works, you should have an understanding of the basic principles of nutrition.

- **Integumentary system:** The integumentary system is the skin. Besides its obvious function in protecting other body systems, the skin is also responsible for regulating the body's temperature and respiration, among other functions. Because you will be in such close contact with the skin of your clients, this is an area requiring careful study.

- **Lymphatic system:** The lymphatic system is sometimes considered part of the cardiovascular system, because its role is to distribute and circulate lymph throughout the body. The lymphatic system includes lymph, the lymph nodes, and lymph vessels.

- **Muscular system:** The muscular system controls the movement of all parts of the body. This system is made up of the various types of muscles present in the body. This is another area that you will need to study carefully; additional information is provided a little later in this chapter.

- **Nervous system:** The nervous system is the hub of awareness. It includes the brain, spinal cord, and the network of nerves threaded through the body. The nervous system is the control center for the body and coordinates all bodily functioning.

- **Reproductive system:** The reproductive system controls human reproduction and includes the genitals and a variety of internal organs and accessory systems.

- **Respiratory system:** The respiratory system controls breathing and includes the nose, mouth, lungs, air passages, the pharynx, trachea, and bronchial tubes.

- **Skeletal system:** The skeletal system is the framework of bones and joints in the body. The skeletal system provides the body's foundation and supports and protects other body systems.

- **Urinary system:** The urinary system produces, stores, and eliminates urine. It includes the kidneys, bladder, and urethra as well as the sphincter muscles.

Energy Systems

Traditional Eastern medicine believes that in addition to the visible physiological systems, the body also has its own energy system, which is sometimes referred to as the *energetic system* or the *meridian system*. The energetic system is called *subtle* because it is not visible to the human eye and is difficult to perceive with other senses. The energetic system forms the body's *aura*, or energy field. The energetic system communicates inside and outside the physical body along *meridian pathways* (energy pathways) and through the *chakras*. The chakras are located at specific parts of the body and are associated with particular organs, body parts, senses, and emotions or areas of consciousness.

The seven chakras begin at the crown and travel down the body. If you are taking the NCETMB examination, you will need to be able to describe the body's energy systems and name and locate the body's chakras. You should also understand standard associations for each chakra.

- **Seventh chakra:** The seventh chakra is also called the *crown chakra*. It is located at the very top of the head and traditionally associated with the brain. This chakra is associated with thought and consciousness.

- **Sixth chakra:** The sixth chakra is also called the *third eye chakra*. It is located between the eyes and is traditionally associated with the eyes, forehead, and temples. This chakra is associated with perception and telepathy.

- **Fifth chakra:** The fifth chakra is also called the *throat chakra*. It is located at the base of the throat and traditionally associated with the upper extremities, neck, and throat. This chakra is associated with communication, expression, and creativity.

- **Fourth chakra:** The fourth chakra is also called the *heart chakra*. It is located in the center of the chest and traditionally associated with the heart, lungs, and circulatory system. This chakra is associated with intuition, love, and relationships.

- **Third chakra:** The third chakra is also called the *solar plexus chakra*. It is located at the solar plexus (midway between the navel and the sternum) and traditionally associated with the digestive system. This chakra is associated with sight and perception (that "gut feeling").

- **Second chakra:** The second chakra is also called the *sacral* or *spleen chakra*. It is located in the center of the abdomen and traditionally associated with the reproductive system. This chakra is associated with passion and sexuality.

- **First chakra:** The first chakra is also called the *root* or *base chakra*. It is located at the base of the spine and traditionally associated with the skeletal system. This chakra is associated with instincts and survival.

EXERCISES: ANATOMY, PHYSIOLOGY, AND BODY SYSTEMS

Directions: Choose the option that best answers the question.

1. The four types of simple epithelial tissues are squamous, cuboidal, columnar, and
   (A) transitional.
   (B) keratinized.
   (C) pseudostratified.
   (D) connective.

   Pseudostratified is a type of simple epithelial tissue that resembles stratified epithelial tissue because the nuclei of cells are located at different heights. Transitional and keratinized are types of stratified epithelial tissue, and connective is an entirely different type of tissue. **The correct answer is (C).**

2. Which of the following is part of the peripheral nervous system?
   (A) Spinal cord
   (B) Cranial nerve
   (C) Brain
   (D) Cerebellum

   The peripheral nervous system consists of nerves that are found outside of the central nervous system, which is made up of the brain (the cerebellum is part of the brain) and the spinal cord. The cranial nerves exit the brain and are therefore part of the peripheral nervous system. **The correct answer is (B).**

ANATOMICAL POSITION AND DIRECTIONAL TERMS

Any time health-care practitioners refer to the human body, they use a universally accepted standard position called the *anatomical position*. In the anatomical position, the human body is standing in an upright position, face forward, with arms at the sides and palms facing front. Using this position as a common orientation point makes it easy for health-care providers to conduct clear and concise discussions about their patients.

Directional terms are universal standards that describe the location of body parts and structures in relation to other structures in the body. Directional terms help to further orient descriptions of human anatomy and also to distinguish different movements of the body. You may find it easier to study directional terms with opposite meanings together.

The terms with which you should be familiar include:

- **Anterior:** Front or situated in front of

- **Posterior:** Rear or situated behind, toward the rear

- **Distal:** Away from, or situated farther from the origin

- **Proximal:** Near or situated closer to the origin

- **Dorsal:** Near the upper surface, or situated toward the back

- **Ventral:** Toward the bottom, or situated toward the belly

- **Superior:** Above or situated over

- **Inferior:** Below or situated under

- **Lateral:** Toward the side, or situated away from the mid-line

www.facebook.com/CareerResource

- **Medial:** Toward the middle, or situated away from the side

- **Rostral:** Situated toward the front

- **Caudal:** Situated toward the back or tail

For purposes of discussion, the body can also be divided into three planes, which is useful for describing specific sections or regions of the body. Planes are created using imaginary lines.

- The *sagittal* or *vertical plane* is created by an imaginary line running vertically through the middle of the body, dividing the body into left and right parts.

- The *coronal* or *frontal plane* is created by an imaginary vertical line dividing the body into front (anterior) and back (posterior) halves.

- The *transverse* or *horizontal plane* is created by an imaginary line running horizontally through the middle of the body; it divides the body into upper and lower halves.

Meridians

Meridians are energy pathways in the body. The concept of the meridians originated with Eastern bodywork modalities and is associated particularly with specialized techniques such as acupuncture. The exact definition and functioning of the meridians varies, depending on the culture you are studying, but in a general sense, they are considered the pathways through which energy and awareness flow through the subtle (non-physical) body.

For the purposes of the NCETMB, you should be able to identify the 6 organ pairs that form the 12 primary meridians in the body. You should also be able to indicate where they are located.

- Bladder ————————> Kidneys

- Gallbladder ————————> Liver

- Heart ————————> Small Intestine

- Lungs ————————> Large Intestine

- Pericardium
  (circulation) ————————> Triple warmer (function rather than a physical organ)

- Stomach ————————> Spleen

EXERCISES: ANATOMICAL POSITION AND DIRECTIONAL TERMS

Directions: Choose the option that best answers the question.

1. In the anatomical position, the body is characterized by all of the following EXCEPT
   (A) lateral thumb position.
   (B) anterior facial position.
   (C) upright body position.
   (D) posterior palms position.

   In the anatomical position, the palms are in the anterior position (facing forward), not the posterior position (facing backward). **The correct answer is (D).**

2. The hand is located at the _____ end of the forearm.
   (A) proximal
   (B) distal
   (C) anterior
   (D) posterior

   Distal means away from, or situated farther from the origin. Proximal means at or near the origin; anterior and posterior refer to the front and back of the body, respectively. **The correct answer is (B).**

SYSTEMS OF SPECIAL NOTE FOR THE MASSAGE THERAPIST

Massage therapists must have a holistic view of the body; that is, you must have a strong understanding of ALL the body systems and the way they interact with one another. For your examination, you should be prepared to answer questions on all of the body's systems. However, due to the amount of practical knowledge you need on both the integumentary and muscular systems, we will look at these systems in a little more detail.

The Integumentary System

Because you will be working in such close proximity to your clients' skin, pay special attention to this topic. *Integumentary* literally means "covering" or "skin." The skin is considered the largest organ in the body and has several key functions, such as providing protection to the internal organs, regulating heat and body temperature, and providing the basic sense of touch.

The skin is made up of two layers: the epidermis, or outer layer, and the dermis, or the subcutaneous layer. The epidermis is multi-layered and comprised of a solid sheet of cells. This layer encases and encloses the body and protects it from foreign invaders such as bacteria. The dermis is made up of a mixture of fibers such as collagen and elastin as well as water and extrafibrillar matrix. The dermis includes a network of cells such as nerves and sweat glands.

Healthy skin is soft, flexible, and somewhat moist. Its texture should be smooth. Skin color will vary, but healthy skin looks healthy; that is, it is even in tone and does not have a yellow, ashy, or red tint. A variety of pathologies

> **TIP**
>
> As you probably recall from your schoolwork, it would be nearly impossible to memorize the meanings of every medical term you might hear or use over the course of your career. Instead, the most effective way to study medical terminology is to learn the meanings of common *prefixes, root words,* and *suffixes.* This allows you to break any unfamiliar medical term down into its parts to understand the meaning.
>
> For example, the word *epidermis* means outermost layer of the skin. If you know that the prefix *epi-* means at, by, or on top of and the root word *dermis* means skin, you can define this word easily.
>
> Using this technique, can you determine what the words *endodermis* and *epidermidis* mean without looking them up?

present with skin disorders such as lesions or tumors. Since you will be in such close contact with the client, you should be able to identify these so you can explain to the client why treatment may not be appropriate.

Problems with nutrition are also frequently reflected in the skin.

The Muscular System

Because soft tissue work involves the muscular system of the body, you should pay special attention to this topic area. *Muscle* is composed of tissue and fibers that are attached by a complex system of *connective tissue,* which is a substance that supports, binds, and connects body structures. The function of muscle is to produce and control force that powers movement of the body. Muscles include *tendons*, which are tough connective tissue that attaches the muscle to bone and allows the body to exert a pulling force.

> **NOTE**
>
> *Fibrous adhesions* result when fascia tissue binds together. This can result from a variety of causes, including surgery, infection, or trauma. Adhesions act as trigger points for pain. One effective treatment of adhesions is myofascial release therapy. *Myofascial* literally means, "Fascia related to the muscles."

Fascia (plural: *fasciae*) is connective tissue that serves a variety of functions, including the wrapping and encasing of individual muscle fibers as well as individual muscles. The body has three layers of fascia: the *superficial* fascia layer that lies directly under the skin and serves as connective tissue between the skin and muscles; *deep* fascia, a strong, densely packed layer that divides and protects the muscles; and *subserous* fascia that lies between deep fascia and the major organs deep inside the body.

Muscle can be classified as one of three types.

1. *Skeletal muscle* makes up the fleshy areas of the body. Skeletal muscle is voluntary because you consciously put it into action. Skeletal muscle attaches to the skeletal frame—bones, skin, and other muscles. Skeletal muscle is also referred to as *striated* muscle.

2. *Cardiac muscle* is found only in the heart. Cardiac muscle propels blood in and out of the heart and powers the circulatory systems.

3. *Smooth muscle* is also called *involuntary* or *nonstriated* muscle. Smooth muscle is located inside the walls of blood vessels and other structures such as the urinary and digestive tracts. Smooth muscle operates automatically, without conscious will.

Skeletal muscle is composed of muscle fibers arranged into bundles called *fascicles*, which form the belly of the muscle. Individual muscle fibers are frequently classified as *fast twitch* or *slow twitch*. Fast twitch fibers are associated with powerful, short bursts of energy that cause rapid fatigue, such as sprinting. Slow twitch fibers are associated with activities of lower intensity and longer duration, such as marathon running. Most people have a predominance of one or the other, based on genetics and activity level.

Some standard terminology is used to describe the direction of muscle fibers.

- *Rectus fibers* run parallel to the long axis of the body or limb; for example, the rectus femoris muscle in the quadriceps.

- *Transverse fibers* run perpendicular to the long axis of the body or limb; for example, the transvere abdominal muscle.

- *Oblique fibers* align at an angle to the long axis of the body or limb; for example, the abdominal obliques.

Structure of Joints

Joints are the locations in the body where bone meets bone. The ends of bones that connect in the joint are called *articulating surfaces*. (Note: Ligaments connect bones to each other, and tendons, which connect muscle to bone, can cross joints.) Joints provide the flexibility that allows the body to move. Joints are classified by the amount and range of motion they permit.

> **TIP**
> No matter which examination you choose to take, you should be able to identify and locate the major muscle groups of the human body, including the upper and lower extremities as well as the abdominals.

- Fixed (*fibrous*) joints do not allow for any movement (or allow only micro-movement), such as those that connect the bones of the skull.

- Slightly moveable (*cartilaginous*) joints allow for a limited range of movement, such as those that connect the bones in the pelvis.

- Synovial (*diarthrotic*) joints move freely within range, such as those at the elbows and knees.

Movable joints in the body are classified as *pivot* joints, *hinge* joints, *ball-and-socket* joints, *gliding* joints, *saddle* joints, and *ellipsoidal* or *condyloid* joints.

- Pivot joints allow for a side-to-side motion. For example, the pivot joints in the cervical spine allow you to turn your head from side to side.

- Hinge joints allow movement similar to the opening and closing of a hinged door. Examples include knees and elbows.

- Ball-and-socket joints allow you to swing the limbs in many different directions. Examples include hip and shoulder joints. These are the most flexible type of joint in the body.

- Gliding joints join two flat bones and allow sideways movement. Examples include some of the bones in the wrists and ankles.

- Saddle joints allow the bones to rock back and forth or from side to side. The only saddle joint in the human body is the location where the thumb meets the wrist/rest of the hand.

- Ellipsoidal or condyloid joints, such as the joint at the base of your index finger, allow bending and extending, rocking from side to side, but rotation is limited.

Cartilage is an elastic substance that cushions the bones at the joints and prevents jarring during motion. Cartilage is also the substance that forms body structures such as the nose and ears. *Ligaments* are fibrous tissue that connect bones to other bones and provide support for the joints. *Bursae* are fibrous sacks that act as a cushion between bones and muscle, tendons, or skin.

EXERCISES: SYSTEMS OF SPECIAL NOTE FOR THE MASSAGE THERAPIST

Directions: Choose the option that best answers the question.

1. In which of the following parts of the body can smooth muscle tissue be found?
   (A) Back muscles
   (B) Heart
   (C) Abdominal muscles
   (D) Iris

   Smooth muscle tissues control body processes outside of our conscious control, including the dilation and constriction of the iris. The heart contains cardiac muscle tissue, and the muscles of the abdomen and back are composed of skeletal muscle tissue. **The correct answer is (D).**

2. Which of the following muscles is found in the back?
   (A) Trapezius
   (B) Iliopsoas
   (C) Pectineus
   (D) Sartorius

   The trapezius is a large muscle that covers parts of the neck, shoulders, and back. The iliopsoas, pectineus, and sartorius are all found in the hip and thigh regions. **The correct answer is (A).**

3. Sudoriferous glands are cutaneous glands of the integumentary system that secrete
   (A) oil.
   (B) sweat.
   (C) follicles.
   (D) sebum.

   The two types of cutaneous glands are sweat-secreting sudoriferous glands and oil- or sebum-secreting sebaceous glands. Follicles are hair-producing structures. **The correct answer is (B).**

TIPS FOR ANSWERING QUESTIONS ON ANATOMY AND PHYSIOLOGY

When answering test questions that deal with anatomy and physiology, you may find it helpful to remember these tips:

- **Anatomy and physiology are interrelated subjects.** Anatomy looks at the structures of the human body while physiology considers how those structures function. Many creative educational materials are available to help you more easily learn about the interrelationship between these subjects. Look in your school textbook, the library, or online for materials such as diagrams or models.

- **Understanding how the body works is essential for selecting and properly executing therapeutic treatment on clients.** Try applying diagnostic tools as you review the diagrams of the human body. For example, if the client's skeletal system shows signs of osteoporosis, what does that mean to you in terms of how you will handle the client?

- **Some systems call for special attention.** You need to know all of the body systems, of course, but you should pay special attention to those body systems that are of the essence for massage therapists and body workers, such as the integumentary and muscular systems.

- **Medical discussions always assume the body is in the anatomical position.** Recognizing the anatomical position is especially important when you are using directional terms, because directional terms describe the locations of structures in the body in relation to other structures or locations in the body.

- **To learn terminology, try using flashcards and a study partner.** You can create flashcards using plain white index cards. Simply write the term on the front of the card and the meaning on the back of the card. Try to find a "study buddy" to work with, perhaps someone who went through your massage program with you. You will maximize your ability to learn if you are quizzing the other person as well as being quizzed yourself.

- **For directional terminology, pair each term with its opposite.** For all other terms, focus on common prefixes, root words, and suffixes. You may find it easier to also match like or opposite items; for example, you may find it easier to remember the meanings of the prefixes *infra*, *inter*, and *intra* if you study them in relationship to each other.

PRACTICE QUESTIONS

Directions: Choose the option that best answers the question.

1. Which of the following make up the most basic level of anatomical organization?
   (A) Atoms
   (B) Molecules
   (C) Cells
   (D) Tissues

2. The function of the mitochondria in cells is to
   (A) store DNA.
   (B) remove waste.
   (C) provide energy.
   (D) synthesize proteins.

3. Which of the following is the BEST definition of an organ?
   (A) A structure that plays a vital role in the functioning of the body
   (B) A body structure that contains one or more of the four tissue types
   (C) A structure that can have either respiratory or circulatory functions
   (D) A body structure containing at least two different types of tissues

4. Which body organ produces bile?
   (A) Spleen
   (B) Liver
   (C) Kidneys
   (D) Pancreas

5. The shoulder complex is comprised of the humerus, the clavicle, and the
   (A) sacrum.
   (B) ilium.
   (C) scapula.
   (D) ischium.

6. Which organ is associated with diabetes?
   (A) Duodenum
   (B) Pituitary gland
   (C) Pancreas
   (D) Adrenal medulla

7. A person is having trouble maintaining normal sleeping patterns. The endocrine system gland most likely involved is the
   (A) parathyroid gland.
   (B) pineal gland.
   (C) adrenal gland.
   (D) thyroid gland.

8. The four classes of macromolecules found in the human body are carbohydrates, lipids, nucleic acids, and
   (A) $H2O$.
   (B) DNA.
   (C) protein.
   (D) $CO2$.

9. The cardiovascular system of the body is comprised of the heart and
   (A) lungs.
   (B) lymphatic vessels.
   (C) muscles.
   (D) blood vessels.

10. The outermost layer of the epidermis is called the stratum
    (A) corneum.
    (B) lucidum.
    (C) granulosum.
    (D) spinosum.

ANSWER KEY AND EXPLANATIONS

1. A	3. D	5. C	7. B	9. D
2. C	4. B	6. C	8. C	10. A

1. **The correct answer is (A).** Atoms are the smallest units of matter found in the body. Molecules are made from atoms, and cells and tissues are more complex than molecules.

2. **The correct answer is (C).** Cell mitochondria converts energy from food into energy that the body can use. The nucleus stores DNA; ribosomes synthesize proteins; and lysosomes remove waste.

3. **The correct answer is (D).** Although the majority of organs are structures containing four main types of tissue, by definition, at least two types of tissue must be present. Choices (A) and (C) are true, but are not the BEST definitions since other structures play important roles in body function, and organs can have other functions besides those related to respiration and circulation.

4. **The correct answer is (B).** The liver has a variety of functions, including the production of bile to aid in digestion. The spleen has certain immune functions; the kidneys help excrete waste; and the pancreas produces hormones and helps with digestion.

5. **The correct answer is (C).** The scapula is more commonly known as the shoulder blade. It connects the humerus of the upper arm to the clavicle, or collarbone. The sacrum, ilium, and ischium are all bones found in the pelvic area.

6. **The correct answer is (C).** The pancreas produces insulin. When an insufficient amount of insulin is produced, diabetes can result. The duodenum helps break down food; the pituitary gland and adrenal medulla release hormones.

7. **The correct answer is (B).** The pineal gland secretes melatonin, which regulates sleep and wake patterns. The parathyroid gland helps regulate calcium levels in the blood and bones; the adrenal gland releases stress-related hormones and plays a role in kidney function; and the thyroid gland helps regulate the body's metabolism.

8. **The correct answer is (C).** Proteins are a type of macromolecule composed of amino acids. H_2O and CO_2 are molecules (not macromolecules) found in the body. DNA is a specific type of nucleic acid.

9. **The correct answer is (D).** The heart pumps blood and the blood vessels transport blood to all areas of the body; together, they make up the cardiovascular system. The lungs and lymphatic vessels are part of the lymphatic system; muscles comprise the muscular system.

10. **The correct answer is (A).** The epidermis consists of five layers; the stratum corneum is the outermost layer. Choices (B), (C), and (D) represent the second, third, and fourth layers of the epidermis, respectively.

SUMMING IT UP

- Anatomy and physiology questions require a fundamental understanding of the human body, its construction, and the ways its systems work. When studying questions pertaining to the human body, focus on the way the systems interrelate with one another.

- Pay close attention to specific details in the questions. Make sure your understanding of common medical terminology is strong.

- While you will, of course, be especially interested in the integumentary and muscular systems, make sure your study of body systems is well-rounded. For both the examination and your practice, it is necessary to have a holistic view of the body and understand how each system affects the others.

CHAPTER 5

Kinesiology

OVERVIEW

- **Characteristics of muscles**
- **Planes of motion**
- **Range of motion**
- **Postural alignment**
- **Tips for answering questions on kinesiology**
- **Practice questions**
- **Answer key and explanations**
- **Summing it up**

Kinesiology is the study of body movement and the body parts involved in movement. This topic is a key area for massage therapists from two perspectives. First, you will find that many of your clients' physical problems originate with or are exacerbated by kinesiological issues like restricted movement, poor postural alignment, and repetitive motion injury. Second, massage therapy is a *physical* profession. In order for you to maintain the ability to pursue this career for the long term, you need to be aware of the positions and movements of your own body, particularly when you are working on clients.

For examination study, at a minimum, you should be able to do the following five things: (1) identify major muscle groups; (2) explain the primary characteristics and actions of different muscle groups; (3) describe general movement patterns, movement of the joints, and the body's range of motion; (4) recognize and describe appropriate postural alignment; and (5) define proprioception and explain what it means.

Although this chapter does not review every detail of these subjects, it highlights important information and gives you some practice questions in these areas. If you are having trouble understanding the information or answering the practice questions, take some time to review your textbooks and notes from school.

The number of questions you will need to answer on kinesiology varies by exam. If you are taking the MBLEx, you will be required to answer a total of 125 questions; of these, about 11 percent, or 14 questions, are on this topic. If you are taking the NCETMB, you will be required to answer a total of 160 questions; of these, between 5 and 10 percent, or 8 to 16 questions, touch on this topic.

CHARACTERISTICS OF MUSCLES

In chapter 4 you reviewed the muscular system in depth. From that study, you will recall that muscle is composed of fibers interwoven with a complex system of connective tissue. Muscle powers all major body functions and movement. It also works with other components in the body to stabilize the body and allow us to stand erect. In short, the role of the muscular system is to produce and control the force that powers movement.

Muscles have unique characteristics, including *irritability*, *contractility*, and *elasticity*.

- *Irritability* (also called *excitability*) is the ability to react to stimuli, such as electrical currents, thermal heat, or nervous impulses.

- *Contractility* is the process of generating tension within the muscle to power movement; for example, when cardiac muscles contract, the heart pumps; when skeletal muscles contract, attached bones are drawn closer together, allowing movement.

- *Elasticity* is muscle's ability to return to its original shape after being stretched.

Muscular Contractions

Muscle contractions are described as *voluntary* and *involuntary*. They originate with the central nervous system in response to conscious thought from the brain (voluntary) or reflexes (involuntary).

Muscle contractions can be described as *concentric, eccentric, isometric*, and *isotonic*.

- During *concentric* contraction, the tension generated is enough to overcome the resistance being applied, and the muscle *shortens* as it contracts. For example, if you perform a bicep curl with a relatively heavy barbell, your bicep muscle will shorten and contract as it responds to the weight load. This is the type of contraction most people think of when they consider muscular contractions.

- During *eccentric* contraction, the tension generated is insufficient to overcome the resistance and the muscle *lengthens* as it contracts. For example, if you place a heavy box gently on the floor rather than allowing it to drop, your bicep muscles will lengthen as they contract in response to the force and movement.

- During *isometric* contraction, the muscle remains the same length. Isometric contraction occurs when the tension matches the load applied to it. For example, if you stood still and held an object such as a box in front of you, the tension and the load would match exactly, and no movement would result.

- During *isotonic* contraction, the tension in the muscle remains constant even though the muscle's length changes. This occurs, for example, when a joint is moved through a range of motion against a fixed resistance. The muscles will shorten or lengthen with the movement but the tension will remain the same.

Muscular contractions allow for the movement of body structures. Muscular contraction may move parts of the skeleton relative to each other (or may move parts of internal organs relative to each other). All movement is classified by the direction in which the affected structures are moved. In human anatomy, movement is described in *planes of motion*, or the direction in which the body part is moved.

EXERCISES: CHARACTERISTICS OF MUSCLES

Directions: Choose the option that best answers the question.

1. One characteristic that all three types of muscle tissue have in common is they all
   (A) are under voluntary control.
   (B) are capable of contracting.
   (C) allow an individual to move.
   (D) perform functions automatically.

Skeletal, cardiac, and smooth muscle tissues can all contract. Skeletal muscles can be controlled voluntarily for the most part and allow an individual to move, while cardiac and smooth muscle tissues are controlled unconsciously (involuntary). **The correct answer is (B).**

2. In which of the following would you find fibrous connective tissue?
   (A) Adipose
   (B) Bone
   (C) Tendons
   (D) Blood

Fibrous connective tissue is made up of tightly packed collagen fibers. It is found in tendons, cartilage, and ligaments. Adipose, bone, and blood are all special types of connective tissue. **The correct answer is (C).**

PLANES OF MOTION

You will recall from your study of anatomy that for purposes of discussion, we use imaginary lines to divide the body into different planes: the lateral or sagittal plane, the frontal or coronal plane, and the transverse plane. These planes correspond to the planes of motions. Humans move in three planes of motion: *sagittal plane, coronal plane,* and *transverse plane*.

- The *sagittal plane* divides the body into left and right sections. Movements in this plane are up-and-down motions called *flexion* and *extension*. Flexion is movement that decreases the angle of a joint (for example, if you straighten your arm and raise it over your head, shoulder flexion occurs). Extension, on the other hand, is movement that increases the angle of a joint (for example, lowering your arm back down is shoulder extension). Many synovial joints are capable of flexion and extension, such as the knee, hip, shoulder, elbow, and wrist.

- The *coronal plane* divides the body into front and back halves. Movement in this plane is sideways and involves moving the body part toward and away from an imaginary center line. This movement is referred to as *abduction* and *adduction*. Abduction moves the body part away from the central line (for example, if you swing your knee outward) while adduction moves the body part toward the central line (for example, if you swing your knee inward). Many joints are capable of abduction and adduction, including the shoulder, hip, and knee.

- The *transverse plane* divides the body into upper and lower halves. Movements in this plane are rotational or twisting in nature, and include *internal* and *external rotation, pronation*, and *supination*. Internal and external rotation involves twisting toward and away from the body. Ball-and-socket joints like the hip, shoulder, and wrist as well as pivot joints such as the neck allow for rotational movement. Pronation is rotational movement in which the palm is turned downward or the sole of the foot is turned outward. Supination is the opposite movement; the palm is turned upward or the foot is turned inward.

- The prefix *hyper-* is sometimes added to indicate movement beyond the normal position, such as *hyperflexion* (flexion beyond the natural range of the joint) and *hyperextension* (extension beyond the natural range of the joint). Hyper-movements can put significant stress on the joints involved.

Ergonomics

Ergonomics is the study of work. More specifically, it is the study of the design and arrangement of the workplace to ensure that work is performed at maximal safety and efficiency. Ergonomics seeks to make work as safe as possible by identifying potential sources of injury and proactively removing or replacing them.

Massage therapy is a physical profession. It involves a near-constant use of the hands and fingers as well as the need to bend and twist over the client. The former may result in repetitive motion disorders, such as carpal tunnel syndrome; the latter might result in a lower back injury.

Understanding ergonomics means being aware of appropriate body mechanics and positioning and being proactive about reducing the physical demands of your job. You might opt to use a hand-held massager for certain therapeutic applications, for example, or replace your massage table with one that is the right height and width for your body.

EXERCISES: PLANES OF MOTION

Directions: Choose the option that best answers the question.

1. Raising your arm in a forward motion is considered what kind of movement?
   (A) Adduction
   (B) Abduction
   (C) Hyperextension
   (D) Hyperflexion

Abduction involves moving the body part away from the body. Adduction involves moving the body part back toward the body. Hypermovements involve overextending the joints. **The correct answer is (B).**

2. What plane divides the body into upper and lower sections?
   (A) Transvere
   (B) Coronal
   (C) Sagittal
   (D) Frontal

The transverse plane divides the body into upper and lower halves. The sagittal plane divides the body into left and right sections. The coronal, or frontal, plane divides the body into front and back halves. **The correct answer is (A).**

RANGE OF MOTION

Joint flexibility is described as a joint's *range of motion* (ROM), or the distance and direction that a particular joint can travel. ROM is a measure of flexibility and it is stated in degrees. Normal ROM means the joint can travel its full distance and direction. Joints with limited ROM have an impaired ability to travel, which may be caused by a mechanical problem or by a condition such as rheumatoid arthritis.

> **NOTE**
> Conditions such as rheumatoid arthritis impair range of motion by causing pain, swelling, and stiffness in the joint.

Range-of-motion exercises can preserve or improve the flexibility and mobility of the joints. They can also reduce stiffness, prevent deformities, and keep the joints supple and flexible.

- Active range of motion (AROM) indicates the distance (or number of degrees) the client can move his or her joints without assistance. AROM exercises can be done without assistance.

- Passive range of motion (PROM) indicates the distance (or number of degrees) joints can be moved with assistance from equipment or another person. (In other words, how far can you move the client's joints when the client is completely relaxed?) PROM exercises are done with the assistance of a therapist or other health-care provider.

TIP

One effective way to study for examinations such as the MBLEx and the NCBTMB is to learn how to study actively. Active study means being actively involved with the material in order to maximize your ability to later recall it. The brain retains more information if it is processed in an active manner. Some ideas for active study include:

- Rewriting and reworking your notes several times. This activity requires you to read and regurgitate the information in a repetitive way. You can also use this opportunity to reorganize material and "fill in the blanks" with any information you missed the first time around.

- Reading the material out loud. For example, you might recite your notes or read essential parts of your textbook into a tape recorder to play back later.

- Creating diagrams that illustrate relationships among the concepts being studied. Association is one of the keys to information retention. In addition, you may recognize previously overlooked relationships in the material you are studying.

Range of motion can be improved in a variety of ways. Of special interest to massage therapists are *stretching* and *reciprocal inhibition*.

Stretching

Regular stretching can improve the body's flexibility and range of motion. When a muscle is stretched, tension is placed on it, which causes the muscle to lengthen. Once the muscle reaches its maximum length, the fibers in the surrounding connective tissue and tendons pick up the tension and begin to align themselves along the same line of force as the tension being applied. In this way, disorganized fibers are realigned and scarred tissue can be rehabilitated.

Assisted stretching is a standard part of sports and rehabilitative massage work as these therapies focus on the prevention and rehabilitation of injuries. Therapeutic stretching is classified as active, active-assisted, active-resisted, passive, and passive-assisted. As part of your studies, you should be able to define each of these terms as well as discuss the care that must be taken to prevent injury to the client during the course of this treatment. You should know when it is appropriate to execute stretching activities and when stretching is contraindicated.

Reciprocal Inhibition

Another way to improve flexibility is the use of *reciprocal inhibition*. In this technique, tension is applied to a particular muscle group (the *antagonist* group) with the intention of forcing the opposing muscle group (the *agonist* group) to release tension and relax. For example, if a client tends to get muscle cramps in the calves (the agonist), the calf muscles are probably over-contracting. The problem can be resolved by helping the client to contract the muscles of the shin (the antagonist).

Reciprocal inhibition is commonly used to relieve muscle cramps and is a standard part of sports massage. By repeatedly undergoing this process, the body eventually unlearns the undesirable response (in our example, over-contracting the calves) in favor of the desired one.

EXERCISES: RANGE OF MOTION

Directions: Choose the option that best answers the question.

1. Which of the following is the BEST definition of flexibility?
   (A) The level of elasticity of the muscles
   (B) The distance the tendons can stretch
   (C) The amount of pliability in the bones
   (D) The range of motion in one or a series of joints

Flexibility is mainly determined by the level of movement that is possible within the joints. Tendons are relatively inflexible, bones are not flexible, and muscles do not play so important a role in overall flexibility as joints. **The correct answer is (D).**

2. One of the primary purposes of the stretch reflex is to
   (A) limit muscle lengthening.
   (B) stimulate a dynamic muscle response.
   (C) maximize muscle lengthening.
   (D) stimulate a static muscle response.

The stretch reflex helps prevent muscle injury by limiting (*not* maximizing) the amount of muscle lengthening. The static reflex and the dynamic reflex are two stages of the stretch reflex. **The correct answer is (A).**

POSTURAL ALIGNMENT

Posture is the position in which the body is held upright against gravity while standing, sitting, or lying down. Good posture means sitting, standing, walking, and lying in the positions that place the least amount of strain on supporting muscles and ligaments. Good posture is the body's ability to maintain the structural integrity of the joints no matter the position the body is in.

> **NOTE**
> Other postural terms you should be able to define and apply include:
> - Balance
> - Biomechanics
> - Center of gravity
> - Equilibrium
> - Gait/gait analysis

Among other benefits, good postural alignment facilitates efficient movement, improved circulation, and favorable organ and muscle functioning. It prevents pain and fatigue associated with imbalances between the left and right sides of the body or between the front and back sides of the body. Imbalances and lack of symmetry occur for different reasons, such as disease, physical injury, or lifestyle. Imbalances often lead to compensatory patterns of muscular contraction, which can worsen problems by further damaging the muscles and tissues involved.

You can help your clients to resolve damaging patterns by engaging in assisted stretching during your massage sessions. The goal of assisted stretching is not only to resolve the current issue but also to prevent further problems down the road by making clients aware of their patterns of movement and helping them to become part of the solution. One of the keys to this heightened awareness is *proprioception*.

Proprioception

Proprioceptors are specialized nerve endings in your joints, muscles, and tendons. Proprioceptors provide a continuous, unconscious stream of sensory input to the central nervous system. This stream of input includes information about the body's spatial positioning, the movement of body parts, and any changes to tension or force on or in the body. The brain uses this information to create an image of where you are and what you are doing; thus, *proprioception* is your sense of how you are oriented in space.

Massage techniques can enhance your clients' proprioception and create better mind-body connections by heightening awareness of movement patterns. Heightened perception can help clients to consciously recognize, for example, common movement patterns, where they hold tension in the body, and so on.

EXERCISES: POSTURAL ALIGNMENT

Directions: Choose the option that best answers the question.

1. A client assumes a slouched posture. The best description for the line of gravity associated with this condition is that it
   (A) passes in front of the cervical spine.
   (B) passes behind the lumbar spine.
   (C) passes in front of the knee joint.
   (D) passes behind the hip joint.

When you slouch, the line of gravity passes through the cervical spine and lumbar spine, behind the hip joint and knee joint, and in front of the ankle joint. **The correct answer is (D).**

2. Reciprocal inhibition is a common occurrence between muscles in agonist/antagonist relationships. It refers to the fact that when one muscle in the pair contracts, the other will
   (A) not be affected.
   (B) increase in size.
   (C) relax.
   (D) contract.

Reciprocal inhibition refers to the fact that when the muscle on one side of a joint contracts, the muscle on the other side of the joint relaxes. This is commonly seen in agonist/antagonist muscle pairs. **The correct answer is (C).**

TIPS FOR ANSWERING QUESTIONS ON KINESIOLOGY

- **Muscles equal force.** While studying the muscular system, remember that muscles produce and control the force that powers the movement of the body. Muscles have unique characteristics and they function in particular ways.

- **Remember how to divide the body.** The imaginary anatomical lines we use to divide the body into different planes also correlate to planes of motion in which we move: the sagittal plane, the coronal plane, and the transverse plane. When reviewing this material, go back to your notes about anatomical structure and positioning. You may find it easier to study that material together.

- **How can you move your own joints?** Range of motion is the distance and direction that a joint can travel. Make a practical study of your own body as you review this material. In what ways can you move different joints on your body, such as your elbow or shoulders? How about your ankles and knees? Can you identify each type of joint? What does your self-study reveal about the motion of each type of joint?

- **Keep your back straight!** Postural analysis will most likely be a common activity once you begin practicing as a massage therapist. You will learn to watch the way clients move and hold their bodies from the moment you meet them. Poor posture can cause a host of problems for a person, including a restricted range of motion, chronic pain, and undue stress on the muscles, joints, and tendons. These problems may be the very reasons the client is seeking help from you. Meanwhile, apply your studies to your own posture. Can it be improved? Why might you be holding your body in particular ways?

PRACTICE QUESTIONS

Directions: Choose the option that best answers the question.

1. Which of the following involves a third-class lever?
   (A) Nodding the head
   (B) Lifting a dumbbell
   (C) Doing a full push-up
   (D) Standing on tiptoes

2. According to the law of action/reaction, what happens if you push on a wall with your hand?
   (A) The wall pushes back on your hand with equal force.
   (B) The wall pushes back on your hand with more force.
   (C) The wall pushes back on your hand with less force.
   (D) The wall yields to the force exerted by your hand.

3. A massage therapist is asking a client about his daily activities. Which of the following basic activities would most likely have the biggest impact on the client's quality of movement?
   (A) Ambulation
   (B) Dressing
   (C) Grooming
   (D) Elimination

4. One action of the trapezius muscle is
   (A) compressing the abdomen.
   (B) elevating the shoulders.
   (C) rotating the scapula.
   (D) flexing the trunk.

5. Muscles are often found in agonist/antagonist muscle pairs. Which of the following muscles is the antagonist for the abdominals (agonist)?
   (A) Posterior deltoids
   (B) Forearm flexors
   (C) Latissimus dorsi
   (D) Spinal erectors

6. A synergist muscle is one that helps
   (A) the muscle shorten.
   (B) maintain posture.
   (C) another muscle move.
   (D) the muscle lengthen.

7. A massage therapist is using range-of-motion (ROM) exercises to help a client recover from a recent wrist injury. Which of the following is an example of a passive ROM exercise?
   (A) Asking the client to move his hand circularly without assistance from the therapist
   (B) Asking the client to lift a small weight without assistance from the therapist
   (C) Moving the client's hand from side to side without assistance from the patient
   (D) Supporting the client's hand while the patient moves his hand from side to side

8. Which of the following is the BEST definition of joint play as it relates to massage therapy?
   (A) Actively moving the joints of clients in ways that the clients cannot
   (B) Using a stretching technique to allow for pain-free joint movement
   (C) Type of joint massage therapy that involves beneficial energy exchange
   (D) Technique designed to help joints surpass their normal range of motion

9. All of the following describe reasons for stretching EXCEPT
   (A) enhancing flexibility.
   (B) relaxing skeletal muscles.
   (C) increasing joint range of motion.
   (D) improving aerobic fitness.

10. Which of the following is a characteristic of good posture in a seated position?
    (A) Feet flat on the floor
    (B) Shoulders rolled forward
    (C) Back slightly arched
    (D) Knees at 45-degree angle

ANSWER KEY AND EXPLANATIONS

1. B	3. A	5. D	7. C	9. D
2. A	4. C	6. C	8. B	10. A

1. **The correct answer is (B).** In a third-class lever, the effort (exerted by the bicep) is located between the fulcrum (elbow) and the resistance (the weight). Nodding the head involves a first-class lever, while choices (C) and (D) involve second-class levers.

2. **The correct answer is (A).** The law of action/reaction states that for every action, there is an equal and opposite reaction. Therefore, a force is exerted by the wall that is equal in magnitude but opposite to the force exerted by your hand.

3. **The correct answer is (A).** Ambulation, or walking, requires the most effort in terms of movement and therefore has the biggest effect on movement quality. Dressing, grooming, and elimination do not require substantial movement and therefore have a lesser effect on movement quality.

4. **The correct answer is (C).** The action of the trapezius muscle (which has a point of origin at the occipital bone and vertebrae and a point of insertion at the clavicle and scapula) is to rotate the scapula. The internal and external obliques compress the abdomen, the sternocleidomastoid elevates the shoulders, and the rectus abdominis compresses and flexes the trunk.

5. **The correct answer is (D).** Agonist/antagonist muscle pairs such as the abdominals and spinal erectors are responsible for moving a limb and returning it to its original position. The anterior deltoids and posterior deltoids, pectorals and latissimus dorsi, and forearm flexors and extensors are other examples of agonist/antagonist muscle pairs.

6. **The correct answer is (C).** Synergist muscles have the same types of movements as other agonist muscles in the body and can therefore help these muscles (and associated joints) move. Choice (B) describes a characteristic of a stabilizer muscle. Choices (A) and (D) describe concentric and eccentric contractions, respectively.

7. **The correct answer is (C).** Passive ROM exercises do not require any client effort. Choices (A) and (D) are examples of active ROM exercises (choice (D) would be classified as active-assistive) and choice (B) is an example of a resistive ROM exercise.

8. **The correct answer is (B).** Joint play is a stretching technique used by massage therapists to allow the client's joints to achieve but not surpass their full range of motion without causing pain. Choice (A) describes a technique known as joint mobilization; choice (B) describes a massage technique known as healing touch.

9. **The correct answer is (D).** Stretching can enhance overall flexibility, help relax tense muscles, and increase the range of motion of joints. However, improving aerobic fitness requires participating in cardiovascular activities such as running or cycling.

10. **The correct answer is (A).** When sitting, the shoulders should be back, the back should be straight, the feet should be flat on the floor, and the knees should be at a 90-degree angle.

SUMMING IT UP

- Kinesiology is all about the body's movement. When studying questions pertaining to kinesiology, be practical. Consider the question in relation to the way your own body works. When the text mentions working a joint through a complete range of movement, try it. Understanding how the concepts apply in a practical manner will make it much easier to answer the examination questions correctly.

- Learn the planes of motion! Questions about anatomy, physiology, pathology, and kinesiology frequently reference body parts using this terminology.

CHAPTER 6

Pathology

OVERVIEW

- **Causes and transmission of disease**
- **Common pathologies**
- **Drugs and drug interactions**
- **Working with particular populations**
- **Tips for answering questions on pathology**
- **Practice questions**
- **Answer key and explanations**
- **Summing it up**

Pathology is the study of the nature and cause of disease. The term *pathology* is also used to describe the manifestation of a condition or disease (e.g., the pathology of dermatitis). Pathology is an important topic for massage therapists due to your close proximity to clients during treatment. You should be able to recognize the signs and symptoms of various conditions and understand how these conditions impact your ability to treat (or avoid treating) clients. This is important for two reasons: (1) you should understand when massage is contraindicated due to the way treatment may affect and interact with a particular condition and (2) you can avoid the spread of disease by recognizing its presence and preventing further transmission.

For examination study, at a minimum you should be able to do the following seven things: (1) discuss the causes of disease and common modes of disease transmission; (2) recognize and describe common pathologies; (3) distinguish conditions that indicate or contraindicate the performance of massage; (4) describe the healing process; (5) identify biological, psychological, and environmental factors that aggravate and alleviate disease; (6) classify drugs and recognize how they might interact with the massage process; and (7) discuss how to work with special populations.

Although this chapter does not review every detail of these subjects, it highlights important information and gives you some practice questions in these areas. If you are having trouble understanding the information or answering the practice questions, take some time to review your textbooks and notes from school.

The number of questions you will need to answer on pathology varies by exam. If you are taking the MBLEx, you will be required to answer a total of 125 questions; of these, about 13 percent, or around 16 questions, are on this topic. If you are taking the NCETMB, you will be required to answer a total of 160 questions; of these, about 13 percent, or around 21 questions, touch on this topic.

CAUSES AND TRANSMISSION OF DISEASE

Disease is defined as a health condition that interferes with the body's normal functioning. Disease is an abnormal state that prevents all or part of the body from functioning properly. Diseases can be recognized by their *symptoms* and *signs*. Symptoms are indicators of illness that are perceived by the sick individual; for example, typical symptoms might include pain, dizziness, itchiness, weakness, or nausea. Signs, on the other hand, are tangible indicators of a condition that can be observed by others. For example, typical signs might include an elevated pulse, high fever, or physical irregularities such as red patches, skin blisters, or lesions.

> **NOTE**
>
> Chronic conditions such as Tay-Sachs disease and cystic fibrosis used to be referred to as genetic *diseases*. Now they are more appropriately referred to as genetic *disorders*.

Diseases can be *acute* or *chronic*. Acute conditions are characterized by a relatively rapid, severe onset of symptoms. Acute conditions, such as chicken pox or pneumonia, are usually short-lived and responsive to therapeutic treatment. Chronic conditions, on the other hand, are those that persist over a long period of time. Although their symptoms may be less severe than an acute phase of the same disease, chronic conditions can be progressive and degenerative, such as rheumatoid arthritis. Chronic conditions can sometimes result in complete or partial disability or even death.

Disease can be caused by any number of conditions, such as exposure to viruses, bacteria, or fungi; trauma; environmental factors such as exposure to asbestos; personal issues such as chemical imbalances or high levels of stress; degenerative processes such as osteoporosis; and so on. In addition, other factors, such as genetics, age, and lifestyle, can predispose a person to certain conditions.

Most diseases can be classified as *infectious*, *non-infectious*, or of unknown origin. Infectious diseases are caused by invading pathogens such as viruses or bacteria. Infectious disease can be transmitted from one person to another either directly or indirectly. Direct contact modes of transmission include touch or via water, food, air, saliva, or blood. Infectious disease can also be transmitted indirectly via *vectors*: animals that carry germs from one person to another, such as insects. Examples of infectious disease include influenza, impetigo, and malaria.

Non-infectious or non-communicable diseases are not caused by pathogens and therefore cannot be passed from one person to another. Rather, non-infectious diseases are caused by any number of factors, such as the environment, nutritional deficiency, lifestyle, and/or genetics. Examples of non-infectious disease include asthma, heart disease, and cancer.

EXERCISES: CAUSES AND TRANSMISSION OF DISEASE

Directions: Choose the option that best answers the question.

1. One example of a chronic condition is
   (A) influenza.
   (B) bone fracture.
   (C) fibromyalgia.
   (D) heart attack.

A chronic condition is one that persists over time, such as fibromyalgia, osteoporosis, diabetes, or epilepsy. In an acute condition, symptoms appear suddenly but will only persist for a relatively short period of time (acute conditions such as bone fractures and heart attacks will require medical intervention). **The correct answer is (C).**

2. All of the following are symptoms of bursitis EXCEPT
   (A) tenderness.
   (B) stiffness.
   (C) inflammation/pain.
   (D) limited range of motion.

Symptoms are subjective indicators of an illness or condition, such as tenderness, stiffness, and pain. Signs are more objective indicators of illness; a limited range of motion is a tangible indicator that a condition may exist. **The correct answer is (D).**

COMMON PATHOLOGIES

Pathologies are best understood in the context of healthy body functioning. In other words, understanding how a body system is designed to function will help you to recognize what happens when functioning is impaired or less than optimal. For your examination, you may be asked to differentiate between normal functioning and functioning in the context of particular diseases or conditions. You may be asked to identify diseases and conditions based both on signs (what you see) and symptoms (what the client feels). You may be asked to indicate if treatment is contraindicated based on the signs, symptoms, or conditions presented. As a massage practitioner, it is your responsibility to know when it is or is not appropriate to treat clients. This part of the examination is meant to test your ability to make this call.

In this section, we will review some common pathologies you may have to deal with in your practice. You should be able to recognize the signs of common conditions and know whether massage is indicated or contraindicated.

Some contraindications apply only to the affected area, while others contraindicate any form of treatment. In addition, some contraindicated conditions may be treatable in consultation with the client's physician. Massage is generally contraindicated if the client presents with the following:

- Acute infectious disease
- High body temperature

> **NOTE**
>
> In health care, an *indication* is a condition that makes a particular treatment or procedure advisable to pursue; likewise, a *contraindication* is a condition that makes a particular treatment or procedure inadvisable or unacceptable to pursue. Some contraindications are *absolute*—inadvisable under all circumstances—while others are *relative*, or acceptable only under certain circumstances.
>
> For massage practitioners, contraindications are conditions under which massage is inappropriate, either locally (on or near the affected body part) or in an absolute sense (the patient should not be treated at all). For example, massage is always contraindicated during an impetigo outbreak *unless* the lesions have completely healed.

- Inflammation (tissue damage, bacterial infestation)
- Intoxication
- Osteoporosis
- Skin problems
- Varicose veins

The following lists of common conditions are not meant to be comprehensive. You should refer back to your school materials for more complete information.

Integumentary (Skin) Conditions

Some of the most common pathologies you will work with include those related to the integumentary system, or the skin. For obvious reasons, massage is contraindicated for clients who present with various skin conditions. Infection can easily invade skin that is compromised (that is, if the client presents with open, broken, or scabbed skin), making massage a high-risk activity for the client. Other conditions, such as impetigo, have a high degree of contagion and can easily spread from the client to you to other clients.

Some of the common infectious skin conditions you should be able to identify and recognize how to deal with include:

- Boils
- Erysipelas (St. Anthony's Fire)
- Fungi (such as ringworm, athlete's foot, jock itch)
- Herpes simplex
- Impetigo
- Lice/mites
- Warts

Some of the common non-infectious skin conditions you should be able to identify and recognize how to deal with:

- Acne
- Eczema
- Hives
- Moles
- Psoriasis

You should also be able to recognize signs of skin cancer as you may get a closer look at some areas of the client's skin than the client can (the back, for example). Finally, you should be able to recognize and handle clients who present with burns, open wounds, or ulcers (bedsores).

Musculoskeletal Conditions

- Bone disorders, such as fractures, osteoporosis, or postural issues
- Connective tissue disorders, such as bunions, bursitis, or cysts
- Joint disorders, such as gout, arthritis, or sprains
- Muscular disorders, such as fibromyalgia, myofascial pain syndrome, shin splints, or muscle cramps
- Neuromuscular disorders, such as carpal tunnel syndrome or herniated discs

Nervous System Disorders

- Alzheimer's disease

- Parkinson's disease

- Herpes zoster (shingles)

Circulatory Conditions

- Pulmonary embolism

- Heart conditions

- Hemophilia

- Hypertension

- Thrombosis

- Varicose veins

Lymph/Immune System Disorders

- Chronic fatigue syndrome

- Edema

- Fever

- HIV/AIDS

- Inflammation

- Lymphoma

Respiratory System Conditions

- Infectious disorders such as bronchitis, common cold, influenza, or pneumonia

- Obstructive pulmonary disease such as asthma or emphysema

Digestive System Conditions

- Disorders of the large intestine such as appendicitis or irritable bowel syndrome

- Disorders of the stomach/small intestine such as Crohn's disease or ulcers

- Other related disorders such as cirrhosis or hepatitis

Endocrine System Disorders

- Diabetes

- Hypoglycemia

Urinary System Conditions

- Bladder/urinary tract disorders such as urinary tract infections

- Kidney disorders such as kidney stones

Reproductive System Conditions

- Breast cancer

- Endometriosis

- Pelvic inflammatory disease

- Pregnancy

The Healing Process

During the healing process, damaged tissue is repaired. The degree of repair and the length of time needed for the healing process to do its work vary greatly depending on the condition in question, the location on the body where the injury or condition occurred, and the severity level of the illness or injury. Healing involves a complex sequence of physiological events, starting with the restoration of damaged tissue at the cellular level. The body then goes through a series of phases, depending on the type and severity of the wound or condition.

In general, conditions of the skin and surface tissue are more easily repaired by the body. Conditions impacting the bones and ligaments usually require a period of immobilization and a lengthier healing time. Conditions affecting muscles and tendons tend to take a significant amount of healing time and generally result in perceptible scarring and weakness. Trauma to the central nervous system is generally irreparable.

For infectious diseases, the healing process cannot begin until the invading pathogens have been destroyed.

For some conditions, friction massage and stretching of the tissue during the healing process can minimize or prevent the formation of scar tissue.

> **NOTE**
>
> Getting ready for your licensing examination is a lengthy process. Occasionally you may find it difficult to maintain your motivation to study. One way to stay motivated is to remind yourself of the ultimate reward for your hard work—the ability to make a living from a discipline you love. You might also set up a reward system for yourself at each milestone in your study; for example, after you have mastered a particularly complex topic like pathology, you might reward yourself with a night out or the purchase of some item you really desire. In addition, keep reminding yourself of how much gratification and pride you will feel when you have successfully achieved your goal.

Aggravating and Alleviating Factors

The healing process can be aggravated or alleviated by factors beyond the body's physiological ability to repair itself. For example, biological factors such as a person's weight, nutrition level, and the presence of secondary conditions such as hypertension or cardiovascular disease can impact the ability to heal. Behavioral factors have a definite impact and include activities such as tobacco use, level of exercise, dietary choices, alcohol consumption, and sexual practices. Psychological and environmental factors such as socioeconomic level, exposure to secondhand smoke, access to medical care, anxiety/depression level, ability to cope with stress, and the strength of the family system can all delay or facilitate the healing process.

EXERCISES: COMMON PATHOLOGIES

Directions: Choose the option that best answers the question.

1. Heat treatment during massage is contraindicated for which of the following conditions?
   (A) Myopia
   (B) Muscular dystrophy
   (C) Myofibrositis
   (D) Multiple sclerosis

For clients with multiple sclerosis, massage is appropriate for stress and pain reduction as well as the maintenance of mobility. However, heat treatments should be avoided as it can trigger MS symptoms or cause symptoms to worsen. For the other conditions listed, heat treatments are not contraindicated. **The correct answer is (D).**

2. During what stage of wound healing do fibroblasts start to enter the site of injury?
   (A) Inflammatory
   (B) Clotting cascade
   (C) Proliferative
   (D) Remodeling

During the proliferative stage of wound healing, fibroblasts enter the area and carry out important functions such as producing collagen. The inflammatory phase (which includes the clotting cascade) helps close the wound and remove debris and bacteria. The remodeling phase follows the proliferative phase. **The correct answer is (C).**

3. For which of the following conditions is massage absolutely contraindicated?
   (A) Irritable bowel syndrome
   (B) HIV
   (C) Deep vein thrombosis
   (D) Pancreatitis

A person with deep vein thrombosis should not receive massage. The increase in blood flow associated with massage might cause a thrombus to detach from a vessel wall, resulting in an embolism. Individuals with irritable bowel syndrome, HIV (as long as the client's overall health is good), and pancreatitis (as long as the condition has been treated by a physician) are all appropriate candidates for massage treatment. **The correct answer is (C).**

4. Which of the following should be avoided when providing massage therapy to a client with scleroderma?
   (A) Warming massage
   (B) Cold therapy
   (C) Massage while sitting up
   (D) ROM exercises

Cold therapy and the application of extreme heat should be avoided when treating an individual with scleroderma. The other treatment options listed may be beneficial or useful in treating the client. **The correct answer is (B).**

DRUGS AND DRUG INTERACTIONS

Massage therapy may be contraindicated when clients are taking certain substances due to potentially harmful interactions between the substance and the treatment. Your goal is always to administer safe and effective therapy to clients. This means you need to be aware of all the client's medical conditions as well as any medications he or she is taking.

One of the ways to determine if the client is taking contraindicated substances is to ask questions during the intake interview. Ask questions such as the following: *What medical conditions do you have? What medications are you taking to treat this? When did you start the medication? What kind of side effects are you experiencing?*

The client's answers can give you a fuller picture of his or her current state of health.

Recreational Drugs

If a client is intoxicated from recreational drugs such as alcohol, marijuana, or other substances, massage is always contraindicated. Massage treatment can intensify the effect of recreational substances such as alcohol by increasing the amount of the substance in the bloodstream. In extreme cases, massage can overtax the liver.

Prescription and Over-the-Counter Medications

Massage therapy is sometimes contraindicated when the client is using prescription or over-the-counter medications, because treatment can exaggerate the effects of certain medications. For example, if a prescription makes the client dizzy, drowsy, or lightheaded, massage can exacerbate that condition, leaving the client feeling in much worse shape than he or she was in before getting on the table. If a prescription is taken to relieve pain, massage can reinforce this effect, potentially causing serious problems for the client.

> **NOTE**
>
> Make sure any client on antibiotics has been taking them for at least three full days before conducting treatment. Otherwise, the underlying bacterial infection may not yet be completely eradicated from the client's system and the massage treatment may spread the infection through the bloodstream.

In addition, the side effects of some medications can be more severe during their first few days of use.

Some medications to watch for include the following:

- Antibiotics
- Antidepressants
- Cardiovascular drugs
- Insulin
- Pain medication (including over-the-counter)

EXERCISES: DRUGS AND DRUG INTERACTIONS

Directions: Choose the option that best answers the question.

1. A client is currently taking painkillers for a medical condition. How should you alter treatment based on this information?
   (A) You should make the treatment more conservative.
   (B) You should avoid irritating the client by asking for feedback.
   (C) You should massage the tissues more aggressively.
   (D) You should ask the client to sit up during treatment.

The biggest risk when treating a client on painkillers is overtreatment. Due to the effects of the drug, the client's tissues will be less sensitive and he or she may not be able to provide you with accurate feedback. Thus, your work should err on the conservative side to avoid the adverse effects associated with overtreating an area. **The correct answer is (A).**

2. You want to find more information about a specific drug. Which of the following references would be the BEST one to use?
   (A) A Web site such as Wikipedia
   (B) A drug reference book for physicians
   (C) A promotional pamphlet from a popular pharmaceutical company
   (D) A personal conversation with a current user of the drug

When researching drugs, you should rely only on authoritative sources accepted by the medical community, such as drug reference books designed for physicians, pharmacists, and other health-care providers. The other sources listed may not provide accurate or sufficient information. **The correct answer is (B).**

WORKING WITH PARTICULAR POPULATIONS

You may work with any number of populations over the course of your career. Some populations require specialized or specific treatment based on underlying conditions. It is important to utilize safe and appropriate accommodations and techniques for all clients. For the examination, you should be able to identify accommodations you may need to make for various populations, including (but not limited to) the following:

- Athletes (healthy and rehabilitating)
- Children (infants and school-age)
- Chronically ill
- Developmentally disabled
- Elderly
- Mentally ill
- Physically disabled
- Pregnant women
- Terminally ill

EXERCISES: WORKING WITH PARTICULAR POPULATIONS

Directions: Choose the option that best answers the question.

1. All of the following are contraindicated massage treatments for pregnant women EXCEPT
   (A) utilizing a prone position after the first trimester.
   (B) kneading on or near the abdominal area.
   (C) practicing heavy percussion movements.
   (D) placing pillows under the knees or head.

Properly trained massage therapists should be able to conduct massage on clients undergoing a normal, non-problematic pregnancy. However, the client should never be placed in a prone (face down) position after the first trimester, you should not knead anywhere near the abdominal area, nor should you use heavy percussion or deep tissue movements. **The correct answer is (D).**

2. All of the following are benefits of conducting massage treatment on the critically ill EXCEPT
   (A) reducing disorientation or confusion.
   (B) providing comfort and relaxation.
   (C) allowing the client to think the treatment is a cure.
   (D) controlling pain or easing physical discomfort.

When working with the critically ill, your goal should be to provide a gentle, caring experience that helps to ease some of the issues the client is experiencing. However, you should never allow the client to think you are providing a cure to his or her condition. **The correct answer is (C).**

TIPS FOR ANSWERING QUESTIONS ON PATHOLOGY

- **It's ALL related.** Anatomy, physiology, and pathology are intimately intertwined topic areas: anatomy defines the structures and systems of the body; physiology describes the body's functioning; and pathology indicates when something has gone awry with a structure, system, or function. You will find it easiest to study each body system as an integrated whole; for example, describe the integumentary system, explain how it functions, then identify common pathologies that you may encounter.

- **Remember that massage exacerbates the effects of any substance.** When considering the interaction between therapeutic massage and medication, remember that one of the benefits of massage is encouraging the movement of blood through the circulatory system. Thus, any substances in the client's system will be pushed through the body, exacerbating their effects.

- **How would you feel?** As you study appropriate treatments for a particular population, try to imagine yourself as a member of that population. Why might certain treatments be indicated or contraindicated, based on a client's condition? For example, imagine you are an athlete rehabilitating from an ankle injury. What treatment approaches would or would not make sense, based on that condition? Visualizing how treatment would feel or be perceived by the client may help you to remember appropriate treatment protocol.

PRACTICE QUESTIONS

Directions: Choose the option that best answers the question.

1. Which of the following is NOT a pathology of the reproductive system?
   (A) Salpingitis
   (B) Bursitis
   (C) Endometriosis
   (D) Prostatitis

2. You are treating a client with a mild case of hemophilia. Which of the following is a good approach to use with this client?
   (A) Inform the client that massage is contraindicated for people with hemophilia.
   (B) Focus on vigorous massage techniques during the therapy session.
   (C) Provide an intense massage but keep the session relatively short.
   (D) Use only gentle massage techniques while treating the client.

3. Black cohosh is an herb used most often to address the symptoms associated with
   (A) depression.
   (B) menopause.
   (C) influenza.
   (D) dementia.

4. Massage is contraindicated during the acute stage of all of the following conditions EXCEPT
   (A) emphysema.
   (B) pneumonia.
   (C) hives.
   (D) common cold.

5. What disorder is often caused by repetitive hand movements?
   (A) Degenerative joint disease
   (B) Scoliosis
   (C) Carpel tunnel syndrome
   (D) Sciatica

6. Which of the following does NOT describe a way in which acute inflammation affects tissues?
   (A) Blood vessels in the area dilate.
   (B) Blood flow to the area increases.
   (C) Plasma flows into the tissues.
   (D) Tissues become less permeable.

7. A client sustained an injury 5 days ago. What stage of healing is she most likely in?
   (A) Acute
   (B) Sub-acute
   (C) Chronic
   (D) Maturation

8. You have located a trigger point on a client's back. When you apply pressure to the trigger point, the client feels pain in her left leg. This is known as
   (A) referred pain.
   (B) reflexive pain.
   (C) retrieved pain.
   (D) represented pain.

9. Which pain-related physiological process occurs immediately after tissue damage?
   (A) Transduction
   (B) Transmission
   (C) Modulation
   (D) Perception

10. In order for a person to feel pain in response to a stimulus, nociceptors must transmit signals
    (A) from the brain.
    (B) from the muscles.
    (C) via the spinal cord.
    (D) via the nerves.

ANSWER KEY AND EXPLANATIONS

1. B	3. B	5. C	7. B	9. A
2. D	4. D	6. D	8. A	10. C

1. **The correct answer is (B).** Bursitis is inflammation of the bursae, sacs containing fluid found in the areas separating tendons from skin or bone. Salpingitis is an infection of the fallopian tubes that leads to inflammation; endometriosis is the abnormal growth of uterine-like cells on the ovaries or other structures; and prostatitis is characterized by inflammation of the prostate gland.

2. **The correct answer is (D).** Therapists can use gentle massage techniques such as the ones used during circulatory massage on individuals with mild cases of hemophilia. More vigorous or intense techniques should not be used as the therapist could cause injury.

3. **The correct answer is (B).** Although discussion of herbal remedies is outside the scope of massage practice, you may find it helpful to recognize some of the most commonly used home herbal remedies. Black cohosh is a member of the buttercup family. It is believed to be an effective herbal remedy to relieve hot flashes, night sweats, and other menopause-related symptoms.

4. **The correct answer is (D).** During the acute stages of many conditions—including emphysema, pneumonia, and hives—a person should not receive massage treatment. Technically it is acceptable for a person with a common cold, which is not an acute condition to receive a massage. However, it is usually best to avoid massage treatments when a client is feeling under the weather.

5. **The correct answer is (C).** Carpel tunnel syndrome is often caused by work involving repetitive hand movements. Symptoms include pain and numbness. Degenerative joint disease may result from aging or injury; scoliosis is typically caused by a congenital defect or injury; and sciatica can result from poor posture, overexertion, or other factors.

6. **The correct answer is (D).** During acute inflammation, vasodilation occurs, additional blood travels to the injured area, plasma flows into the tissues, and the tissues become more permeable, not less.

7. **The correct answer is (B).** The acute stage of healing commences immediately after an injury. The sub-acute stage usually begins several days later and can last for several weeks. The maturation and chronic stages follow the sub-acute stage.

8. **The correct answer is (A).** The correct term for this phenomenon is referred pain: pain arises in the trigger point, but the individual feels the sensation of pain in another part of the body.

9. **The correct answer is (A).** Transduction occurs when an unpleasant stimulus is converted into electrical energy. Transmission, modulation, and perception are the three steps of the pain process occurring after transduction.

10. **The correct answer is (C).** When tissue is damaged or in danger of being damaged, nociceptors detect this condition and send a signal along the spinal cord. Once the signal reaches the brain, it is processed and the individual experiences the sensation of pain.

SUMMING IT UP

- **Pathology is the study of disease.** This is a key area on your examination due to the close proximity in which you will work with others. It is critical that you recognize the signs and symptoms of various conditions so that you understand when massage treatment is indicated or contraindicated.

- **Massage treatment is not always appropriate.** In situations where treatment is contraindicated, you must recognize if the contraindication is absolute or if it applies only conditionally. You must also recognize when it is best to refer a client to a different kind of health practitioner.

- **People are not one-size-fits-all.** As a professional who provides services to the public (and possibly to the public at large), you will likely work with a large cross-section of the population. You will need to be able to recognize how treatment must be modified and customized to be appropriate for clients in various conditions.

CHAPTER 7

Therapeutic Massage and Bodywork Assessment

OVERVIEW

- **Client consultation and intake procedures**
- **Assessment techniques and treatment plans**
- **Client recordkeeping**
- **Tips for answering questions on therapeutic massage and bodywork assessment**
- **Practice questions**
- **Answer key and explanations**
- **Summing it up**

Therapeutic massage and bodywork assessment is the process by which you gather relevant information about the client and plan an effective course of treatment based on your findings. During the assessment process, you will collect information in a number of ways. You will get some information directly from the client via intake forms or answers to your questions. You will gather other data from your observations of the client's physical condition and the physical assessments you conduct.

Implementing a systematic assessment process is essential for therapists for a number of reasons. First and foremost, a methodical approach allows you to thoroughly evaluate each client to ensure that the course of treatment is advisable and not contraindicated by some underlying condition. The assessment should clearly indicate if massage is a good treatment choice or if you should refer the client to a different type of health-care provider. Second, an organized approach enables you to efficiently determine the root causes of the client's symptoms so that you can quickly plan an appropriate treatment. Finally, the care you take will reinforce for the client that you are a serious health-care professional. It will also confirm that both you and the client are operating from the same set of expectations for treatment.

For examination study, at a minimum, you should be able to do the following five things: (1) explain how to appropriately conduct a client consultation; (2) describe the assessment methods used during client evaluation, including observational, palpatory, and other techniques; (3) identify postural alignment and physical holding patterns in the body; (4) integrate your findings and formulate an appropriate course of treatment; and (5) describe techniques for orderly and professional client recordkeeping.

Although this chapter does not review every detail of these subjects, it highlights important information and gives you some practice questions in these areas. If you are having trouble understanding the information or answering the practice questions, take some time to review your textbooks and notes from school.

The number of questions you will need to answer on therapeutic massage and bodywork assessment varies by exam. If you are taking the MBLEx, you will be required to answer a total of 125 questions; of these, about 17 percent, or around 21 questions, are on this topic. If you are taking the NCETMB, you will be required to answer a total of 160 questions; of these, about 18 percent, or around 28 questions, touch on this topic.

History of Massage in the West

Although it is widely known that therapeutic massage originated in the Eastern cultures of Asia, it is not always recognized that massage has also had a long history in the Western parts of the world as well. The first Western peoples known to have practiced some form of therapeutic massage were the ancient Greeks. By 300 B.C.E., the practice of massage was widely accepted across Greece, thanks in large part to a priest-physician named Aesculapius, who developed the practice of gymnastics as a combination of exercise and massage. Via the Greeks and later the Romans, the practice of massage gained popularity throughout Europe. Although practice declined sharply in the Middle Ages, massage reemerged during the Renaissance due to a renewed interest in science and medicine.

As interest in massage continued to grow over the centuries, many medical practitioners incorporated it into their treatment regimens. In some places, massage came to be the preferred method for maintaining personal health and treating diseases. In the seventeenth and eighteenth centuries, Swedish physiologist Per Henrik Ling pioneered a system of movements called *Medical Gymnastics* and founded the Royal Swedish Central Institute of Gymnastics. In time, Ling's system, later known as *Swedish Movements* or the *Swedish Movement Cure*, spread through Europe. In the mid-1800s, brothers Charles Fayette and George Henry Taylor introduced Ling's system in the United States and further increased the visibility of massage with the general public and among medical professionals.

As the nineteenth century progressed, the practice of massage continued to be refined and further established as a medicinal approach. Some notable achievements included those of Dr. Johann Mezger, who introduced the concept of scientific massage, and Dr. Douglas O. Graham, who pioneered Swedish massage in the United States. By the end of that century, massage practice had accelerated into a popular, serious business.

However, at the beginning of the twentieth century, the British Medical Association uncovered widespread abuses in the education and practice of massage therapy. These discoveries undermined the credibility of the massage industry and caused a significant decline in practice.

Over time, the practice of massage slowly regained some of its footing as new techniques like Connective Tissue Massage and Deep Transverse Friction massage were developed. In the 1960s, the United States saw a notable upsurge of interest in massage treatment as many people turned to massage and other therapies as alternatives to traditional medicine.

Today, with the emergence of new practices, such as chiropractic medicine, as well as the accreditation of massage schools and the proliferation of professional affiliations, the practice of therapeutic massage has slowly but surely regained its standing as a viable treatment field.

CLIENT CONSULTATION AND INTAKE PROCEDURES

During your initial meeting with the client, you should plan to spend a few minutes gathering data to evaluate the client's physical condition and determine if massage treatment is appropriate. Standard intake forms allow the client to easily provide you with relevant information such as full name, address, emergency contact, and insurance provider (if applicable). In addition, intake forms encourage clients to provide a complete health history by requiring them to answer questions about current or past medical conditions; previous surgeries or procedures; current or past medications; allergies that might impact treatment; and any relevant symptoms, signs, or concerns.

TIP

Clients may not always be entirely forthcoming about their health history or they may refuse to answer relevant questions about their current physical condition. In such situations, even if the client appears healthy, you should refuse to conduct treatment, as you have no way of knowing what underlying conditions may be present.

Once the client has completed the intake forms, you can conduct an interview to clarify the information and delve further into the reasons for treatment. It is critical to follow up on any issue that may contraindicate treatment, or to get clarifying information about any conditions, procedures, or medications that are unfamiliar to you. An effective way to learn more is to ask the client appropriate follow-up questions during the interview, for example: *"I see you are taking such-and-such medication; can you tell me more about the condition being treated with this medication? How long have you been taking this substance? How does it make you feel?"*

The intake interview is also an opportunity to ask the client questions about his or her current lifestyle, as day-to-day activities or recent events or traumas may provide some indication as to what may be causing or aggravating the condition for which the client is seeking treatment.

As part of the intake process, you can also use a simple anatomical diagram to allow clients to indicate exactly where on the body they are experiencing pain or other symptoms. You can follow up by asking appropriate questions about the issue, such as, *"How long have you had this condition? Is there anything that gives you relief from the pain?"* You should assess the patient's level of pain or discomfort by having the client rate his or her pain level on a scale of 1 to 10. Later you can use this as a marker to gauge the effectiveness of the treatment.

EXERCISES: CLIENT CONSULTATION AND INTAKE PROCEDURES

Directions: Choose the option that best answers the question.

1. An intake form can be used to gather complete information about all of the following EXCEPT
   (A) the client's insurance provider.
   (B) the client's medical history.
   (C) a list of the client's allergies.
   (D) the effects of the client's medications.

   Although the intake form can be used to gather a wide variety of details about the client, the effects of his or her medication are generally too broad and complicated to be listed on a form. In this case, you should ask the client follow-up questions about his or her medications or consult with the client's primary physician. **The correct answer is (D).**

2. A new client you are interviewing for the first time refuses to divulge certain sensitive details about his medical history, but is quite insistent upon getting a massage. How should you proceed?
   (A) Give him a massage with whatever information you have.
   (B) Decline to work on the client if he will not cooperate.
   (C) Demand that he tell you what you need to know.
   (D) Seek further information from others who know the client.

   If the client refuses to provide pertinent information about his medical history or condition, you should decline to perform any work. Working on a patient without his or her full medical history may be dangerous, as he or she may have an underlying condition that may contraindicate massage. **The correct answer is (B).**

ASSESSMENT TECHNIQUES AND TREATMENT PLANS

Massage therapists use a variety of assessment techniques when evaluating clients.

- **Observation/visual input:** What do you observe when you look at the client? Does the client appear healthy? What do the client's posture, *gait* (manner of walking), and movements tell you about the client's body structure and potential functional issues?

- **Palpatory input:** What observations can you make as you physically manipulate the client's body? Do you notice any trigger or tender points in the muscle tissues or joints? If the client is complaining of pain or discomfort, can you pinpoint the source? Does the client's temperature seem high? What is the client's pulse rate? Do you detect any abnormalities in sensation level? Assess the client's soft tissues and bony landmarks and look for trigger points, endangerment sites, or adhesions.

- **Auditory and olfactory input:** What kind of input are you getting from your other senses? Do you hear any clicking noises or other sounds that might indicate a potential problem? Any sounds heard during assessment may help you to identify the source of the problem and localize treatment. Do you smell anything odd or out of the ordinary? Though smell is not itself a diagnostic tool, many practitioners learn to recognize the presence of distinct odors.

- **Energetic input:** What kind of energy are you sensing in the client? For energy practitioners, this is often a literal, objective assessment tool. For other, more traditional practitioners, the energy input is not diagnostic but rather refers to the "vibe" you get from the client.

- **Intuitive input:** What is your intuition telling you about the client? Are you getting the sense the client is not being fully honest with you? Do you intuitively sense the client's root issue?

Range-of-Motion Assessment

Assessing the client's *range of motion* (ROM) is an essential part of the initial evaluation. Range-of-motion assessment allows you to identify potential problems with joints and surrounding tissues. ROM assessment includes the following:

- **Active movement:** What happens when the client moves each of his or her limbs through a particular range of motion? Can this be accomplished easily and without pain?

- **Passive movement:** What happens when you move the client's limbs through their full range of motion? Do you encounter any resistance or catches? Does the client seem to hesitate or feel pain?

- **Resisted movement:** What happens when you apply resistance against the client's movements? Does the client experience weakness or pain?

> **NOTE**
>
> Can you locate and name the body's bony landmarks? You will need to be able to identify these for the examination.

Postural Analysis and Physical Holding Patterns

As part of the client assessment, you will analyze the client's *posture* and *physical holding patterns*. Postural analysis allows you to identify the possibility of muscular imbalances or other symmetry deviations that can cause or contribute to pain or discomfort. Postural difficulties can result in compensatory patterns or muscular adaptations that eventually cause the client pain, dysfunction, and/or restricted motion by putting undue stress on the skeleton, joints, or muscles.

You can conduct a postural analysis informally with a visual inspection or you might conduct the analysis more formally using a plumb line and a postural analysis grid chart. Make sure you view the client from the front, both sides, and the back.

You will also look for physical (also called somatic) holding patterns. These are less-than-optimal movement patterns that can develop over time due to muscular or skeletal imbalances, lack of symmetry, or injury. For example, if a client suffered a knee injury at some point and the injury never healed properly, you might notice issues with the client's gait. Eventually, maladaptive holding patterns can cause musculoskeletal or other types of pain.

One example of a physical holding pattern is *muscle guarding*. This is the practice of unconsciously holding a muscle in a partially contracted state. This condition can occur for any number of reasons (such as a skeletal imbalance or fear of reinjuring a damaged muscle) and can result in tenderness, soreness, and pain.

All of the information you gather during the assessment will be used to determine if massage is appropriate treatment for the client. If it is indicated, you can use the information you have collected to formulate the client's treatment plan.

Formulating the Treatment Plan

Treatment plans should be individualized to the client; they should be appropriate for the client's overall condition and designed to address the specific issues or problems the client is experiencing. The treatment plan is essentially a blueprint of the expected end result and how you intend to get there. Your treatment plan should cover:

- Recommended number and frequency of massage sessions

- Massage techniques to be utilized

- Particulars of treatment: length of sessions, specificity to body part, and so on

- Additional modalities, such as hot stones or hydrotherapy

- Treatment goals and anticipated timeline

- Referrals or recommendations for other care providers, either instead of or in conjunction with massage treatment

EXERCISES: ASSESSMENT TECHNIQUES AND TREATMENT PLANS

Directions: Choose the option that best answers the question.

1. Information regarding a client's temperature or pulse rate would be considered
   (A) intuitive input.
   (B) observational input.
   (C) palpatory input.
   (D) energetic input.

   A client's temperature or pulse rate would be considered palpatory input, which refers to information ascertained from physically manipulating a patient's body. **The correct answer is (C).**

2. When you physically move a client's limb, what range of motion are you using?
   (A) Passive
   (B) Active
   (C) Resisted
   (D) Precipitated

   When you physically move a client's limb, you are performing a passive range of motion movement. **The correct answer is (A).**

3. Pain and discomfort associated with postural difficulties is most often related to
   (A) muscular adaptations.
   (B) skeletal defects.
   (C) vitamin deficiencies.
   (D) genetic dispositions.

   The pain and discomfort commonly associated with postural difficulties is most often related to muscular adaptations. It is also frequently related to compensatory patterns. Pain and discomfort results from the undue strain muscular adaptations and compensatory patterns place on the client's skeleton, muscles, or joints. **The correct answer is (A).**

4. The primary influencing factor of a treatment plan is the client's
   (A) ability to afford treatment.
   (B) goals and desires.
   (C) understanding of treatment.
   (D) physical issues/needs.

   Physical issues/needs are the most important factor in the development of a treatment plan. Your blueprint for treatment should be based primarily on the client's physical condition and address the needs created by this condition. Although the client's goals and desires are important, they would generally be a secondary consideration. **The correct answer is (D).**

NOTE

Recent research suggests that you can enhance your ability to retain the information you are studying simply by varying the places in which you study. For example, if you typically study at the kitchen table, you may find that you can remember more about a topic if you study in another room in your house (your living room, for example) or at the local library.

Researchers believe the change in surroundings enhances retention because the brain creates associations between the material being studied and the location/conditions under which it is reviewed. If you study in unique circumstances, the brain can more easily access the content later due to these associations.

CLIENT RECORDKEEPING

In some states, massage therapists are required to create and update records for their clients. In other states, record-keeping is not required but is still highly recommended. Diligent recordkeeping ensures that you always have access to complete information about the client, including notes you make before, during, and after treatment. Keeping records also prevents situations in which the client has to answer the same questions over and over again.

If you work with other health-care providers or if you or your clients will be reimbursed by a health insurance company, you may be required to share your records with others. This is one of the key reasons your client records should be professional, thorough, and follow all recordkeeping protocols.

- **Intake forms:** Client intake forms allow you to quickly gain a substantive amount of information about the client. You can buy preprinted intake forms from a medical supply store or you can create your own. Regardless, any intake form you use should be professional, concise, and ask the client to provide only information that is relevant to treatment.

- **SOAP note:** The acronym SOAP stands for *Subjective, Objective, Assessment*, and *Planning*. SOAP is a four-part documentation format used by many different kinds of health-care providers to document and track client/patient progress. Each part of a SOAP note has a distinct purpose.

  o **Subjective:** The subjective section is a summary of the client's commentary regarding his or her condition. This includes statements made at the initial interview and during and after treatment. It provides a summary of symptoms, potential origins of problems, and the client's perception of pain, impact of other activities, and so on. This section might also include comments shared by the client's other health-care providers.

  o **Objective:** The objective section is a summary of your observations of the client. This includes findings from the different assessments you have completed as well as the results of any tests or evaluations.

  o **Assessment:** The assessment section is a record of your findings, the treatment conducted, and the client's response to the treatment. This section compares the client's response to the treatment against the goals and also indicates progress (or lack thereof).

  o **Planning:** The planning section is a summary of suggestions for future treatment, follow-up care, and instructions for the client.

EXERCISES: CLIENT RECORDKEEPING

Directions: Choose the option that best answers the question.

1. Which part of the SOAP system is based solely on information you receive directly from the client or other health-care providers the client has seen?
   (A) Subjective
   (B) Objective
   (C) Assessment
   (D) Planning

   The subjective portion of the SOAP system is based entirely on information you receive directly from the patient or other health-care providers he or she has seen. This includes client commentary and any relevant information you receive from other medical professionals who have treated the client. **The correct answer is (A).**

2. The assessment portion of the SOAP system would include all of the following EXCEPT
   (A) the treatment conducted.
   (B) the client's response to treatment.
   (C) post-treatment instructions.
   (D) a record of findings.

   The assessment portion of the SOAP system would NOT contain the client's post-treatment instructions. This information would be included in the planning portion. **The correct answer is (C).**

TIPS FOR ANSWERING QUESTIONS ON THERAPEUTIC MASSAGE AND BODYWORK ASSESSMENT

- When you are assessing clients for treatment, you are pulling together everything you have learned about massage therapy so far. You are reviewing the client's anatomy and body structures, checking for pathologies and contraindications, and identifying physical conditions that can benefit from the application of therapeutic massage. Based on this assessment, you will formulate an individualized treatment plan. Therefore, much like the previous chapter, as you study this topic, you will have the most success if you draw from and integrate your knowledge of related subject matter. For example, consider the integumentary system. You know what it is, what it is made of, and how it works. You can recognize common pathologies that impact the skin. Now, you can also determine how those pathologies might impact the treatment plan for the client. It is much easier to remember information if you can make it follow a logical path.

- The acronym SOAP is an excellent way to remember the four different aspects that must be considered in any client record. An acronym can act as a *mnemonic,* which is a technique for improving memory. Some other mnemonic strategies you might apply to this material involve creating a pattern out of rhyming words (similar to a poem or song), creating a visual of the information, or writing a story based on a list related to the content. What are some mnemonics you can use for the information in this section?

PRACTICE QUESTIONS

Directions: Choose the option that best answers the question.

1. Following her session, a client schedules a follow-up appointment based on your recommendation. In which portion of the SOAP system would this information be recorded?
   (A) Subjective
   (B) Objective
   (C) Assessment
   (D) Planning

2. When you assess a client's gait, you are observing his
   (A) spinal posture.
   (B) manner of walking.
   (C) ability to balance.
   (D) degree of flexibility.

3. During the intake interview, a new client tells you he is currently taking an over-the-counter medication with which you are unfamiliar. How should you proceed?
   (A) Decline to treat the client.
   (B) Begin the massage session.
   (C) Suggest the client switch to a different medication.
   (D) Learn more about the medication before continuing.

4. In assessing a client, you determine that she would benefit from hydrotherapy. On the treatment plan, this would be noted as
   (A) an additional modality.
   (B) one of the particulars of treatment.
   (C) a massage technique to be utilized.
   (D) a referral or recommendation.

5. The Swedish Movement Cure was developed by
   (A) George Henry Taylor.
   (B) Per Henrik Ling.
   (C) Johann Mezger.
   (D) Douglas O. Graham.

6. Postural analysis is primarily used to identify
   (A) physical holding patterns.
   (B) existing injuries.
   (C) muscular imbalances.
   (D) muscle guarding.

7. The practice of massage in the Western hemisphere originated with the
   (A) Romans.
   (B) Greeks.
   (C) Swedish.
   (D) English.

8. Which type of input is generally considered to be an objective diagnostic tool only for certain types of practitioners?
   (A) Palpatory
   (B) Energetic
   (C) Observational
   (D) Olfactory

9. Which portion of the SOAP system is intended to serve as a summary of your observations about the client?
   (A) Subjective
   (B) Objective
   (C) Assessment
   (D) Planning

10. Which of the following techniques was introduced by Dr. Johann Mezger?
    (A) Scientific massage
    (B) Connective tissue massage
    (C) Medical gymnastics
    (D) Deep transverse friction massage

ANSWER KEY AND EXPLANATIONS

1. D	3. D	5. B	7. B	9. B
2. B	4. A	6. C	8. B	10. A

1. **The correct answer is (D).** Any future appointments, follow-up care, or client instructions should be included in the planning portion of the SOAP system.

2. **The correct answer is (B).** Gait refers to a client's ability to walk. You can observe the client's gait from the moment he or she walks in the door.

3. **The correct answer is (D).** When a client indicates he is taking an unfamiliar medication, you should get more information about the medication before beginning or continuing with treatment. It is critically important to ensure that the medication in question does not contraindicate massage.

4. **The correct answer is (A).** As hydrotherapy is not a form of massage, this treatment would be noted on a treatment plan as an additional modality.

5. **The correct answer is (B).** The Swedish Movement Cure was developed by Per Henrik Ling, who was also responsible for inventing the Medical Gymnastics system and founding the Royal Swedish Central Institute of Gymnastics.

6. **The correct answer is (C).** Postural analysis is primarily used to identify muscular imbalances, as well as symmetry deviations.

7. **The correct answer is (B).** The practice of massage in the Western hemisphere originated with the Greeks. Western interest in massage was largely cultivated by the development of gymnastics by a Greek priest-physician named Aesculapius.

8. **The correct answer is (B).** Energetic input is generally considered to be an objective diagnostic tool only for those practitioners who specialize in energy-based massage techniques.

9. **The correct answer is (B).** The objective portion of the SOAP system is intended to serve as a summary of your observations about the client.

10. **The correct answer is (A).** Dr. Johann Mezger introduced the scientific massage technique.

SUMMING IT UP

- **Treatment begins with assessment.** Before you can begin working on a client, you must first learn as much about the client and his or her condition, concerns, and therapeutic goals as possible. The various assessment methods available to you are designed to help you create a clear picture of your client that can be used to determine the most appropriate course of action.

- **Assessment works both ways.** The client is not the only one who will be assessed at the outset of your professional relationship. The client will also be judging you as a therapeutic professional. A thorough assessment system will encourage the client to view you as a competent, reliable health-care provider. Instilling this confidence in your clients will go far toward fostering the client/therapist relationship.

- **Developing a treatment plan.** Again, the primary goal of assessment is to develop an appropriate treatment plan. The information you gather during the assessment will help you to design a treatment strategy that is specifically tailored to the client with whom you are working.

CHAPTER 8

Therapeutic Massage and Bodywork Application

OVERVIEW

- **Holistic principles and mind-body practice**
- **Effects of massage**
- **Soft tissue techniques**
- **Chief positioning and draping**
- **Massage and bodywork tools**
- **Client self-care**
- **Standard precautions**
- **Body mechanics for therapists**
- **Tips for answering questions on therapeutic massage and bodywork application**
- **Practice questions**
- **Answer key and explanations**
- **Summing it up**

Therapeutic massage and bodywork application is the apex of what you have been working toward: the integration and application of knowledge and skills in the performance of safe, hygienic, beneficial treatment on clients. Therapeutic application has both theoretical and practical components. It is just as important for you to understand, for example, the physiological and psychological effects of treatment on clients as it is for you to be able to carry out effective soft tissue manipulation.

Other significant practical components of therapeutic application include appropriate client draping and positioning and following standard precautions to create a safe and hygienic environment. Part of your practice will be teaching clients how to be more proactive about self-care, such as stress management and relaxation techniques. Finally, you will want to practice your own brand of self-care by making sure you are following guidelines for appropriate body mechanics so that you do not injure yourself in the course of your work.

For examination study, at a minimum, you should be able to do the following six things: (1) discuss the theoretical underpinnings of massage practice, including the mind-body connection and the holistic nature of treatment; (2)

describe the benefits of soft tissue manipulation; (3) explain appropriate client draping and positioning; (4) identify and describe soft tissue and related techniques; (5) discuss appropriate body mechanics for the therapist; and (6) apply standard precautions necessary for a safe and hygienic practice.

Although this chapter does not review every detail of these subjects, it highlights important information and gives you some practice questions in these areas. If you are having trouble understanding the information or answering the practice questions, take some time to review your textbooks and notes from school.

The number of questions you will need to answer on therapeutic massage and bodywork application varies by exam. If you are taking the MBLEx, you will be required to answer a total of 125 questions; of these, about 17 percent, or around 21 questions, are on this topic. If you are taking the NCETMB, you will be required to answer a total of 160 questions; of these, about 22 percent, or around 35 questions, touch on this topic.

HOLISTIC PRINCIPLES AND MIND-BODY PRACTICE

For health-care practitioners, *holistic* means consideration of all aspects of a person's being—physical, mental, and emotional—when providing treatment to that person. Massage therapy is considered a holistic practice because it impacts so many aspects of the client. In addition, massage therapy is not just about treating symptoms but rather is about establishing the root cause of problems and resolving them in order to restore balance and alignment to the body.

The *mind-body connection* is about the interaction between the psyche and the physical body; it is based on the idea that everything that happens to one also impacts the other. Just as the mind processes pain experienced physically, the body responds to how you feel and what you think. For example, if you are feeling stressed or depressed, you might experience back pain, headaches, or exhaustion. You might develop insomnia or experience a change in appetite. These physical manifestations can be addressed through massage treatment; similarly, experiencing the release and relaxation of massage can help ease feelings of stress or other emotions.

You can facilitate mind-body healing with clients by helping them to become more aware of the link between the way they feel and their physical holding patterns. You can promote client self-care using tools such as meditation or relaxation or visualization and guided imagery.

Stress and the Body

The human body responds to *stress* (real or perceived threats) in an automatic, complex chain of reactions which result in the release of hormones such as adrenaline and cortisol into the bloodstream. Adrenaline surges increase heart rate, elevate blood pressure, and boost energy levels so that the body is able to respond physically when necessary. Cortisol is the primary stress hormone; when released into the bloodstream, it increases sugar (glucose) levels and enhances the brain's ability to utilize this substance. Cortisol curbs nonessential bodily functions like the digestive and reproductive systems and triggers mood, motivation, and fear responses in the brain.

Constant exposure to cortisol and other stress hormones can cause or increase the severity of a variety of health conditions. Some of the known issues resulting from constant stress include:

- Heart disease
- Issues with digestion and nutrition; obesity
- Increase in anxiety and depression; memory impairment
- Problems with relaxation and sleep
- Worsening of conditions of the skin, such as psoriasis or eczema

The Relaxation Response

One of the best solutions to the problems caused by chronic stress is known as the *relaxation response*. The relaxation response is activated by the parasympathetic branch of the nervous system in the body. It is exactly what it sounds like: the body responding to some activity or stimuli by releasing tension, slowing down, and relaxing into a calmer and more restful state. The relaxation response can be triggered by a number of different activities, such as meditation, guided imagery, and, of course, therapeutic massage. As a skilled bodyworker, you can help your clients to access this state of balance and relaxation.

The Mind-Body Connection

Although psychological counseling is out of the scope of practice for massage therapists, the mind-body connection is still a relevant concept. The mind-body connection is the belief that the mind and the body do not operate separately but rather form an integrated whole. In other words, anything that affects one also affects the other. Many people pursue alternative health therapies such as meditation, yoga, and massage, in order to forge a stronger mind-body connection.

The mind-body connection is based on the work of William Reich, who pioneered the theory that emotional energy can be locked into a person's tissues and eventually be the cause of physical dysfunction and pain. Following this logic, the mind-body connection also means that any mental or emotional distress or pain experienced over the course of one's life has also been experienced on some level by the physical body.

For example, being exposed to an emotional situation may manifest itself as a tendency to hold tension in a particular part of the body, such as by clenching the jaw or tensing the upper back. This tension may result in chronic pain. Touch therapies such as massage can release this pain but may also make clients feel emotional without understanding why. If a client responds emotionally during a session, you should stop and ask if the client needs anything, such as privacy, a tissue, a bottle of water, or an end to the session. If you feel overwhelmed by the client's response, you might refer that person to a more appropriate mental health practitioner.

EXERCISES: HOLISTIC PRINCIPLES AND MIND-BODY PRACTICE

Directions: Choose the option that best answers the question.

1. Taking a holistic approach to health care means focusing on
   (A) the client's spiritual needs.
   (B) external factors affecting the client's condition.
   (C) all aspects of the client's being.
   (D) the client's personal energies.

   Practitioners who approach clients from a holistic perspective must consider all aspects of the person's being, including his or her physical, mental, and emotional states. **The correct answer is (C).**

2. Feelings of extreme stress can result in maladaptive
   (A) musculoskeletal asymmetry.
   (B) physical holding patterns.
   (C) range of motion.
   (D) repetitive movement injuries.

   Because the body manifests what the mind thinks and feels, experiencing emotions such as extreme stress can result in maladaptive physical holding patterns. **The correct answer is (B).**

EFFECTS OF MASSAGE

Massage therapy has many positive effects on clients, both physically and psychologically/emotionally. Physically, massage treatment relaxes tight muscles, promotes the flow of the circulatory and lymphatic systems, promotes healthy release of toxins, and facilitates physical and postural awareness for clients.

From a physical perspective, massage can

- improve circulation.

- promote healthier skin.

- alleviate pain and tension.

- reduce muscular tension and stress.

- improve flexibility and mobility.

Massage also has psychological and emotional benefits. Remember, psychological and emotional issues can manifest themselves in the body in physical ways. For example, a client might be suffering from an aching back or a stiff neck as a result of holding in emotional tension. The physical manipulations of massage can trigger the release of these emotions.

From a psychological perspective, massage can

- facilitate the release of emotional tension.

- induce a sense of relaxation and well-being.

- reduce feelings of anxiety and depression.

Due to the implications of touch and the strong mind-body connection inherent to bodywork practices, you may find that some of your clients respond quite emotionally to treatment. It is essential that you recognize how to most appropriately handle such situations using both verbal and nonverbal communication (give the client a moment to compose himself/herself, provide a tissue, offer to discontinue treatment, ask if the client would like to be alone for a few minutes, etc.).

Regular massage can promote a greater degree of alertness, a more balanced sense of well-being, and the ability to deal more effectively with stress. Remember, though, your focus should *always* be on the physical treatment of the client. The psychological benefits of massage are secondary to the physical effects of treatment. Dealing with emotional issues is firmly outside your scope of practice.

EXERCISES: EFFECTS OF MASSAGE

Directions: Choose the option that best answers the question.

1. The circulatory benefits of massage include all of the following EXCEPT
   (A) improving circulation.
   (B) detoxifying blood.
   (C) increasing blood flow.
   (D) reducing cholesterol.

   Though massage has many circulatory benefits, it is not an effective means of reducing cholesterol. **The correct answer is (D).**

2. During a session, your client suddenly becomes very emotional. How should you respond?
   (A) Ignore her and continue the massage.
   (B) Stop the massage and leave the room.
   (C) Use your communication skills to alleviate the situation.
   (D) Reprimand her for her behavior.

   In the event that a client becomes emotional during a massage, you should use your verbal and nonverbal communication skills to gently diffuse the situation and determine the most appropriate course of action. **The correct answer is (C).**

SOFT TISSUE TECHNIQUES

Certain soft tissue techniques form the basis for a variety of therapeutic modalities. In order to be an effective massage therapist, you should be able to perform and understand the purpose of these techniques.

- **Static touching/holding:** Static touching and holding involves placing the hands or fingers on the client's body without moving them. Static holding allows the client to adjust to your touch.

- **Gliding (effleurage):** Gliding involves smooth sliding movements of the hands over the entire body or over particular body parts. Gliding allows the client to become used to your touch. It also warms up tissue prior to more involved work.

- **Kneading (petrissage):** Kneading involves lifting, rolling, squeezing, and stretching movements. Kneading is useful for working out adhesions and stretching and loosening the muscles and fascia.

- **Percussion (tapotement):** Percussion involves striking the client's body in a rapid motion. Percussion might include slapping, pinching, or pounding movements, for example. Percussion should be used only in appropriate applications.

- **Friction:** Friction involves the application of pressure in specific ways; for example, circular friction is a common movement. Friction loosens scar tissue and adhesions and is useful for stretching and the promotion of flexibility.

- **Compression (pumping):** Compression is a form of friction in which a pumping motion is directed at the belly of the muscle.

- **Rocking:** A form of vibration involving a gentle swaying of the body or of particular body parts.

- **Shaking:** A form of vibration involving a gentle trembling of the body or of particular body parts.

- **Traction:** Traction involves the use of a drawing or pulling force and is useful for alleviating pain.

- **Vibration:** Vibration involves a continuous shaking or trembling movement using either the hands or an electrical apparatus. Vibration can be stimulating or relaxing, depending on the application and the speed of the strokes.

Other Techniques

Other common techniques you should understand and be able to perform during treatment include:

- Range-of-motion movements

- Relaxation techniques

- Stretching techniques

EXERCISES: SOFT TISSUE TECHNIQUES

Directions: Choose the option that best answers the question.

1. Which soft tissue technique involves lifting, rolling, squeezing, and stretching movements?
   (A) Percussion
   (B) Kneading
   (C) Compression
   (D) Gliding

   Kneading, also called petrissage, involves lifting, rolling, squeezing, and stretching movements. **The correct answer is (B).**

2. The percussion technique is primarily based on
   (A) striking of the body.
   (B) swaying of the body.
   (C) a pumping motion.
   (D) smooth sliding movements.

   The percussion technique is primarily based on rapid striking of the body. **The correct answer is (A).**

CLIENT POSITIONING AND DRAPING

Positioning

As you get ready to begin a massage session, instruct the client to assume a comfortable position on the massage table. Position the client so that the body part upon which you will work is in front of you, close to you, and facing upward. Depending on the treatment, the client may be lying face up or face down. You may need to assist the client in assuming an appropriate position.

Once the client is on the table, his or her comfort is of the utmost importance. Some clients may experience difficulty if they attempt to lie in a certain position without support. In such cases, use cushions and/or bolsters for added support. You may choose any type of cushion, as long as it is clean, properly covered, and washable. When the client is face up, you can add support by placing bolsters under the knees. If the client is face down, you can place the bolsters under the ankles. No matter where you place the bolsters, make sure they are under the sheet so that they do not come in direct contact with the client's skin.

Some downward-facing clients may also benefit if you place extra support under the chest, as this will help support the cervical spine. For this form of support, the client's chest should be lifted three to four inches off the table while the head rests comfortably forward. Clients who suffer from severe low back pain may require extra support under the abdomen when lying face down. In this case, the client's abdomen should be lifted about six to eight inches off the table. Those who have trouble lying back with their head resting on the table will likely require extra support both for the head and neck as well as the small of the back and the back of the legs.

In some cases, you may need to accommodate for clients who cannot lie on the massage table at all. In such cases, you will need to work with the client in a seated position.

Draping

Draping refers to the use of linens to keep the client appropriately covered during the course of the massage session. Draping properly ensures the client's warmth, comfort, and privacy. Proper draping, which is often required by law, is also an important part of maintaining appropriate client boundaries.

> **NOTE**
> The massage therapist is responsible for providing clean linens for every client.

In most cases, the treatment session begins when the client and therapist begin the intake interview. Once the interview is complete, you can show the client around the treatment room. The client will need to know, for example, where to hang clothes and how to get on the table. You should leave the room so that the client can get undressed in private. The client will disrobe to his or her comfort level and get on the table, under the clean sheets you have provided. After a few minutes, you can reenter the room to begin the session.

Keeping the client warm at all times during the session is very important, as a person who is chilled is virtually incapable of relaxing. Ideally, you should try to maintain a continuous awareness of the client's level of comfort. Even if the treatment room is kept at a generally mild temperature, some clients may become too cool or too warm. Remember to monitor the client's comfort level and adjust the draping as needed. For example, an electric mattress pad or a flannel blanket can be useful for warming a client who cools easily.

If you practice in a state that requires you to be licensed, be aware that you may be subject to certain regulations that apply specifically to draping practices. Such laws often require that certain body parts be kept covered at all times. In some states, you may be allowed to temporarily remove draping while working on, for example, gluteal muscles or breast tissue.

After the massage is completed, clients should be allowed to get up and redressed following a procedure that will ensure safety and protect his or her privacy.

EXERCISES: CLIENT POSITIONING AND DRAPING

Directions: Choose the option that best answers the question.

1. As you are about to begin a massage, the client tells you that he wishes to proceed without draping. How should you respond?
   (A) Remove the draping at his request.
   (B) Ignore him and begin the massage.
   (C) Tell him the draping must be kept on.
   (D) Suspend the massage session and ask him to leave.

   In this situation, you should make sure the client understands that draping is not optional. When applicable, you can let the client know you are legally required to follow proper draping protocol and that such rules are in place for the client's safety and protection. **The correct answer is (C).**

2. For clients requiring extra support of the cervical spine, you can place a bolster under the
   (A) abdomen.
   (B) head.
   (C) chest.
   (D) neck.

   When working with clients who need extra support for their cervical spine when lying in a downward-facing position, extra support should be placed under the chest. **The correct answer is (C).**

MASSAGE AND BODYWORK TOOLS

Many massage and bodywork tools are available to assist you in providing treatment. More advanced tools such as ultrasound require specialized training and expertise and so are considered outside the scope of massage therapy. However, some of the other tools you might use with clients include:

- Electric and manual massagers
- Hot/cold packs
- Rollers
- Stones

Hot/Cold/Hydrotherapy Applications

Some therapeutic treatments involve the use of hot and cold agents, either alone or alternating, or the application of water in some way. You will need to understand how to safely use these modalities. Some treatments are beyond the scope of massage practice, so you should also know what you can and cannot do for your clients.

- *Hydrotherapy* involves the use of water during treatment. Water can be used in its normal state (cold or hot) or in the form of steam or ice. The effects of water treatment vary greatly depending on the particular application.

- *Heat therapy* involves the application of heat to some part of the client's body. The treatment may take the form of dry heat, such as a heating pad or sauna, or moist heat, such as a heating pack or steam bath. Heat therapy is used to increase circulation and promote relaxation. Heat treatment should not be used on any area that is inflamed.

- *Cryotherapy* involves the application of cold to the client's body. The treatment may take the form of an immersion bath, ice massage, or application of a cold pack. Cold therapy is used to improve circulation and reduce inflammation. It can have either a stimulating or depressive effect depending on the length of treatment.

EXERCISES: MASSAGE AND BODYWORK TOOLS

Directions: Choose the option that best answers the question.

1. All of the following treatment devices are considered to be within the scope of practice for massage therapy EXCEPT
   (A) rollers.
   (B) ultrasound.
   (C) hot stones.
   (D) electric massagers.

   Ultrasound is outside the scope of practice of massage therapy because it requires specialized training and expertise. **The correct answer is (B).**

2. A client presents with localized redness and swelling. Given that the results of your assessment indicate that massage is appropriate, what treatment might be appropriate for soothing this area?
   (A) Hot stone therapy
   (B) Roller therapy
   (C) Heat therapy
   (D) Cryotherapy

   Redness and swelling are generally signs of inflammation. Cryotherapy can help to soothe inflammation. **The correct answer is (D).**

CLIENT SELF-CARE

Part of treatment is educating clients on activities that promote self-care. When possible, you can help your clients to better manage their health by teaching them stress management and relaxation techniques. Encourage clients to pay attention to how they feel and what they are doing with their bodies.

Some key elements of self-care include the following:

- **Awareness:** One of the key ways you can assist your clients in taking better care of themselves is to help them become more aware of themselves. Through your treatment, you can teach clients about their typical physical holding patterns, movement patterns, and issues with gait, body alignment, and so on.

- **Decreasing pain:** In the event they are injured or experiencing pain due to some other condition, clients should know and follow the *Rest-Ice-Compression-Elevation* (RICE) technique.

- **Increasing safety:** Corresponding closely to an increase in awareness, clients can also increase personal safety simply by learning to move and hold the body correctly.

- **Modifying activity:** When a client's daily activities lend themselves to the possibility of injury, you can help them consider ways to make those activities safer.

- **Stretching:** Showing clients the appropriate way to stretch and encouraging them to stretch frequently promotes maximal flexibility and an increase in range of motion.

- **Strengthening:** Clients should recognize that they can maintain their health if they engage in activities designed to improve cardiovascular health and increase strength and endurance, such as cardiovascular exercise and weight-lifting.

- **Self-massage:** You can help clients to relieve muscle pain and soreness between treatment sessions by showing them how to perform some basic self-massage techniques.

- **Relaxation:** Sharing relaxation methods, such as breathing exercises and visualization techniques, can help clients learn to become calmer and deal more effectively with stress.

EXERCISES: CLIENT SELF-CARE

Directions: Choose the option that best answers the question.

1. A client could most increase his or her physical endurance through
   (A) stretching exercises.
   (B) self-massage activities.
   (C) strengthening exercises.
   (D) breathing techniques.

   A client's physical endurance would best be increased through strengthening exercises such as weight-lifting. **The correct answer is (C).**

2. Which element of self-care could be used to improve flexibility and range of motion?
   (A) Self-massage
   (B) Breathing exercises
   (C) Strengthening
   (D) Stretching

   Stretching is the primary way for a client to improve his or her flexibility and range of motion. **The correct answer is (D).**

STANDARD PRECAUTIONS

Safety and hygiene are important everywhere, but are paramount for those working in a health-care field. Recognizing and identifying potentially hazardous conditions will allow you to offer a safe and effective practice to clients. A large number of diseases are caused by the transmission of infectious organisms like viruses, bacteria, and fungi. Since it is impossible to completely cleanse the environment of these microorganisms (also called *pathogens*), it is best to focus instead on reducing their numbers as much as possible in order to prevent the spread of disease.

You can remove pathogens from surfaces and objects in three primary ways.

1. **Sterilization:** The most effective means of pathogen removal is sterilization. This method completely destroys all living organisms on surfaces and objects and is commonly used in environments such as operating rooms in hospitals. Due to the degree of difficulty and the time required to effectively sterilize any environment, however, this method is generally not used in massage practices.

2. **Disinfection:** A method of pathogen removal that is almost as efficient as sterilization is disinfection. This method effectively destroys all pathogens except for bacterial spores. Disinfectant substances are powerful and can be used on all surfaces and objects. Some commonly used disinfectants include ammonia compounds, phenols, chlorine bleach, and alcohol. Professional-strength disinfectants are particularly potent and should be used with great caution. They should not be used as hand cleaners, as they may cause skin damage.

3. **Sanitation:** The most commonly practiced method for decontamination in massage practices is sanitation. Sanitation practices remove a significant number of the pathogens that normally accumulate on surfaces. In most cases, sanitation can be achieved using water and soap or some other form of detergent.

One of the most important and commonly practiced forms of sanitation among massage therapists is thorough hand washing. During thorough hand washing, you vigorously scrub your hands with soap (antibacterial, preferably) and warm water. After briefly wetting the hands, apply the soap and work it into a lather. Scrub for up to thirty seconds, making sure to reach all parts of the hands, including the areas between the fingers and thumbs, around the nails and cuticles, and along the forearm. When scrubbing is complete, rinse the hands and dry them with a clean towel. You should wash your hands before and after every session.

On occasion, you might encounter certain circumstances under which special hygienic precautions may be indicated. Normally, massage is not performed if a highly infectious or contagious disease is present and you should not be exposed to bodily fluids in the normal course of events. However, sometimes these situations occur. Under those circumstances, the additional risk needs to be handled appropriately.

In some cases, it is the client who is at an increased risk. Some clients may present with substantially weakened immune systems and may be particularly vulnerable to any pathogens to which they are exposed. Proper hygienic precautions on your part are of vital importance for you and clients alike.

Universal Precautions

Universal precautions are standard practices utilized in health-care settings to avoid contact with others' bodily fluids. Universal precautions are designed with the assumption that all blood and bodily fluids present risk for blood-borne diseases such as HIV and hepatitis. They are intended to control the spread of infection by protecting individuals from exposure to blood or to bodily fluids that might contain blood.

Some of the universal precautions that apply to massage treatment are discussed below.

- **Hand-washing:** Thorough hand-washing is mandatory before and after every session. Hands and other skin surfaces should be washed immediately in the event that you come in contact with blood or other bodily fluids.

- **Gloves:** You may need to wear gloves for a variety of reasons.

  o If you have an injury or sore on the hands, you should wear gloves to work on clients. However, note that if you develop skin lesions or weeping dermatitis, you should not practice massage until your condition improves.

  o If there is even a remote possibility of direct contact with a client's bodily fluids, mucous membranes, non-intact skin, or items or surfaces contaminated with blood or bodily fluids, wear gloves.

o If you wear gloves, put them on before beginning the task and remove them immediately once the task is completed. Discard the gloves and immediately wash your hands.

- **Linens:** If any linen becomes soiled with blood or other bodily fluids, collect it carefully, without undue agitation.

  o Store the linen in a leak-proof bag until you can transport it to the laundry or a soiled linen container.

  o Although there is little risk of catching disease from soiled linen, you should still follow hygienic and common-sense methods for storing and processing linens. Handle soiled linens the minimal amount necessary.

  o Wash linens in hot water with appropriate detergents. Dry using a heated dryer as heat kills germs. Contaminated linens can be treated by adding one cup of chlorine bleach to the wash water.

- **Surfaces:** Walls and floors are generally not associated with disease transmission. As such, it is not so important to sanitize or disinfect such surfaces, except in the event of accidents or spills. However, it is still advised to clean these surfaces regularly using appropriate products.

Sanitizing Objects and Surfaces

You can sanitize most of the objects used in your practice with a *wet sanitizer*. This is a receptacle that contains disinfectant solution and is large enough to allow complete immersion of objects. Prefabricated wet sanitizers are available for purchase and come equipped with a cover that prevents the solution from becoming contaminated. Some states may regulate the type of receptacle used for this purpose.

Before you immerse any objects in the wet sanitizer, wash them with hot water and soap. Rinse the objects thoroughly in order to prevent contamination. After being immersed in the wet sanitizer, the objects should be removed and rinsed again. Then dry them with a clean towel and place them in a dry sanitizer until they are once more needed for use.

Another way to sanitize objects is to use moist heat. In this process, the objects are placed in boiling water (212° Fahrenheit) for about twenty minutes. Finally, many hospitals and other medical facilities utilize a device known as an *autoclave*, which sterilizes objects using high-pressure steam.

You should also maintain clean surfaces in your practice for both disease control and aesthetic purposes. All surfaces should be cleaned and sanitized on a regular basis.

Some of the surfaces that require regular sanitary attention include:

- **Floors:** Carpets should be vacuumed regularly and shampooed as needed. Solid floors should be swept daily, sanitized with detergent and water, and disinfected.

- **Massage tables and bolsters:** Remove oils from these surfaces using a spray-cleaner or soap and water, then disinfect them.

- **Restrooms:** All restroom surfaces should be sanitized with detergent and water and then disinfected with a commercial disinfectant. A chlorine bleach solution may also be used. When using a disinfectant, spray the surface and wipe dry. Afterwards, spray the surface again and allow it to air dry. Ensure that the restroom is properly stocked with appropriate paper products as well as liquid antibacterial soap.

- **Other surfaces:** All other surfaces in the treatment area should be sanitized either with soap and water or with commercial cleaning solution.

EXERCISES: STANDARD PRECAUTIONS

Directions: Choose the option that best answers the question.

1. Which of the following most accurately describes disinfection?
   - (A) It is commonly used to remove pathogens from surgical instruments.
   - (B) It completely destroys all pathogens.
   - (C) Its most common form is hand washing.
   - (D) It destroys all pathogens except bacterial spores.

   Disinfection practices destroy all pathogens except bacterial spores. Only sterilization can destroy all pathogens. **The correct answer is (D).**

2. Sanitization via moist heat involves the use of
   - (A) heated chemicals.
   - (B) an autoclave.
   - (C) boiling water.
   - (D) steam cleaning.

   Sanitization via moist heat involves the use of boiling water. In this process, the object to be sanitized is placed in boiling water for approximately twenty minutes. **The correct answer is (C).**

BODY MECHANICS FOR THERAPISTS

In addition to attending to the physical needs of your client during each session, you must also be aware of your own body. Poor posture, bad techniques, and improper workplace design can all lead to stress and strain on your body, increasing the possibility that you will injure yourself.

Before you can begin to develop a system for ensuring your physical health in the workplace, you must understand the basic sciences involved. *Body mechanics*, commonly known as *biomechanics*, refers to the mechanics of the body's muscular activity and movement. Proper body mechanics increase strength and energy and decrease the likelihood of injury. *Kinesiology* is the study of the way the body moves as well as the body parts involved in each movement. You have already learned how to apply kinesiology to your practice; you should also take care to apply it to yourself.

The importance of observing and improving your body mechanics is critical because proper movement patterns decrease the possibility of injuries that may affect your ability to do your job and, in turn, may affect your business. You must take as good care of yourself as you do your clients.

Ergonomics is concerned with the way people interact with systems, equipment, and each other in the workplace. It is about designing work environments that optimize both your physical well-being and your ability to be productive.

Ergonomics has three basic principles, as follows:

1. Work activities should be designed so as to allow the worker to assume a number of different, healthy, and safe postures.

2. When performing work activities, exert muscular force using the largest suitable muscle groups available.

3. When performing work activities, hold the joints around the midpoint of their range of motion. This is especially important when considering the use of the upper limbs, head, and neck.

One of your primary concerns in the treatment area should be the height of your massage table. Your table should be situated at the correct height for you to comfortably work on the client without needless bending and stretching. Your table should be adjustable so that you can adjust it based on the size of the client, when necessary.

When working on a client, stay in a neutral-spine position. Keep your back straight, knees slightly bent, elbows close to the body, and wrists relaxed. Avoid placing all of your pressure on your thumbs. Try to work from the center of your pelvis and let your legs do the heavy work.

Since your hands are your primary tools of trade, you need to take especially good care of them. Avoid exaggerated wrist angles by staying behind the massage movements instead of on top of them. Do not hyperextend your wrists or use the heel of the hand when applying compressive forces. Use your forearms and elbows to do pressure work or to perform deep, gliding strokes. When you need to apply pressure with your fingers or thumbs, do so using the palmar side of these extremities, rather than the tips.

Of course, some of your physical needs may not be readily identifiable until you are actually working on a client. For this reason, it is important to remain conscious of your body and body movements at all times during a session. If you notice that a certain movement causes discomfort or pain, stop immediately and readjust your posture or change the technique.

Finally, remember to pace yourself. Massage is a physical profession and it is easy to burn out. Though it may seem worthwhile to do as many massages as possible every day, remember that massage is strenuous work. The key to longevity in this type of career is to pace yourself carefully. Avoid taking on more than you can handle.

EXERCISES: BODY MECHANICS FOR THERAPISTS

Directions: Choose the option that best answers the question.

1. The study of how the body moves and the body parts used in each movement is referred to as
   (A) kinesiology.
   (B) body mechanics.
   (C) ergonomics.
   (D) biomechanics.

   Kinesiology is the study of the body's movements.
   The correct answer is (A).

2. When working on clients, you should exert force from your legs instead of your torso because
   (A) you can reach farther with this technique.
   (B) the legs are a larger muscle group.
   (C) doing so prevents overextension of the arms.
   (D) doing so negates the need to adjust table height.

   You will recall that one of the principles of ergonomics is the dependence on large muscle groups to exert force when possible. The legs are the largest muscle group in the body. **The correct answer is (B).**

TIPS FOR ANSWERING QUESTIONS ON THERAPEUTIC MASSAGE AND BODYWORK APPLICATION

- **Follow the logic:** The application of therapeutic massage and bodywork is the pivotal moment of your studies. It is here that you integrate everything you have learned for use on both your examination and your massage table. To achieve the highest degree of success, follow the logical chain of information, from your initial study of anatomy and body systems to your review of kinesiology and body mechanics to your experience with therapeutic assessment and application.

- **Focus on the basics:** Most massage modalities have their roots in the fundamental soft tissue techniques discussed in this chapter. Pay careful attention to these techniques in your studies.

- **Remember the client:** Many of the concepts covered in this chapter involve your interactions with the client. With this in mind, it may be helpful to remember the client-centric point of view as you answer the examination questions. When presented with scenarios, consider each answer carefully, and select the one that is best for the client. Always consider the *client's needs* first.

PRACTICE QUESTIONS

Directions: Choose the option that best answers the question.

1. Which of the following soft tissue techniques is also known as effleurage?
   (A) Percussion
   (B) Gliding
   (C) Friction
   (D) Traction

2. Which of the following is NOT true of heat therapy?
   (A) It can improve circulation.
   (B) It can be applied in dry and moist forms.
   (C) It can reduce inflammation.
   (D) It can promote relaxation.

3. The use of scientific information to optimize the workplace is referred to as
   (A) body mechanics.
   (B) ergonomics.
   (C) biomechanics.
   (D) kinesiology.

4. If you have a minor paper cut on your hand, you should
   (A) wash your hands frequently to keep them clean.
   (B) cancel your appointments until the cut heals.
   (C) conduct treatment without using that hand.
   (D) put on gloves before touching a client.

5. Which soft tissue technique involves the use of a drawing or pulling force?
   (A) Friction
   (B) Rocking
   (C) Kneading
   (D) Traction

6. You are treating a client who suffers from severe low back pain and is unable to lie face down on the table without support. When placing support, how far off the table should the abdomen be elevated?
   (A) 1–2 inches
   (B) 2–4 inches
   (C) 4–6 inches
   (D) 6–8 inches

7. The main purpose of following proper draping protocols is to
   (A) meet legal and ethical requirements.
   (B) keep the client comfortable.
   (C) maintain client boundaries and privacy.
   (D) All of the above

8. During a session, you suddenly notice that you experience pain when performing a certain stroke. How should you respond?
   (A) Continue the session and ignore the pain.
   (B) Switch to a different stroke that does not cause pain.
   (C) Tell the client you are taking a quick break.
   (D) Discontinue the massage and cancel any remaining appointments.

9. The most effective method of destroying pathogens is through
   (A) disinfection.
   (B) moist heat.
   (C) sterilization.
   (D) sanitation.

10. Which soft tissue technique involves a pumping motion aimed at the belly of the muscle?
    (A) Compression
    (B) Kneading
    (C) Percussion
    (D) Rocking

ANSWER KEY AND EXPLANATIONS

1. B	3. B	5. D	7. D	9. C
2. C	4. D	6. D	8. B	10. A

1. **The correct answer is (B).** Effleurage is another name for gliding, which involves smooth sliding movements of the hands over the body or body part.

2. **The correct answer is (C).** Heat therapy does not reduce inflammation. Inflammation can be reduced with cryotherapy.

3. **The correct answer is (B).** The use of scientific information to optimize the workplace is called ergonomics.

4. **The correct answer is (D).** In the event that you develop a skin lesion on your hand, you should always wear gloves before touching the client. This method protects both the client and you.

5. **The correct answer is (D).** Traction involves using a drawing or pulling force.

6. **The correct answer is (D).** Clients who suffer from severe low back pain often require extra support under the abdomen when lying face down. When this type of support is provided, the client's abdomen should be elevated 6–8 inches off the table.

7. **The correct answer is (D).** Meeting legal and ethical requirements, keeping the client comfortable, and maintaining client boundaries and privacy are all among the reasons for following proper draping protocols.

8. **The correct answer is (B).** If you experience pain when performing a certain stroke, you should immediately switch to another stroke that does not cause any pain. Ignoring this problem could be potentially harmful to your health.

9. **The correct answer is (C).** The most effective means of destroying pathogens is sterilization. Sterilization is the only method capable of destroying all of the pathogens on an object.

10. **The correct answer is (A).** Compression involves a pumping motion aimed at the belly of the muscle.

SUMMING IT UP

- **Study the components of therapeutic application.** Therapeutic application has both theoretical and practical components. Massage therapy involves more than just physical manipulation of the client's body. There are many other concerns that play just as important a role in massage therapy as the physical work you do on the client.

- **Massage therapy includes both mind and body.** Psychology and mental well-being have a significant effect on our physical health. Massage therapy is a modality that works with the physical body, though it can have indirect effects on the client's mental and emotional state.

- **Remember the client's needs AND your needs.** The practice of massage therapy requires you to pay close attention to the needs of your clients. It is imperative that clients feel comfortable and secure at all times. At the same time, you must also take precautions to ensure YOUR health and safety.

CHAPTER 9

Professional Standards and Legal and Business Practices

OVERVIEW

- **Professional standards**
- **Legal practices**
- **Business practices**
- **Tips for answering questions on professional standards and legal and business practices**
- **Practice questions**
- **Answer key and explanations**
- **Summing it up**

Professional standards and legal and business practices are the principles upon which your practice must be built. Appropriate operational standards and professional practices are vital. The choices you make and the business operations you follow form the very foundation of the your practice. Your goal should be to establish and maintain the most professional, safe, and trustworthy environment possible, so that both your client/therapist relationships and business will flourish.

The professional standards and legal and business practices questions on the massage therapy examinations cover a fairly broad range of topics. The focus of these questions varies by exam; however, some of the topics you should expect to encounter include the following:

- Business and strategic planning
- Ethical behavior and choices
- Federal and state laws pertaining to massage therapy
- Office management
- Patient confidentiality
- Professional boundaries
- Scope of practice
- Sexual misconduct
- The therapeutic relationship

For examination study, at a minimum, you should be able to do the following four things: (1) recognize and discuss the standard parameters of ethical behavior and professional boundaries for massage therapists; (2) explain the nature of the therapeutic relationship between the therapist and the client; (3) identify basic federal and state laws applicable to your practice; and (4) describe core business practices concepts and strategies required for success. In addition, if you plan to take an NCE examination, you should also be able to recognize and describe the elements of the Code of Ethics and Standards of Practice published by the National Certification Board for Therapeutic Massage and Bodywork (NCBTMB).

Although this chapter does not review every detail of these subjects, it highlights important information and gives you some practice questions in these areas. If you are having trouble understanding the information or answering the practice questions, take some time to review your textbooks and notes from school.

The number of questions you will need to answer on professional standards and legal and business practices varies by exam. If you are taking the MBLEx, you will be required to answer a total of 125 questions; of these, about 13 percent, or around 16 questions, are on this topic. If you are taking the NCETMB, you will be required to answer a total of 160 questions; of these, about 12 percent, or around 15 questions, touch on this topic.

PROFESSIONAL STANDARDS

Ethical Behavior

Ethics are defined as standards of conduct and moral judgment, or a system or code of morals. Ethics are important in any profession. However, due to the intimate nature of the client/therapist relationship, the making of ethical—or morally right—choices is critically important for massage therapists.

For your examination, you should understand what is meant by ethical behavior. You should also be familiar with a variety of the concepts related to ethics:

- **Boundaries:** Recognizing legal, professional, and personal boundaries

- **Confidentiality:** Understanding your obligation to protect client information

- **Informed consent:** Allowing the client to participate in treatment decisions

- **Right of refusal:** Allowing the client to stop treatment at any time

- **Scope of practice:** Recognizing the limits that apply to your practice (i.e., what you can and cannot do)

Code of Ethics

A code of ethics provides a blueprint for professional behavior that members of a profession are expected to follow. For bodyworkers, a code of ethics is designed to protect both the practitioner and the client by explicitly outlining expectations for behavior. For example, members of the American Massage Therapy Association (AMTA) are expected to follow the AMTA Code of Ethics; individuals certified by NCBTMB are expected to adhere to the NCBMTB Code of Ethics. (Reprinted in full for your convenience in *Appendix A: NCBTMB Code of Ethics and Standards of Practice.*)

In general, agreeing to abide by a code of ethics means you

- are committed to providing the highest quality of professional care.

- are educated and qualified to render professional services.

- recognize the limitations of your discipline and refer clients when they are better served by other health-care professionals.

- provide treatment only when it is likely to be advantageous to the client.

- keep up with the profession and continue to grow your skills and knowledge.

- make ethical, nondiscriminatory decisions and conduct your practice with honesty and integrity.

- protect your clients by all means possible.

- respect the rights of your clients, recognize boundaries, and refuse to engage in inappropriate behaviors.

Ethical Violations

In most cases, the top ethical concern for massage therapists is sexual misconduct. Because massage therapy and bodywork involve physical contact with a client who may be unclothed, sexual feelings may arise in either the practitioner or the client. In the course of providing massage therapy or bodywork, it is critically important to avoid any form of sexual misconduct. Some approaches to avoiding sexual misconduct include wearing professional apparel, avoiding any sexual conversation or behavior, abstaining from engaging in a sexual relationship with a client, and observing the appropriate dressing regulations.

Not all ethical violations are so blatant as sexual misconduct. Some other tips for maintaining high ethical standards at your practice include giving clients a fair value for their money, refraining from cancelling appointments other than in the event of an emergency, and paying your bills in a timely manner.

Boundaries

A *boundary* is a delimiting point (a border or a limit). In professional practice, boundaries can be legal, professional, and personal.

- Legal boundaries are determined by a governing body. For massage therapists, legal boundaries are generally defined by your *scope of practice*, which is the outline of the things you are and are not allowed to do. Legal boundaries are generally determined by the governing body that regulates practices in your state.

- Professional boundaries are the rules that govern your professional behavior. Most professional organizations publish guidelines for members associated with that profession. For example, if you are certified by NCBTMB, you are expected to abide by the NCBMTB Code of Ethics and Standards of Practice. If you are a member of the American Massage Therapy Association (AMTA), you are expected to abide by the AMTA's Code of Ethics and Standards of Practice. (And so on and so forth.) No matter your professional affiliation, however, you should expect to behave professionally around all clients at all times.

- Personal boundaries are one's personal "safety zone."

Confidentiality

A key ethical consideration for massage therapists and other health-care workers is confidentiality. As part of your practice, you will gain access to a considerable amount of information about clients. Under no circumstance should you disclose this information to nonprofessional parties.

In some cases, it may be necessary to share information about a client with a fellow therapist or with some other health-care provider (the client's doctor, for example). Even under such circumstances, however, you need to make sure you have obtained the client's consent to speak with that person.

Health Insurance Portability and Accountability Act (HIPAA)

Among the most important laws affecting massage therapy practices is the Health Insurance Portability and Accountability Act (HIPAA). HIPAA laws were first introduced in 1996. HIPAA governs the privacy and security of personal health information. HIPAA grants clients/patients guaranteed access to their medical files and also governs the ways in which medical professionals may use that information. According to HIPAA, health-care providers are required to let their clients know how their personal information is secure. In addition, health-care providers are required to obtain the client's express consent prior to sharing information with an insurance company, medical professionals, or other third parties. Careful observation of HIPAA laws is critical, as these regulations are taken very seriously and any violation may have severe consequences for your practice.

Informed Consent

Informed consent is defined as a client's agreement to undergo treatment with a full understanding of all risks involved. Informed consent means the client is the one who makes the ultimate decision as to whether or not to pursue the treatment. In order to provide informed consent, the client must understand the treatment goals and purpose, benefits and risks, potential consequences, and the time and money involved. It is your responsibility to ensure that the client has this information.

Right of Refusal

The *right of refusal* works both ways. First, clients have the right to refuse treatment for any reason, at any time. That means if the client wishes you to stop treatment midway, you must honor that decision. Second, you have the right to refuse to treat a client for any reason (you might, for example, refuse to treat a client who presents with a contraindication, or one who appears to be under the influence of drugs or alcohol).

Scope of Practice

As already mentioned, another important consideration is your *scope of practice*. Due to its intimate nature, the massage profession has definite limitations, and you must never go beyond them.

In addition, you should avoid doing or saying anything beyond your level of training. For example, you will not diagnose conditions nor prescribe or suggest medications for clients. You should also refrain from performing procedures for which you are not appropriately trained, abstain from giving unsolicited or unqualified advice, and avoid asking clients invasive questions about their personal lives.

Standards of Practice

Standards of practice provide explicit guidance in how to present yourself and conduct your business. Standards of practice generally cover legal and ethical requirements, business practices, professionalism, roles and boundaries, sexual misconduct, and confidentiality.

If you become certified by NCBTMB, you agree to abide by the NCBTMB Standards of Practice. If you are a member of AMTA, you agree to abide by the AMTA Standards of Practice. Other organizations may have similar published standards, so that members are fully aware of expectations for behavior and professionalism.

In addition, some states may provide additional ethical standards to be followed.

Client/Therapist Relationship

The core element of any massage practice is the client/therapist relationship. Many of the concepts discussed in this chapter impact your ability to successfully forge relationships with your clients. For example, if a therapist fails to respect boundaries, maintain confidentiality, or stay within the bounds of professional practice, that therapist cannot really expect to build trusting relationships with clients. On the other hand, a therapist who acts in a trustworthy manner builds trustworthy relationships.

An important point to keep in mind is the *power differential* that exists in the client/therapist relationship. This power differential favors you, as you are considered the expert health-care professional in this situation; the client is seeking your advice and paying for your services. In addition, consider that your role involves standing fully clothed over a client who is generally in a prone position and some state of undress.

As you interact with each client, be vigilant about any unhealthy developments in your relationship. Some clients may become overly dependent on you to meet emotional needs, a phenomenon known as *transference*. This dependence often stems from unresolved issues relating to previous personal relationships. *Countertransference* is the opposite situation, in which you project your issues or conflicts onto the client. Both situations are unhealthy and you will need to be mindful to ensure they do not occur.

Another client/therapist relationship pitfall to avoid is taking on *dual roles* or *dual relationships*. Dual relationships occur when you enter into an additional relationship with a client while continuing to act as the client's therapist. For example, if the client becomes a personal friend or gets involved with you on a business level (for example, if you barter services with each other), that is considered a dual role. Engaging in dual roles can be risky, because it becomes easier to cross boundaries.

Assuming an employer/employee relationship with a client when bartering your massage treatment services for some other form of service is risky because it can lead to complications surrounding the value of each person's time and worth. As the therapist, it is your responsibility to maintain the proper boundaries in your relationship with the client, so you should avoid taking on any dual roles that might confuse this relationship.

Finally, becoming romantically involved with a client is the most dangerous dual role of all and should always be avoided. If you find yourself wishing to enter into a romantic relationship with a client, you should end the professional relationship and seek supervision or guidance before proceeding.

Communication

An important part of any job, but particularly one in which you interact with the public, is the ability to communicate well. For the massage therapist, this means really listening to your clients and taking cues from them (from what they say with words as well as what they say with nonverbal cues).

During a session, you may engage in conversation with a client who wishes to talk; however, if the client seems to be avoiding conversation, you should remain quiet and allow the client to relax. When you do converse with a client, be sure to keep the conversation professional and try to keep it focused on the massage and how the patient is feeling.

Interviewing Clients

Your primary communication goal before, during, and after a treatment is to build and maintain a good rapport with the client. The most important portion of communication between practitioner and client occurs when the two first meet. The client's first impression of you is critical to the relationship. Therefore, when you enter the treatment room, be sure that your full attention is on the client and engage in conversation. Offer a caring handshake and address the client by his or her first name. Remember to make regular eye contact as you discuss the client's condition and treatment, as this will serve to communicate your interest in the client. You can also communicate interest by acknowledging the client's input during the conversation. You should also be sure that the client understands that you are committed to respecting his or her confidentiality. Finally, keep in mind that approaching your client from a humanistic point of view that focuses on the client's needs, interests, and values can have a significant impact on the success of the communication and rapport-building process. Remember, for example, that each client is unique, possesses varying individual skills, and desires success.

EXERCISES: PROFESSIONAL STANDARDS

Directions: Choose the option that best answers the question.

1. After developing a comprehensive, multifaceted treatment plan with a client, she decides that she wants to stop in the middle of the procedure. At this point you should
   (A) continue the procedure until the contract is fulfilled.
   (B) encourage the client to continue.
   (C) tell her that she will still have to pay the full price.
   (D) stop the procedure immediately.

   Regardless of how much effort you and the client have put into developing a treatment plan, if the client asks you to stop treatment, you should stop immediately. This is known as the client's right of refusal. **The correct answer is (D).**

2. You are interviewing a potential new client who was referred to you by her husband, who is an existing client. During the course of the interview, the client asks you a few questions about her husband's treatment. How should you respond?
   (A) Answer her questions truthfully.
   (B) Give fabricated answers to protect the husband's privacy.
   (C) Politely let her know you cannot share that information.
   (D) Scold her for prying into her husband's business and ask her to leave.

   Under no circumstances should you share personal information about a client, even when the party asking for that information is a close family member. **The correct answer is (C).**

LEGAL PRACTICES

A wide variety of laws and legal regulations govern the operation of a massage therapy practice. Federal, state, and local governments all issue and enforce various laws that may impact your practice in some way. Strict observance of the laws is critical to operating a successful practice. Breaking or bending the law in any way can not only hurt your business, it can also cost you your practice and land you in serious legal jeopardy.

Government bodies at the federal, state, county, and municipal levels can all impact your particular practice. Below are a few of the ways these bodies impact the profession in general.

- **Federal government:** The federal government grants certain organizations the authority to accredit massage therapy schools, which allows for the distribution of financial aid grants to students who attend such schools.

- **State government:** State governments frequently regulate the practice of massage therapy within the state. Others do not govern the practice of massage therapy at all.

- **County government:** County governments may regulate the practice of massage therapy in unincorporated areas not governed by municipal government. County governments may also be responsible for the enforcement of zoning and health regulations in these areas. Most importantly for massage therapy practices, county governments also keep records of business names and grant businesses the right to use them.

- **Municipal government:** Municipal (local) governments regulate business operations within their limits. In addition, municipal governments deal with health concerns as well as zoning and parking laws. Some municipal governments, particularly large city governments, may enact their own laws specifically regarding the practice of massage therapy or may even prohibit it.

Individuals who apply for a massage license may be subject to regulations pertaining to the licensure process. As per these requirements, you may need to present your employment history, references, a recent photo, fingerprints, and confirmation from a physician that you do not have any communicable diseases. In addition, as already discussed, you may be subject to specific rules in regards to required education.

Some municipal governments enact laws that regulate the physical properties of business establishments. Such laws are generally concerned with lighting, bathrooms, signage, health codes, and more. Other requirements and restrictions established by these governments, such as dress codes, licensing fees, medical examinations, or background checks, may also apply.

Additional Legal Information

Other legal matters to keep in mind include the following:

- **Business classification:** As a business entity, you will need to register as a sole proprietorship, partnership, corporation, or some other form of business classification. Each classification includes specific tax requirements and legal responsibilities.

- **Business licensing:** Most municipal governments require businesses to be licensed. Local governments use these licenses as a record of local businesses and the goods and services they provide. Business licensure generates funds for the local treasury and helps to ensure that all zoning laws are being observed.

- **Contractual relationship:** Massage therapists enter into verbal and written contracts on a daily basis. Most commonly, this involves contracts between the practitioner and the client for services provided. This also involves contracts for services from third parties for various goods and services.

- **Fictitious name statement:** Business owners who make up a name for their business are required to submit that name to the county government. There may be a fee for this registration and you will probably have to make sure no other business already uses that name.

- **Local taxes:** Based on the regulations established by your municipal government, you may be required to pay local taxes on your business property, which means the value of your property will be assessed and you will pay a percentage of that value annually. You may also be subject to other forms of taxation, such as a sewer tax.

- **Taxpayer identification number:** Any business owner who hires employees, incorporates, or enters into a partnership must obtain a taxpayer identification number for tax purposes.

- **Zoning law:** Zoning laws dictate where you can and cannot operate a business within a municipality. Most municipal governments require certain types of businesses to be located in areas zoned for such businesses.

Not all massage regulations cover all forms of bodywork. In states where massage is regulated, each specific regulation either directly defines the forms of massage and bodywork meant to be included in that regulation, or else it indicates a broad definition of massage applies. In the case of those regulations with only a broad definition of massage, the decision as to whether the definition in question applies to a specific form of bodywork is usually left to the discretion of a special board or commission.

EXERCISES: LEGAL PRACTICES

Directions: Choose the option that best answers the question.

1. HIPAA is primarily concerned with
   (A) certification.
   (B) privacy.
   (C) malpractice.
   (D) taxation.

   HIPAA requires health-care providers to guard the personal information of clients/patients. **The correct answer is (B).**

2. The authority to accredit massage therapy schools is granted to certain organizations by which level of government?
   (A) Federal
   (B) State
   (C) County
   (D) Municipal

   The federal government is responsible for granting certain organizations the authority to accredit massage therapy schools. **The correct answer is (A).**

BUSINESS PRACTICES

Once you have earned your massage license, there are a wide variety of ways you can put your license to use. You may choose to work for someone else, or you may start your own business. Where the law allows, you may choose to work out of your home or open an office. You can also opt to work as a traveling massage therapist who practices at various sites as needed, or you might take a job at a hospital or other medical facility. Some massage therapists also work in spas, resorts, salons, or on cruise ships. However you choose to conduct business, it is important for you to have a fundamental understanding of both traditional business practices and the business of massage.

Business Concerns

Massage therapists who work for someone else are generally paid on a regular schedule and sometimes earn a percentage of the fees charged for their services. Employers provide all essential needs for the practice, handle taxes, and may provide added benefits, such as health insurance or vacation time.

Some massage therapists choose to work as independent contractors, which means working out of someone else's office on agreed-upon terms, for a negotiated fee. As an independent contractor, you are considered self-employed, so you may have to provide your own materials and supplies. Your clients may be either referred to you or scheduled for you. You will also be responsible for paying your own taxes, including federal and state income tax, social security tax, and self-employment tax.

Massage therapists who own their business and/or employ others are usually subject to other types of taxes, such as state unemployment tax or sales tax, if they sell products through the business.

As with any job, when you agree to be an employee or independent contractor, you must be sure that the exact details of your agreement are clearly stated in writing. All of the responsibilities and expectations of both employee and employer should be outlined in advance of an agreement.

Business Plan

If you decide you want to start your own business, you should first prepare a business plan, which constitutes your vision for your business, what you expect to accomplish, and how you intend to get there. A traditional business plan includes estimated expenses, immediate goals, and a mission statement, which is a brief written explanation of the intent of your new business. Some prospective business owners look at the long-term potential and create five- and ten-year business plans.

When writing a business plan, consider everything from how to advertise to whether you will use a linen service. Your community's Small Business Administration (SBA) or Chamber of Commerce can help you to determine all of the considerations at hand so that your business plan is thorough and complete.

Marketing Plan

One of the key components of any good business plan is a marketing plan. Marketing is based on four principal elements: *product, place, price, promotion*. When developing a marketing plan, think about the services your business will offer, where you will practice, the price points you will work in, and how you intend to promote your business. Some of the many methods of marketing you may choose to pursue include:

- Advertising on the Internet, TV, radio, or in print
- Handing out business cards
- Listing in the phonebook/Yellow Pages
- Offering discounts/gift certificates
- Pinning fliers on bulletin boards
- Providing promotional massages
- Setting up a Web site
- Soliciting word-of-mouth recommendations

Business Recordkeeping

One of the most important aspects of running your own business involves business records. Whether you do your recordkeeping via computer or by hand, maintaining an accurate record of your income and expenses is vital. Keep in mind that every expense you incur can potentially be used as a tax deduction. Keep all of your business receipts as these are tangible documentation of your expenses. If you are audited by the IRS, such documentation will be critical.

If you think that you would not do a good job at recordkeeping, consider some alternatives. If you have the funding, you might invest in software or hire a bookkeeper to do the work.

Client Recordkeeping

Your client records are crucial for maintaining familiarity with clients and for tracking their progress. These records contain highly confidential personal and medical information as well as the history of your treatment. You will need to keep these records organized and safe. Consider investing in a fire-proof filing cabinet that locks.

Note that client records may be needed when billing insurance companies for services rendered.

Insurance

No massage therapy practice can afford to be without insurance. Insurance protects you and your business from various risks that could threaten your financial well-being. As you begin your new venture, there are a number of different types of insurance you will need to consider.

- **Professional liability insurance:** Professional liability insurance protects you against claims made by clients who allege that your professional negligence resulted in injury or damage to them. Most professional liability insurance provides defense coverage (meaning the insurance company will defend you against warranted lawsuits) as well as indemnity (meaning the insurance company will pay the judgment levied against you, up to the amount agreed upon in your policy). Claims generally not covered by professional liability policies include those dealing with sexual misconduct. Some insurance carriers may pay for your defense in the event of a sexual misconduct allegation, but none will cover the judgment. Professional liability coverage is complex. Many practitioners obtain professional liability insurance through one of the major professional massage organizations, such as the American Massage Therapy Association (AMTA) or Associated Bodywork and Massage Professionals (ABMP). Coverage can also be purchased independently.

- **Business owners insurance:** Business owners insurance (frequently called a business owner policy, or BOP) is designed to meet the needs of small business owners. It includes a combination of property and liability insurance which is designed to protect your property and equipment due to losses from events such as fire or theft. In addition, most business insurance covers liability claims from third parties, such as slip-and-fall claims. Some policies also provide time element coverage, which covers lost income and expenses if your practice needs to be closed due to a covered cause of loss. Business insurance is generally obtained through major insurance companies, via an insurance agent.

- **Disability insurance:** Disability insurance provides income in the event that you are unable to work for a period of time due to a covered injury or illness. Generally, you must be disabled for some period of time (several weeks to several months) before you can collect on such a policy. This type of insurance is often expensive and difficult to obtain. Your decision on whether to purchase disability insurance should be based on how much you rely on a continued income.

- **Medical/health insurance:** Many different types of health insurance policies are available, offering various degrees of coverage for a wide range in price. The most basic and inexpensive policies offer coverage for hospital costs. More comprehensive and costly policies may cover hospital visits, routine procedures, medications, and more. Medical insurance can be purchased individually or as part of a group policy. Many of the major professional associations offer some form of group medical insurance in which you can enroll at discounted prices.

Professional Networking

The relationships you build and maintain with other health-care professionals are an important factor in the potential success of your practice. First and foremost, building relationships with other health-care professionals can increase the number of referrals you receive. If local physicians, chiropractors, physical therapists, and others know you and trust your work, they are likely to refer their patients/clients to you. Similarly, such relationships give you comfort and trust when referring your clients to other types of providers.

In addition, it is important to maintain relationships with fellow massage therapists, especially those who specialize in modalities other than your own.

Employees

When an established practice is ready to grow, one of the most critical steps in the expansion process is hiring employees. Growing your staff will give you expanded ability to serve clients. However, employing others adds another level of complexity to your business. You must keep payroll records, withhold the proper taxes, prepare tax returns, buy workers compensation insurance, and more. If you reach this level in your business, it is important to remember that potential employees should be

- licensed and willing to follow the rules and regulations of your practice.

- ethical individuals who are willing to interact with clients courteously and professionally.

- hard working and willing to participate in continuing education and professional growth opportunities.

- self-motivated and honest.

EXERCISES: BUSINESS PRACTICES

Directions: Choose the option that best answers the question.

1. The best way to prevent a financial crisis if your business is audited is to
   (A) hire an accountant.
   (B) store emergency funds separately.
   (C) keep all your business receipts.
   (D) purchase the right insurance.

   The best way to prevent a financial crisis if your business is audited is to keep all your business receipts, as these receipts serve as physical documentation of your business transactions. Such documentation can be invaluable in this situation. **The correct answer is (C).**

2. A written document that outlines the purposes and goals of a new business is known as a
   (A) business plan.
   (B) mission statement.
   (C) letter of intent.
   (D) marketing plan.

   A business plan is a written document outlining the purposes and goals of a new business. **The correct answer is (A).**

TIPS FOR ANSWERING QUESTIONS ON PROFESSIONAL STANDARDS AND LEGAL AND BUSINESS PRACTICES

When answering test questions that deal with professional standards and legal and business practices, you may find it helpful to remember these tips.

- **Read the questions carefully.** Many professional standards and legal and business practices questions will present a brief scenario and ask you to indicate how you should proceed in that situation. Be sure to read each question carefully so that you fully understand exactly what is going on in each scenario. Misreading a scenario can lead you to an incorrect response.

- **Take time to think critically.** When you encounter a scenario-based question, carefully read the scenario and take a moment to think it over. Do not rush to select an answer. Many of these questions require common sense to answer correctly, so stop and think about the situation before you answer.

- **Study the terminology.** Many professional standards and legal and business practices questions will be based directly on specific terminology and concepts discussed in the chapter. As you study, be sure to pay close attention to key terms. Understanding these concepts will go a long way toward improving your performance.

- **Conduct your own research.** Many of the business and legal concepts discussed in the chapter are touched only briefly. To gain a better understanding, try researching them further using other resources. Topics such as taxes and insurance can be complex with local implications too specific to be covered in generalities. Look to appropriate outside sources for help.

PRACTICE QUESTIONS

Directions: Choose the option that best answers the question.

1. During his treatment session, a client reveals that he has recently been experiencing serious mood swings. You believe he may be suffering from depression and indicate as much. Which of the following are you violating?
   (A) Code of ethics
   (B) Standards of practice
   (C) Confidentiality laws
   (D) Scope of practice

2. If you accidentally injure a client during treatment, legal costs associated with the injury may be covered by your
   (A) health insurance.
   (B) business insurance.
   (C) liability insurance.
   (D) disability insurance.

3. Exchanging a massage for bookkeeping services is an example of
   (A) ethics violation.
   (B) dual roles.
   (C) countertransference.
   (D) scope of practice.

4. Jane Smith is opening a new massage practice called "Contemporary Relaxation." Jane must submit a fictitious name statement to the
   (A) federal government.
   (B) state government.
   (C) county government.
   (D) massage board.

5. Product, place, price, and promotion are elements of
   (A) bookkeeping.
   (B) marketing.
   (C) business planning.
   (D) professional communication.

6. A new client arrives at your practice with severe back pain. Upon examination, you believe the client has a medical problem that is unlikely to respond to massage treatment. Massage is not contraindicted, however. Your best response at this point should be to
   (A) treat the client and allow her to think the treatment will resolve the issue.
   (B) try to change the client's mind about the treatment by providing a definitive diagnosis.
   (C) suggest appropriate alternatives and let the client choose how to move forward.
   (D) immediately decline to move forward with the treatment.

7. As you work on a client, he becomes flirtatious and asks you personal questions. How should you respond?
   (A) Be flirtatious in return.
   (B) Discontinue the massage.
   (C) Reprimand the client.
   (D) Diplomatically ask him to be more appropriate.

8. Reacting to a client who seems to have become emotionally involved with you is considered
   (A) self-disclosure.
   (B) countertransference.
   (C) outside scope of practice.
   (D) dual transfer.

9. Your professional liability insurance will NOT cover the cost of judgment against you in cases of
   (A) malpractice.
   (B) gross incompetence.
   (C) accidental injury.
   (D) sexual misconduct.

10. The issuance of which of the following helps to generate funds for a municipal government's treasury?
    (A) Taxpayer identification number
    (B) Business identity
    (C) Business license
    (D) Fictitious name statement

ANSWER KEY AND EXPLANATIONS

1. D	3. B	5. B	7. D	9. D
2. C	4. C	6. C	8. B	10. C

1. **The correct answer is (D).** By suggesting that the client may be suffering from depression, you are violating the scope of practice. You are not a physician or psychologist and should therefore not be diagnosing the client's mental condition. You might suggest that the client seek help from a mental health-care provider, but you should go no further than that.

2. **The correct answer is (C).** Legal costs associated with injuries sustained by the client during treatment might be covered by your professional liability insurance, which protects you against claims alleging professional error.

3. **The correct answer is (B).** Exchanging a massage for bookkeeping services is an example of dual roles. In this instance, your relationship with the client consists of both a client/therapist relationship and an employer/employee relationship.

4. **The correct answer is (C).** New business owners who choose an original name for a business must submit a fictitious name statement to the county government.

5. **The correct answer is (B).** Product, place, price, and promotion are the principle elements of marketing.

6. **The correct answer is (C).** Since you have determined massage is unlikely to improve the client's condition, you should share your thoughts with the client and suggest more appropriate alternatives. However, because massage is not contraindicated, the client has the option to continue with the treatment if she prefers.

7. **The correct answer is (D).** If a client becomes flirtatious and begins acting inappropriately, you should ask him to keep the conversation appropriate. Engaging in any sexually charged conversation could be construed as sexual misconduct and should be avoided.

8. **The correct answer is (B).** Reacting to a client who has become too emotionally dependent on you is countertransference.

9. **The correct answer is (D).** Professional liability insurance providers generally do not provide coverage for allegations of sexual misconduct.

10. **The correct answer is (C).** The issuance of business licenses helps to generate funds for the municipal government's treasury. It also helps the local government ensure that all zoning laws are being observed.

SUMMING IT UP

- Professional standards and legal and business practices questions require a fundamental understanding of the ethical requirements, traditional standards of practice, common business practices, and legal obligations associated with massage therapy and bodywork.

- Pay close attention to specific details in the questions. Make sure your understanding of ethics, standards, and business terminology is strong.

- Keep in mind that learning and understanding the information presented in this chapter is important not only for the exam, but also for your practice. In order to operate a successful massage therapy practice, you will need to understand and satisfy all of the requirements discussed.

PART IV

TWO PRACTICE TESTS

PRACTICE TEST 2
Massage and Bodywork Licensing Examination (MBLEx)   161

PRACTICE TEST 3
National Certification Examination for Therapeutic Massage and Bodywork (NCETMB)   183

ANSWER SHEET PRACTICE TEST 2: MASSAGE AND BODYWORK LICENSING EXAMINATION (MBLEX)

1. Ⓐ Ⓑ Ⓒ Ⓓ   26. Ⓐ Ⓑ Ⓒ Ⓓ   51. Ⓐ Ⓑ Ⓒ Ⓓ   76. Ⓐ Ⓑ Ⓒ Ⓓ   101. Ⓐ Ⓑ Ⓒ Ⓓ
2. Ⓐ Ⓑ Ⓒ Ⓓ   27. Ⓐ Ⓑ Ⓒ Ⓓ   52. Ⓐ Ⓑ Ⓒ Ⓓ   77. Ⓐ Ⓑ Ⓒ Ⓓ   102. Ⓐ Ⓑ Ⓒ Ⓓ
3. Ⓐ Ⓑ Ⓒ Ⓓ   28. Ⓐ Ⓑ Ⓒ Ⓓ   53. Ⓐ Ⓑ Ⓒ Ⓓ   78. Ⓐ Ⓑ Ⓒ Ⓓ   103. Ⓐ Ⓑ Ⓒ Ⓓ
4. Ⓐ Ⓑ Ⓒ Ⓓ   29. Ⓐ Ⓑ Ⓒ Ⓓ   54. Ⓐ Ⓑ Ⓒ Ⓓ   79. Ⓐ Ⓑ Ⓒ Ⓓ   104. Ⓐ Ⓑ Ⓒ Ⓓ
5. Ⓐ Ⓑ Ⓒ Ⓓ   30. Ⓐ Ⓑ Ⓒ Ⓓ   55. Ⓐ Ⓑ Ⓒ Ⓓ   80. Ⓐ Ⓑ Ⓒ Ⓓ   105. Ⓐ Ⓑ Ⓒ Ⓓ
6. Ⓐ Ⓑ Ⓒ Ⓓ   31. Ⓐ Ⓑ Ⓒ Ⓓ   56. Ⓐ Ⓑ Ⓒ Ⓓ   81. Ⓐ Ⓑ Ⓒ Ⓓ   106. Ⓐ Ⓑ Ⓒ Ⓓ
7. Ⓐ Ⓑ Ⓒ Ⓓ   32. Ⓐ Ⓑ Ⓒ Ⓓ   57. Ⓐ Ⓑ Ⓒ Ⓓ   82. Ⓐ Ⓑ Ⓒ Ⓓ   107. Ⓐ Ⓑ Ⓒ Ⓓ
8. Ⓐ Ⓑ Ⓒ Ⓓ   33. Ⓐ Ⓑ Ⓒ Ⓓ   58. Ⓐ Ⓑ Ⓒ Ⓓ   83. Ⓐ Ⓑ Ⓒ Ⓓ   108. Ⓐ Ⓑ Ⓒ Ⓓ
9. Ⓐ Ⓑ Ⓒ Ⓓ   34. Ⓐ Ⓑ Ⓒ Ⓓ   59. Ⓐ Ⓑ Ⓒ Ⓓ   84. Ⓐ Ⓑ Ⓒ Ⓓ   109. Ⓐ Ⓑ Ⓒ Ⓓ
10. Ⓐ Ⓑ Ⓒ Ⓓ   35. Ⓐ Ⓑ Ⓒ Ⓓ   60. Ⓐ Ⓑ Ⓒ Ⓓ   85. Ⓐ Ⓑ Ⓒ Ⓓ   110. Ⓐ Ⓑ Ⓒ Ⓓ
11. Ⓐ Ⓑ Ⓒ Ⓓ   36. Ⓐ Ⓑ Ⓒ Ⓓ   61. Ⓐ Ⓑ Ⓒ Ⓓ   86. Ⓐ Ⓑ Ⓒ Ⓓ   111. Ⓐ Ⓑ Ⓒ Ⓓ
12. Ⓐ Ⓑ Ⓒ Ⓓ   37. Ⓐ Ⓑ Ⓒ Ⓓ   62. Ⓐ Ⓑ Ⓒ Ⓓ   87. Ⓐ Ⓑ Ⓒ Ⓓ   112. Ⓐ Ⓑ Ⓒ Ⓓ
13. Ⓐ Ⓑ Ⓒ Ⓓ   38. Ⓐ Ⓑ Ⓒ Ⓓ   63. Ⓐ Ⓑ Ⓒ Ⓓ   88. Ⓐ Ⓑ Ⓒ Ⓓ   113. Ⓐ Ⓑ Ⓒ Ⓓ
14. Ⓐ Ⓑ Ⓒ Ⓓ   39. Ⓐ Ⓑ Ⓒ Ⓓ   64. Ⓐ Ⓑ Ⓒ Ⓓ   89. Ⓐ Ⓑ Ⓒ Ⓓ   114. Ⓐ Ⓑ Ⓒ Ⓓ
15. Ⓐ Ⓑ Ⓒ Ⓓ   40. Ⓐ Ⓑ Ⓒ Ⓓ   65. Ⓐ Ⓑ Ⓒ Ⓓ   90. Ⓐ Ⓑ Ⓒ Ⓓ   115. Ⓐ Ⓑ Ⓒ Ⓓ
16. Ⓐ Ⓑ Ⓒ Ⓓ   41. Ⓐ Ⓑ Ⓒ Ⓓ   66. Ⓐ Ⓑ Ⓒ Ⓓ   91. Ⓐ Ⓑ Ⓒ Ⓓ   116. Ⓐ Ⓑ Ⓒ Ⓓ
17. Ⓐ Ⓑ Ⓒ Ⓓ   42. Ⓐ Ⓑ Ⓒ Ⓓ   67. Ⓐ Ⓑ Ⓒ Ⓓ   92. Ⓐ Ⓑ Ⓒ Ⓓ   117. Ⓐ Ⓑ Ⓒ Ⓓ
18. Ⓐ Ⓑ Ⓒ Ⓓ   43. Ⓐ Ⓑ Ⓒ Ⓓ   68. Ⓐ Ⓑ Ⓒ Ⓓ   93. Ⓐ Ⓑ Ⓒ Ⓓ   118. Ⓐ Ⓑ Ⓒ Ⓓ
19. Ⓐ Ⓑ Ⓒ Ⓓ   44. Ⓐ Ⓑ Ⓒ Ⓓ   69. Ⓐ Ⓑ Ⓒ Ⓓ   94. Ⓐ Ⓑ Ⓒ Ⓓ   119. Ⓐ Ⓑ Ⓒ Ⓓ
20. Ⓐ Ⓑ Ⓒ Ⓓ   45. Ⓐ Ⓑ Ⓒ Ⓓ   70. Ⓐ Ⓑ Ⓒ Ⓓ   95. Ⓐ Ⓑ Ⓒ Ⓓ   120. Ⓐ Ⓑ Ⓒ Ⓓ
21. Ⓐ Ⓑ Ⓒ Ⓓ   46. Ⓐ Ⓑ Ⓒ Ⓓ   71. Ⓐ Ⓑ Ⓒ Ⓓ   96. Ⓐ Ⓑ Ⓒ Ⓓ   121. Ⓐ Ⓑ Ⓒ Ⓓ
22. Ⓐ Ⓑ Ⓒ Ⓓ   47. Ⓐ Ⓑ Ⓒ Ⓓ   72. Ⓐ Ⓑ Ⓒ Ⓓ   97. Ⓐ Ⓑ Ⓒ Ⓓ   122. Ⓐ Ⓑ Ⓒ Ⓓ
23. Ⓐ Ⓑ Ⓒ Ⓓ   48. Ⓐ Ⓑ Ⓒ Ⓓ   73. Ⓐ Ⓑ Ⓒ Ⓓ   98. Ⓐ Ⓑ Ⓒ Ⓓ   123. Ⓐ Ⓑ Ⓒ Ⓓ
24. Ⓐ Ⓑ Ⓒ Ⓓ   49. Ⓐ Ⓑ Ⓒ Ⓓ   74. Ⓐ Ⓑ Ⓒ Ⓓ   99. Ⓐ Ⓑ Ⓒ Ⓓ   124. Ⓐ Ⓑ Ⓒ Ⓓ
25. Ⓐ Ⓑ Ⓒ Ⓓ   50. Ⓐ Ⓑ Ⓒ Ⓓ   75. Ⓐ Ⓑ Ⓒ Ⓓ   100. Ⓐ Ⓑ Ⓒ Ⓓ   125. Ⓐ Ⓑ Ⓒ Ⓓ

Massage and Bodywork Licensing Examination (MBLEx)

Directions: Choose the option that best answers the questions.

1. Which of the follow is NOT a benefit of massage on the muscular system?
   (A) Improved blood flow
   (B) Increased nutrients
   (C) Improved range of motion
   (D) Increased growth

2. When you are scheduling appointments, you should
   (A) book only as many as you can handle without becoming burnt out.
   (B) treat as many clients as you can in order to maximize your profits.
   (C) schedule as few as possible so as to maximize your time with each client.
   (D) try to treat an equal number of clients each day.

3. Which of these BEST describes how massage improves skin's color and tone?
   (A) It relaxes the muscles.
   (B) It improves the flow of lymph.
   (C) It improves mobility.
   (D) It improves skin circulation.

4. The primary purpose of asking a client about his or her lifestyle during the intake interview is to
   (A) gather personal background data on the client.
   (B) estimate how much exercise the client gets on a regular basis.

   (C) make the client feel more comfortable talking with you.
   (D) learn about any activities or traumas that may indicate the cause of pain.

5. During an intake interview, a client reveals that he has a certain skin condition. You are not intimately familiar with the condition, but you do not believe it would contraindicate massage. Which of the following is the MOST important step you should take next?
   (A) Agree to perform the massage.
   (B) Ask the client follow-up questions.
   (C) Consult a physician or other reliable source.
   (D) Tell the client to fill out paperwork.

6. Massage therapists can obtain discounted group health insurance if they apply for it through a(n)
   (A) professional massage organization.
   (B) HMO.
   (C) insurance company.
   (D) local hospital system.

7. Which of the following is considered a cause of spina bifida?
   (A) Extreme stress
   (B) Genetic mutation
   (C) Low levels of blood glucose
   (D) Abnormal growth in the brain

8. All of the following are physiological effects of massage EXCEPT
   (A) it helps clients became more aware of how they deal with tension.
   (B) it increases the flow of lymph and blood throughout the body.
   (C) it helps injured muscles feel better and heal more quickly.
   (D) it improves and aids in the digestive process.

9. Which of the following statements describes an eccentric muscle contraction?
   (A) A muscle lengthens as it contracts.
   (B) A muscle heats up as it contracts.
   (C) A muscle shortens as it contracts.
   (D) A muscle cools down as it contracts.

10. Which of the following is NOT part of the lymphatic system of the body?
    (A) Spleen
    (B) Thymus
    (C) Bone marrow
    (D) Pancreas

11. Which of the following disorders is caused by herpes zoster?
    (A) Shingles
    (B) Measles
    (C) Rubella
    (D) Mumps

12. Which of these BEST describes how massage improves the body's immune system?
    (A) By making the skin softer and more supple
    (B) By relaxing the organs in the digestive system
    (C) By giving connective tissue more flexibility
    (D) By improving the flow of lymph in the body

13. You can assess a client's passive range of movement by
    (A) instructing the client to perform a basic movement task.
    (B) applying resistance against the client's movements.
    (C) asking the client to move his or her limb through its range of movement.
    (D) moving the client's limb through its range of movement yourself.

14. Following the initial session, the plan you develop for future treatments should be based primarily on the
    (A) client's level of satisfaction.
    (B) degree of success of initial treatment.
    (C) changes in the client's physical condition.
    (D) client's goals and desires.

15. All of the following are purposes of stretching EXCEPT
    (A) enhancing flexibility.
    (B) relaxing skeletal muscles.
    (C) increasing joint range of motion.
    (D) improving aerobic fitness.

16. Which of the following marketing methods would likely reach the largest audience?
    (A) Newspaper ad
    (B) Phone book ad
    (C) Billboard ad
    (D) Television ad

17. The friction technique can be used to
    (A) warm up the client's tissues.
    (B) loosen scar tissue and adhesions.
    (C) acclimate the client to your touch.
    (D) work out adhesions and loosen muscles.

18. The left atrium of a heart is receiving less blood than it should. This issue is MOST likely related to which of the following?
    (A) Pulmonary vein
    (B) Right atrium
    (C) Coronary sinus
    (D) Right ventricle

19. A weak and painless muscle test would indicate a
    (A) disruption of nerve supply, circulation, or energy.
    (B) torn ligament or fracture.
    (C) first- or second-degree muscle strain.
    (D) severed muscle or loss of enervation.

20. Which of these BEST describes Thai massage?
    (A) It includes a series of assisted body positionings, stretching, and rocking.
    (B) It is a form of healing based on channeling universal energy.
    (C) It is a system of special breathing and relaxation techniques performed in conjunction with several methods of rebalancing alignment.
    (D) It is built on the premise that every cell in the body has equal and opposite poles.

21. Which of these BEST describes Swedish massage?
    (A) It is a type of bodywork performed expressly for medical purposes.
    (B) It is a massage modality based on established osteopathic techniques.
    (C) It is a form of therapeutic massage that is primarily focused on relaxation.
    (D) It is primarily made up of deep pressure specifically applied to deep tissues.

22. Which of the following is the primary influencing factor in determining the dynamics of the client/therapist relationship?
    (A) Confidentiality
    (B) Dual roles
    (C) Transference
    (D) Power differential

23. Which of the following would constitute a violation of HIPAA regulations?
    (A) Sharing personal information with another professional
    (B) Engaging in a sexual relationship with a client
    (C) Refusing to allow a client to see his medical records
    (D) Giving a preferred client a free massage

24. Some candidates who apply for a massage therapy license may be required to provide confirmation from a physician that he or she
    (A) is physically capable of performing a massage.
    (B) has been properly vaccinated.
    (C) is free of communicable diseases.
    (D) has no history of cardiac issues.

25. Sanitizing objects by means of moist heat requires
    (A) high-pressure steam.
    (B) decontamination chemicals.

    (C) immersion in boiling water.
    (D) the use of a disinfectant agent.

26. In which portion of your SOAP notes would you compare the client's treatment response to your initial goals?
    (A) Subjective
    (B) Objective
    (C) Assessment
    (D) Planning

27. Where are the effects of massage MOST immediately experienced?
    (A) The skin
    (B) The internal organs
    (C) The glands
    (D) The digestive system

28. Which of the following is NOT an important body structure used to test for anterior knee pain?
    (A) Anterior cruciate ligament
    (B) Posterior cruciate ligament
    (C) Achilles tendon
    (D) Meniscal cartilage

29. All of the following are muscles of the back and shoulder EXCEPT the
    (A) latissimus dorsi.
    (B) zygomaticus major.
    (C) teres minor.
    (D) rhomboid major.

30. Which of the following is a characteristic of healthy fascia?
    (A) Dry surface
    (B) Flexibility
    (C) Rough texture
    (D) Firmness

31. What is the name of the joint found at the top of the shoulder?
    (A) Acromioclavicular joint
    (B) Calcaneocuboid joint
    (C) Sacroiliac joint
    (D) Tarsometatarsal joint

32. In the skeletal system, what bone runs parallel to the radius?
    (A) Humerus
    (B) Tibia
    (C) Fibula
    (D) Ulna

33. Which type of insurance is designed to provide you with a supplemental income in the event that you are unable to work because of an injury or illness?
   (A) Medical
   (B) Business interruption
   (C) Liability
   (D) Business

34. Which of these actions should a massage therapist NOT take with a client suffering from inflammation?
   (A) Therapeutically touching an inflamed muscle
   (B) Holding a pressure point near an inflamed joint
   (C) Using spreading massage on an inflamed joint
   (D) Massaging a proximal area to the inflamed area

35. Massage can affect women of childbearing age by
   (A) shortening the length of menstruation.
   (B) postponing the onset of menopause.
   (C) making it easier to conceive.
   (D) reducing the pain of labor.

36. Massage plays an integral role in the modern health system of which of these Asian countries?
   (A) Japan
   (B) South Korea
   (C) Vietnam
   (D) China

37. As you are finishing a session, your client asks you to go to dinner with her. How should you respond?
   (A) Accept her invitation immediately.
   (B) Go with her only if she is not interested in pursuing a romantic relationship.
   (C) Refer her to another therapist before beginning a new relationship.
   (D) Politely decline the invitation on ethical grounds.

38. All of the following are true of draping EXCEPT that it
   (A) maintains the client's boundaries.
   (B) is used to keep the client warm.
   (C) should cover both the client and table.
   (D) is required by law in all states.

39. When the client's passive range of movement suddenly comes to an abrupt, painful stop, he or she would likely be described as exhibiting which type of abnormal end feel?
   (A) Hard
   (B) Empty
   (C) Firm
   (D) Spasm

40. Which of the following is an accurate description of kyphosis?
   (A) Improper tension between knee and leg joints
   (B) Abnormal convexity of thoracic area of spine
   (C) Abnormal protrusions of seventh cranial nerve
   (D) Decreased metabolism of proteins

41. Physical holding patterns may result from all of the following EXCEPT
   (A) skeletal imbalances.
   (B) asymmetry.
   (C) genetic disposition.
   (D) previous injuries.

42. Capillaries in the body are usually instantly but temporarily dilated when a massage therapist applies
   (A) kneading.
   (B) light percussion.
   (C) fiction.
   (D) light strokes.

43. The various synovial joints of the body allow for different types of movement. Ball-and-socket joints allow for all of the following types of movement EXCEPT
   (A) adduction.
   (B) flexion.
   (C) rotation.
   (D) gliding.

44. Which of the following is NOT a proper treatment for scleroderma?
   (A) Anti-inflammatory agents
   (B) Massage of lower extremities
   (C) Immunosuppressive therapy
   (D) Cryotherapy and extreme heat

45. A massage therapist is asking a client about Activities of Daily Living (ADLs). Which of the following basic ADLs would most likely have the biggest impact on a client's quality of movement?
    (A) Ambulation
    (B) Dressing
    (C) Grooming
    (D) Elimination

46. Fascia is composed of a matrix, collagen, and
    (A) muscles.
    (B) blood.
    (C) nerves.
    (D) elastin.

47. Condyloid joints are capable of all of the following types of movement EXCEPT
    (A) rotation.
    (B) flexion.
    (C) extension.
    (D) adduction.

48. An abnormal hard end feel may be an indication of
    (A) acute bursitis.
    (B) synovitis or soft tissue edema.
    (C) muscular, capsular, or ligamentous shortening.
    (D) degenerative joint disease.

49. All of the following massage techniques causes sedative effects EXCEPT
    (A) kneading.
    (B) light friction.
    (C) stroking.
    (D) light percussion.

50. A synergist muscle is a muscle that helps
    (A) the muscle shorten.
    (B) maintain posture.
    (C) another muscle move.
    (D) the muscle lengthen.

51. Placing extra support under the chest might increase the comfort levels of clients who
    (A) suffer from low back pain.
    (B) have difficulty remaining on the table for an extended period.
    (C) require added support for their cervical spine region.
    (D) are significantly overweight.

52. An object is traveling along a flat surface at a constant speed. According to the law of inertia, the object will
    (A) change directions but maintain speed.
    (B) slow down over time.
    (C) travel at a constant speed.
    (D) speed up but stay in the same direction.

53. Which of these BEST describes how a prolonged period of percussive movements can affect the nervous system?
    (A) All nerve centers are excited.
    (B) Local nerves are anesthetised.
    (C) All nerve centers are sedated.
    (D) Local nerves are stimulated.

54. If you discover during postural analysis that a client's bilateral landmarks are noticeably higher on one side than the other, you can conclude that he or she exhibits a deviation off which plane of division?
    (A) Lateral
    (B) Frontal
    (C) Sagittal
    (D) Transverse

55. Which of the following types of businesses involves sharing profits with stockholders?
    (A) Partnership
    (B) Corporation
    (C) Sole proprietorship
    (D) Limited liability company

56. All of the following are benefits that massage has on the digestive system EXCEPT
    (A) it increases digestive juices.
    (B) it relaxes organs.
    (C) it decreased muscle cramps.
    (D) it reduces nausea.

57. Lomi-Lomi, a form of massage that includes rhythmic dances and ceremonial music, originated in which South Pacific culture?
    (A) Samoan
    (B) Polynesian
    (C) Hawaiian
    (D) Tahitian

58. Gait refers to a client's ability to
    (A) stretch.
    (B) walk.
    (C) stand.
    (D) pivot.

59. You are interviewing a new client who seems very enthusiastic about getting a massage. Believing that his condition contraindicates massage, you decline to treat him. In response, the client offers you a substantial payment in addition to your normal fee if you will treat him anyway. In this situation, you should
    (A) immediately accept the money and treat the client.
    (B) warn the client of the danger involved, but treat him anyway.
    (C) offer to refer the client to another therapist.
    (D) refuse the client's offer and maintain your stance.

60. The relaxation response is activated by elements of which body system?
    (A) Endocrine
    (B) Circulatory
    (C) Nervous
    (D) Lymphatic

61. Which of the following is a primary cause of whiplash?
    (A) Decalcification of bones around the neck structure
    (B) Improper curvature of the upper spinal cord
    (C) Autoimmune disorders
    (D) Movement of the neck beyond its normal range of motion

62. Which of the following is an accurate description of scleroderma?
    (A) Degeneration of connective tissue surrounding skin and organs
    (B) Destruction of the central nervous system
    (C) Hypo-release of pancreatic enzymes
    (D) Inflammation of joints closest to the patella

63. At what age does the anterior fontanel typically close?
    (A) 6 months
    (B) 12 months
    (C) 18 months
    (D) 24 months

64. You are giving a client an intense, strategically planned full-body massage. With most of the session completed, the client suddenly asks you to stop. At this point, you should
    (A) stop the massage immediately.
    (B) encourage the client to continue.
    (C) warn the client that she'll still have to pay full price if you stop now.
    (D) ignore the client and finish the massage since you are almost done anyway.

65. Which of the following physical changes occurs during adulthood?
    (A) Strength increases over time.
    (B) Flexibility decreases over time.
    (C) Fertility increases over time.
    (D) Body fat decreases over time.

66. The use of percussion may involve any or all of the following movement EXCEPT
    (A) pounding.
    (B) squeezing.
    (C) pinching.
    (D) slapping.

67. In order to avoid hyperextending your wrists, you should be particularly mindful of your body mechanics when
    (A) performing deep, gliding strokes.
    (B) applying compressive force.
    (C) kneading or rocking.
    (D) using circular friction.

68. According to the law of action-reaction, what happens if you push on a wall with your hand?
    (A) The wall pushes back on your hand with equal force.
    (B) The wall exerts more force back on your hand.
    (C) The wall pushes back on your hand with less force.
    (D) The wall yields to the force exerted by your hand.

69. Which of these benefits of massage is enhanced by using heat treatments?
    (A) An anaesthetic effect on muscles
    (B) The dilation of blood vessels
    (C) The reduction of inflammation
    (D) An improvement in deep breathing

70. Which of the following is NOT a characteristic of trigger points?
    (A) They occur in the muscles.
    (B) They cause pain when touched.
    (C) They can be caused by injury.
    (D) They are palpable lumps.

71. Which of the following is a sign of varicose veins in a client?
    (A) Bulging, blue veins, usually in the legs
    (B) Bulging, blue veins, usually on the face
    (C) Small, spindly red veins in the arms
    (D) Small, spindly red veins on the back

72. If, during postural analysis, you observe that a landmark appears to be located either more anterior or posterior of the client's body than normal, you can determine that the deviation is off which plane of division?
    (A) Transverse
    (B) Sagittal
    (C) Frontal
    (D) Lateral

73. Which of the following benefits of massage is MOST responsible for relieving pain?
    (A) The release of endorphins
    (B) The regulation of respiration
    (C) The improvement of lymph flow
    (D) The increase of nutrients in muscles

74. In what part of the female reproductive system does egg fertilization occur?
    (A) Endocervical canal
    (B) Uterus
    (C) Fallopian tubes
    (D) Ovaries

75. One of the primary purposes of the stretch reflex is to
    (A) limit muscle lengthening.
    (B) stimulate a dynamic muscle response.
    (C) maximize muscle flexibility.
    (D) stimulate a static muscle response.

76. By week 9 to week 12 of gestation of a human fetus
    (A) the tooth buds appear.
    (B) the eyebrows appear.
    (C) movement can be felt.
    (D) heartbeat can be heard.

77. During a session, your client begins speaking suggestively and making sexual innuendo. How should you respond?
    (A) Engage the client in an equally suggestive manner.
    (B) Ignore the client and continue the massage.
    (C) Gently return the conversation to the massage.
    (D) Suspend the massage and reprimand the client.

78. Which type of abnormal end feel is described as when the range-of-motion movement is ended with a squishy or yielding feeling?
    (A) Empty
    (B) Springy block
    (C) Soft
    (D) Firm

79. A plumb line is a simple tool commonly used during assessment of the client's
    (A) active range of motion.
    (B) posture.
    (C) passive range of motion.
    (D) gait.

80. Which important contributor to the development of massage established the Royal Swedish Central Institute of Gymnastics?
    (A) Johann Mezger
    (B) Charles Fayette Taylor
    (C) Mathias Roth
    (D) Per Henrik Ling

81. Which of these BEST describes how massage can help people who are bedridden or confined to wheelchairs?
    (A) Massage can give clients a feeling of sedation.
    (B) Massage can improve circulation and blood flow.
    (C) Massage can improve respiration throughout the body.
    (D) Massage can reduce feels of nausea.

82. While massaging a new client, you notice that he seems to be reluctant to engage in any conversation beyond answering your basic questions. In this situation, you should
    (A) gently encourage him to be more open and responsive.
    (B) try engaging him more aggressively.
    (C) remain quiet and allow him to relax.
    (D) ignore him and carry on with your attempts at conversation.

83. Which soft tissue technique is used to warm up tissue and allow the client to become used to your touch?
    (A) Static touching
    (B) Percussion
    (C) Friction
    (D) Gliding

84. Which of the following usually occurs after trauma to a long bone?
    (A) Systematic embolism
    (B) Pulmonary embolism
    (C) Air embolism
    (D) Fat embolism

85. Which of the following statements about isometric muscle contractions is true?
    (A) The muscle does not shorten during this contraction.
    (B) The body performs this contraction while running.
    (C) The muscle shortens during this contraction.
    (D) The body performs this contraction while lifting weights.

86. The organ of the digestive system that removes water and salt from wastes before they are expelled from the body is the
    (A) anus.
    (B) stomach.
    (C) esophagus.
    (D) colon.

87. Rocking and shaking are both unique forms of which soft tissue technique?
    (A) Friction
    (B) Compression
    (C) Kneading
    (D) Vibration

88. Which of the following massage modalities became popular in Western culture in the late 1800s?
    (A) Swedish massage
    (B) Thai massage
    (C) Reflexology
    (D) Shiatsu

89. The flushing of a client's skin during massage specifically indicates
    (A) increased elasticity.
    (B) improved digestion.
    (C) increased blood flow.
    (D) improved glandular activity.

90. When testing a client's active movement ability during range-of-motion assessment, you should be observing
    (A) what happens when the client moves his or her limbs through a certain range of motion.
    (B) what happens when you move the client's limbs through a certain range of motion.
    (C) whether the client hesitates when you move one of his or her limbs.
    (D) how the client reacts when you apply resistance against his or her movement.

91. Which of the following BEST describes the strain-counterstrain technique?
    (A) The client is positioned to release a muscle or tendon.
    (B) The massage therapist locates trigger points through palpation.
    (C) The client contracts muscles while in a specific position.
    (D) The massage therapist does not allow the joint to move.

92. Which of the following is true about a client who suffers from migraines?
    (A) The client should be treated with therapeutic touch, but not massage.
    (B) The client should be treated in a dimly lit room.
    (C) The client may have little or no limb movement.
    (D) The client may need extra back support, but no bolstering.

93. A person sustained an injury 5 days ago. What stage of healing is he/she most likely in?
    (A) Acute
    (B) Subacute
    (C) Chronic
    (D) Maturation

94. A person assumes a slouched posture. Which of the following correctly describes the associated line of gravity?
    (A) It passes in front of the cervical spine.
    (B) It passes behind the lumbar spine.
    (C) It passes in front of the knee joint.
    (D) It passes behind the hip joint.

95. One example of a problematic posture is sway back posture. Which of the statements below is true of sway back posture?
    (A) The head is extended forward.
    (B) The pelvis is tilted backward.
    (C) The head is extended backward.
    (D) The pelvis is tilted forward.

96. All of the following are bones of the leg and knee EXCEPT the
    (A) tibia.
    (B) patella.
    (C) humerus.
    (D) femur.

97. Four groups of spinal nerves are
    (A) parietal, occipital, temporal, frontal.
    (B) olfactory, optic, abducens, and trigeminal.
    (C) cervical, thoracic, lumbar, and sacral.
    (D) motor, sensory, autonomic, and automatic.

98. What role does the diaphragm play in respiration?
    (A) It filters the air that is inhaled through the nasal passages.
    (B) It expands or contracts to change the volume of the lungs.
    (C) It exchanges oxygen from the air with waste carbon dioxide.
    (D) It brings oxygen to all of the tissues and organs of the body.

99. The release of which of the following hormones is associated with the onset of puberty in both males and females?
    (A) Testosterone
    (B) Estrogen
    (C) GnRH
    (D) Androgens

100. Which of the following is the BEST definition of joint play as it relates to massage therapy?
    (A) It is actively moving the joints of clients in ways that the clients cannot.
    (B) It is a type of joint massage therapy that involves beneficial energy exchange.
    (C) It is using a stretching technique to allow for pain-free joint movement.
    (D) It is a technique designed to help joints surpass their normal range of motion.

101. Which of the following involves a third-class lever?
    (A) Nodding the head
    (B) Lifting an arm weight
    (C) Doing a full push-up
    (D) Standing on the balls of the feet

102. Which of the following is the BEST definition of flexibility?
    (A) It is the level of elasticity of the body's muscles.
    (B) It is the distance that the tendons can stretch.
    (C) It is the amount of pliability that the bones have.
    (D) It is the range of motion in one or a series of joints.

103. Which of the following is an accurate description of scoliosis?
    (A) Deterioration of muscle cells in the neck
    (B) Degeneration of lymph nodes
    (C) Lateral curvature of the spine
    (D) Improper connection of ligaments

104. Which of the following is the correct etiology of multiple sclerosis?
    (A) Degeneration of the cornea
    (B) Degeneration of small blood vessels
    (C) Degeneration of myelin sheaths
    (D) Degeneration of ligaments

105. All of the following are conditions that can be improved through massage EXCEPT
    (A) sciatica.
    (B) arthritis.
    (C) neuralgia.
    (D) influenza.

106. Which of the following is a physiological effect of massage?
(A) Increased heart rate
(B) Improved bone density
(C) Increased metabolism
(D) Improved eyesight

107. Which of the following BEST describes how massage can benefit the respiratory system?
(A) Massage can help heal respiratory infections.
(B) Massage can help strengthen the diaphragm.
(C) Massage can help improve deep breathing.
(D) Massage can help improve lung function.

108. Assessment information you gather from palpatory input is attained through
(A) sight.
(B) touch.
(C) intuition.
(D) sound.

109. Which portion of SOAP may contain information provided by the client's other health-care providers?
(A) Subjective
(B) Objective
(C) Assessment
(D) Planning

110. Some of the earliest known records of massage can be found in an ancient Chinese text called the
(A) San-Tsai-Tou-Hoei.
(B) Cong Fou.
(C) Laws of Manu.
(D) Ayur-Veda.

111. The federal government authorizes various organizations to award accreditation to massage therapy schools in order to facilitate
(A) the distribution of federal aid grants.
(B) uniformity of the educational curriculum.
(C) the regulation of certification standards.
(D) adherence to federal massage therapy laws.

112. Misrepresenting your educational achievements to your clients would be a direct breach of
(A) your scope of practice.
(B) the client's boundaries.
(C) client confidentiality.
(D) the code of ethics.

113. After being washed, linens should be dried in a heated dryer because
(A) they are more sanitary than other dryers.
(B) the heat kills any remaining germs.
(C) there is less chance of contamination than with air drying.
(D) they dry the moist linens more quickly.

114. In order to ensure your own safety when working on a client, you should do all of the following EXCEPT
(A) bend your knees slightly.
(B) hold your elbows away from your body.
(C) keep your back straight.
(D) relax your wrists.

115. What is the definition of supination?
(A) Turning the feet inward
(B) Turning the feet outward
(C) Turning the palms downward
(D) Turning the palms upward

116. The disinfection method of decontamination is capable of destroying all forms of pathogens EXCEPT
(A) fungi.
(B) viruses.
(C) bacteria.
(D) bacterial spores.

117. When you are working with the financial records of your practice, it is important to remember that all of your business expenses can be claimed as
(A) tax deductions.
(B) business assets.
(C) tax exemptions.
(D) proprietary assets.

118. An athlete is warming up. He grabs his right ankle with his right hand and then uses his hand to bend and stretch his leg. What type of stretch is this?
(A) Aerobic
(B) Passive
(C) Active
(D) Anaerobic

119. Any unusual clicks or pops that you hear while manipulating a client's body could be classified as which type of assessment input?
(A) Palpatory
(B) Auditory
(C) Observational
(D) Intuitive

120. Which assessment technique is generally NOT considered diagnostic for most massage practitioners?
(A) Auditory input
(B) Energetic input
(C) Intuitive input
(D) Palpatory input

121. Which of these BEST describes how massage can help a person suffering from sciatica?
(A) A massage directly over the root of the nerve will decrease swelling.
(B) A massage to nearby muscles will anesthetise the root of the nerve.
(C) A massage directly over the root of the nerve will sedate the client.
(D) A massage to nearby muscles will reduce pain in the general area.

122. Which of the following is the most common form of skin cancer in humans?
(A) Malignant melanoma
(B) Basal cell carcinoma
(C) Squamous cell carcinoma
(D) Kaposi's sarcoma

123. Which structure of the respiratory system splits into two branches known as the bronchi?
(A) Alveolar sacs
(B) Larynx
(C) Pharynx
(D) Trachea

124. What is one of the main purposes of resisted range-of-motion exercise with respect to muscles?
(A) Boosting length
(B) Improving flexibility
(C) Increasing strength
(D) Decreasing discomfort

125. Which type of massage movement improves blood flow in the deeper arteries and veins?
(A) Friction
(B) Compression
(C) Kneading
(D) Stroking

ANSWER KEY AND EXPLANATIONS

1. D	26. C	51. C	76. A	101. B
2. A	27. A	52. C	77. C	102. D
3. D	28. C	53. B	78. C	103. C
4. D	29. B	54. D	79. B	104. C
5. C	30. B	55. B	80. D	105. D
6. A	31. A	56. A	81. B	106. C
7. B	32. D	57. C	82. C	107. C
8. A	33. B	58. B	83. D	108. B
9. A	34. C	59. D	84. D	109. A
10. D	35. D	60. C	85. A	110. B
11. A	36. D	61. D	86. D	111. A
12. D	37. D	62. A	87. D	112. D
13. D	38. D	63. C	88. A	113. B
14. C	39. D	64. A	89. C	114. B
15. D	40. B	65. B	90. A	115. D
16. D	41. C	66. B	91. B	116. D
17. B	42. D	67. B	92. B	117. A
18. A	43. D	68. A	93. B	118. B
19. A	44. D	69. B	94. D	119. B
20. A	45. A	70. C	95. D	120. B
21. C	46. D	71. A	96. C	121. D
22. D	47. A	72. C	97. C	122. B
23. C	48. D	73. A	98. B	123. D
24. C	49. D	74. C	99. C	124. C
25. C	50. C	75. A	100. C	125. C

1. **The correct answer is (D).** Massage benefits the muscular system in many ways including by improving blood flow, improve improving range of motion, and increasing nutrients. Massage does not, however, increase muscle growth.

2. **The correct answer is (A).** When you are scheduling your appointments, you should remember to book only as many as you can handle without becoming burnt out. Many massage therapists ultimately enjoy only relatively short careers in the field because they quickly become burnt out from overbooking. Pacing yourself properly can help to ensure a long and fruitful career.

3. **The correct answer is (D).** One of the main benefits of massage is increased and improved circulation. Since massage improves circulation at the skin's surface, its use often gives the skin a brighter color because of the increased blood flow near the surface.

4. **The correct answer is (D).** The primary goal of asking the client about his or her lifestyle during the intake interview is to learn about any regular activities or recent traumas that may be causing or contributing to his or her present condition.

5. **The correct answer is (C).** Whenever you encounter a client with a condition you are unfamiliar with, you should always research the condition by consulting a physician or some other reliable source before deciding how to proceed.

6. **The correct answer is (A).** Massage therapists can obtain discounted group health insurance through special plans provided by professional massage organizations.

7. **The correct answer is (B).** Although scientists do not know exactly what causes spina bifida, many believe that genetic mutation is the primary cause of the disease. The disorder occurs during the development of the embryo and is most likely due to genetic and environmental factors.

8. **The correct answer is (A).** When clients realize how they deal with stress and improve their ability to cope with stress, they are realizing a psychological benefit of passage. The other benefits listed are all physiological effects of massage.

9. **The correct answer is (A).** The two types of isotonic muscle contractions are eccentric and concentric. Eccentric means a muscle lengthens as it contracts, concentric means it shortens as it contracts, and neither definition addresses muscle temperature.

10. **The correct answer is (D).** The spleen, thymus, and bone marrow are all part of the lymphatic system. The pancreas is part of the body's endocrine system, not the lymphatic system.

11. **The correct answer is (A).** Shingles, which is a highly contagious and very painful disease, is caused by the herpes zoster infection.

12. **The correct answer is (D).** Massage helps improve the body's immune system by improving the flow of the lymph throughout the body. Since the lymph helps to keep the body free of waste and harmful microorganisms, it affects the body's immune system.

13. **The correct answer is (D).** The client's passive range of movement is assessed by moving the client's limb through its range of movement yourself.

14. **The correct answer is (C).** Whether you are developing the initial treatment or any additional treatments, the client's physical condition is always your primary concern. During reassessment following the initial treatment, you should look for any changes, positive or negative, that have occurred as a result of the first treatment.

15. **The correct answer is (D).** Stretching can enhance overall flexibility, help relax tense muscles, and increase the range of motion of joints. However, improving aerobic fitness requires participating in aerobic activities such as running or cycling.

16. **The correct answer is (D).** Of the marketing methods listed, a television ad would likely reach the largest audience.

17. **The correct answer is (B).** The friction technique is commonly used to loosen scar tissues and adhesions, as well as to promote flexibility through stretching.

18. **The correct answer is (A).** The four pulmonary veins of the heart supply blood from the lungs to the left atrium. The right atrium pumps blood into the right ventricle, the coronary sinus helps supply

blood to the right atrium, and the right ventricle supplies blood to the pulmonary artery.

19. **The correct answer is (A).** A weak and painless muscle test is generally an indication of a disruption of nerve supply, circulation, or energy to the involved muscle.

20. **The correct answer is (A).** Thai massage, which is traditionally performed on the floor, primarily consists of a series of assisted body positionings, similar to those of yoga, along with rocking and stretching techniques.

21. **The correct answer is (C).** Swedish massage is a form of therapeutic massage that is primarily focused on relaxation.

22. **The correct answer is (D).** The power differential is the primary influencing factor in determining the dynamics of the client/therapist relationship. Any shifts in the power differential can alter or even totally reverse the client/therapist relationship.

23. **The correct answer is (C).** Refusing to allow a client to see his medical records would be a violation of HIPAA regulations. HIPAA requires medical professionals to guarantee their clients access to their medical records. In addition, sharing personal information about a client with another professional would not be expressly prohibited by HIPAA regulations unless specifically done so without the client's permission.

24. **The correct answer is (C).** Based on the standards of the organization to which you are submitting your application for licensure, you may be required to provide confirmation from a physician that you are free of communicable diseases that you could pass on to your clients.

25. **The correct answer is (C).** When objects are sanitized using the moist heat method, they are immersed in boiling water for approximately twenty minutes.

26. **The correct answer is (C).** When using the SOAP system, you would compare the client's treatment response to your initial goals in the assessment portion.

27. **The correct answer is (A).** The skin is the part of the body that experiences the most immediate effects of massage. Massage causes the skin

to become softer and more supple, and it helps improve blood flow and nutrition to the skin.

28. **The correct answer is (C).** The Achilles tendon is not stressed in any of the eight major tests for knee pain because it is not part of the knee.

29. **The correct answer is (B).** The zygomaticus major is a muscle of the face, not a muscle of the back.

30. **The correct answer is (B).** Healthy fascia is able to move relatively easily because it is slippery, flexible, and smooth.

31. **The correct answer is (A).** The acromioclavicular (or AV) joint is found at the top of the shoulder between a portion of the scapula and the clavicle. Choices (B) and (D) are found in the feet and choice (C) is found in the pelvic region.

32. **The correct answer is (D).** The ulna and the radius are the two bones in the forearm that are located parallel to each other. The humerus is the long bone of the upper arm, and the tibia and fibula are the two bones of the lower leg that run parallel to each other.

33. **The correct answer is (B).** Business interruption insurance, also known as disability insurance, is designed to provide you with a source of income if you become unable to work due to an injury or illness.

34. **The correct answer is (C).** Massage therapists should not use a spreading massage directly over an inflamed joint or an inflamed muscle because it could spread an injury. A massage therapist may use therapeutic touching directly over the inflamed area.

35. **The correct answer is (D).** Women who get massage before labor often have shorter and less painful labors. Massage can also help some of the symptoms of PMS, such as water retention and irritability.

36. **The correct answer is (D).** Massage remains a key component of modern health care in China, widely practiced in hospitals and other medical facilities across the country.

37. **The correct answer is (D).** Engaging in any sort of social activity with a client would be in direct

violation of the code of ethics. As such, you should politely decline the invite on ethical grounds.

38. **The correct answer is (D).** Although many of those states that regulate the practice of massage therapy do have specific laws requiring the use of proper draping methods, not all states have such legal requirements.

39. **The correct answer is (D).** When the client exhibits a spasm end feel, the passive range of movement of the joint being assessed will come to an abrupt end and the client will usually experience pain.

40. **The correct answer is (B).** Kyphosis is the abnormal convexity of the thoracic area of the spine. Kyphosis, which can often cause a hunchback in people who suffer from it, causes weakness and tightness in the shoulders and upper back that could be alleviated by massage.

41. **The correct answer is (C).** Physical holding patterns are not genetically inherited. Rather, they develop over time as a result of skeletal or muscular imbalances, asymmetry, stress, or injury.

42. **The correct answer is (D).** Capillaries in the body are usually instantly but temporarily dilated when a massage therapist applies light strokes. Deep stroking causes the capillaries to stay dilated for a longer period, and the area on the skin becomes flushed.

43. **The correct answer is (D).** Ball-and-socket joints such as the hip are capable of all types of motion except gliding. These movements include adduction, abduction, flexion, extension, and rotation.

44. **The correct answer is (D).** Cryotherapy, or cold therapy, and extreme heat should be avoided when treating scleroderma. This is because extreme temperatures can exacerbate the condition.

45. **The correct answer is (A).** Ambulation, or walking, requires the most effort in terms of movement and would therefore likely have the biggest effect on movement quality. Dressing, grooming, and elimination would not require a substantial amount of movement by the client, and would therefore likely have a lesser effect on movement quality.

46. **The correct answer is (D).** Fascia is a connective tissue found throughout the body that is composed of a gelatinous matrix, strong collagen fibers, and elastin, which is made up of stretchable elastic fibers. Fascia does not contain muscles, blood, or nerves.

47. **The correct answer is (A).** Condyloid joints such as the wrist joint are capable of flexion, extension, adduction, and abduction, but are not capable of rotation.

48. **The correct answer is (D).** An abnormal hard end feel is often an indication of degenerative joint disease. It may also be a sign of fracture or a joint with loose components.

49. **The correct answer is (D).** Light percussion does not provide a sedative effect the way kneading, light friction, and stroking (especially stroking over reflex areas) do.

50. **The correct answer is (C).** Synergist muscles have the same types of movements as other agonist muscles in the body, and can therefore help these muscles (and associated joints) move. Choice (B) describes a characteristic of a stabilizer muscle, and choices (A) and (D) describe concentric and eccentric contractions, respectively.

51. **The correct answer is (C).** The comfort level of clients who require extra cervical spine support can usually be increased by placing added support under the chest.

52. **The correct answer is (C).** The law of inertia states that bodies in motion tend to stay in motion while bodies at rest tend to stay at rest. This means the object described will continue traveling in a straight line at a constant speed until some other force interferes with its motion.

53. **The correct answer is (B).** A longer period of percussive movements can anesthetise local nerves. A short period of percussive movements can stimulate nerve centers.

54. **The correct answer is (D).** In cases where the client presents with bilateral landmarks that are noticeably higher on one side of the body than the other, it can be concluded that he or she exhibits a deviation off the transverse plane.

55. **The correct answer is (B).** Corporations, the largest and most complex of the business models listed here, typically share their profits with shareholders.

56. **The correct answer is (A).** Massage helps the digestive system by relaxing the muscles and organs, decreasing cramps, and reducing nausea. Massage does not, however, increase the flow of digestive juices.

57. **The correct answer is (C).** A deeply spiritual massage modality that incorporates traditional music and dance, Lomi-Lomi was developed by ancient Hawaiians, possibly as long as 5,000 years ago.

58. **The correct answer is (B).** Gait refers to a client's ability to walk. Assessing the client's gait is an important part of the postural analysis and overall assessment.

59. **The correct answer is (D).** The NCBTMB Code of Ethics states that massage therapists should refuse any gifts meant to influence their decisions, especially in cases where accepting a particular gift would only be for personal gain and not the welfare of the client. In this scenario, you should refuse the client's offer and maintain your stance against providing treatment.

60. **The correct answer is (C).** The relaxation response is activated by the parasympathetic branch of the body's nervous system.

61. **The correct answer is (D).** Whiplash is usually caused by a sudden or jerky movement that causes the neck to move beyond its normal range of motion. For example, many car accident victims suffer from whiplash because of the rapid deceleration resulting from the impact.

62. **The correct answer is (A).** Scleroderma is a disease characterized by deterioration of connective tissue surrounding skin and organs.

63. **The correct answer is (C).** A baby is normally born with two fontanels, or soft spots: the anterior fontanel and the posterior fontanel. The posterior fontanel usually closes by 8 weeks, but the anterior fontanel does not typically close until 18 months, although this closure can occur at as early as 9 months.

64. **The correct answer is (A).** According to the NCBTMB Code of Ethics, massage therapists are required to respect the client's right to terminate his/her treatment at any time, regardless of prior consent. As such, you should stop the massage immediately.

65. **The correct answer is (B).** As people get older they tend to become less flexible physically. In addition, strength decreases, fertility decreases, and body fat increases.

66. **The correct answer is (B).** The percussion technique may involve pounding, pinching, and/or slapping. Squeezing movements are generally associated with kneading.

67. **The correct answer is (B).** You should pay particularly close attention to your body mechanics when applying compressive force, as you can easily hyperextend your wrists when such force is applied improperly.

68. **The correct answer is (A).** The law of action-reaction states that for every action there is an equal and opposite reaction. Therefore, when your hand exerts force on the wall, the wall exerts the same amount of force back onto your hand.

69. **The correct answer is (B).** When a heat treatment is added to a massage treatment, it increases the dilation of the blood vessels in the body. Cold treatments, not hot treatments, reduce inflammation and anesthetise muscles.

70. **The correct answer is (C).** Trigger points are lumps in skeletal muscle that can be palpated, or felt, and they are painful to the touch. These points, however, cannot be attributed to injury.

71. **The correct answer is (A).** Varicose veins are characterized by bulging, blue veins that are usually found in the legs. Massage therapists must use caution around these veins, as they should not be massaged.

72. **The correct answer is (C).** Whenever an observed landmark appears to be positioned anterior or posterior of the client's body, the deviation can be said to be off the frontal plane.

73. **The correct answer is (A).** One of the ways that massage helps relieve pain is through the release of endorphins, which are chemicals that stop pain in

the body. Although the benefits of massage include improved lymph flow, the regulation of respiration, and the increase of nutrients in the muscles, these benefits are not so directly linked with relieving pain.

74. **The correct answer is (C).** An egg is released in the ovaries and travels down the fallopian tubes, where fertilization may occur. A fertilized egg will develop into a fetus in the uterus, and the endocervical canal is located between the vagina and the uterus.

75. **The correct answer is (A).** The stretch reflex helps prevent muscle injury by limiting the amount of muscle lengthening. The static reflex and the dynamic reflex are the two stages of the stretch reflex.

76. **The correct answer is (A).** During weeks 9 to 12 of gestation, some of the changes include the appearance of tooth buds, the production of red blood cells by the liver, and the ability of the baby to make a fist. The changes described in choices (B), (C), and (D) do not occur until about week 20 of gestation.

77. **The correct answer is (C).** It is critically important for massage therapists to avoid engaging in any behavior that may be construed as sexual misconduct. With that in mind, when a client tries to engage you sexually in any way, you should refuse his or her advances. In this case, the best way you could respond would be to gently return the conversation to the massage.

78. **The correct answer is (C).** A soft end feel is usually indicated when the movement is ended with a squishy or yielding feeling. This type of end feel is often associated with synovitis or soft tissue edema.

79. **The correct answer is (B).** Plumb lines are commonly used to aid in the assessment of the client's posture, along with a postural analysis grid chart.

80. **The correct answer is (D).** Per Henrik Ling, in addition to introducing a system of movements known as Medical Gymnastics, also established the influential Royal Swedish Central Institute of Gymnastics.

81. **The correct answer is (B).** People who are always forced to sit or lie down could develop circulation problems in their lower limbs because those limbs are not often used. Massage can help people with poor circulation in their legs by massaging the legs and encouraging more flow to the area. Although the other choices listed are benefits of massage, they do not pertain specifically to people who are bedridden or who use a wheelchair.

82. **The correct answer is (C).** Not all clients will be interested in conversing with you as you work on them. If a client is generally quiet and gives only very brief replies to your questions, you should remain quiet and allow the client to relax.

83. **The correct answer is (D).** Gliding, which simply involves sliding your hands over the entire body or certain body parts, is normally used to warm up tissues and allow the client to become used to your touch.

84. **The correct answer is (D).** Often a fat embolism occurs because of trauma that occurred to the long bone. When the marrow fat is exposed to the bloodstream, it can travel to the kidneys, lungs, or brain.

85. **The correct answer is (A).** An isometric muscle contraction occurs when a muscle is engaged but it does not change length. A good example of an isometric contraction is holding an object out directly in front of you and keeping the arm straight. Muscles do shorten and lengthen during isotonic contractions, and lifting weights and running are both activities that involve isotonic muscle contractions.

86. **The correct answer is (D).** The colon absorbs water, potassium, and some vitamins from waste before it is expelled from the body through the anus. The esophagus is a tube that transports food to the stomach, where it is broken down and partially digested before entering the small intestine. Eventually, waste is excreted through the anus.

87. **The correct answer is (D).** Rocking and shaking are both specific variations of vibration, which involves a continuous shaking or trembling movement.

88. **The correct answer is (A).** During the late 1800s, massage was becoming more popular in countries

in Europe and in other Western companies. The Swedish massage was the most popular modality at the time.

89. **The correct answer is (C).** Flushing, or a pink color, on the skin indicates increased blood. As blood flow increases in the capillaries near the skin's surface, the red color of the blood shows through the skin.

90. **The correct answer is (A).** When you test a client's active movement ability while assessing his or her range of motion, you should be observing what happens when the client moves his or her own limbs through a certain range of motion.

91. **The correct answer is (B).** In the strain-counterstrain technique, the massage therapist uses palpation to locate trigger points in the muscle. Then, the therapist helps the client adjust his or her position to reduce the strain on the muscles.

92. **The correct answer is (B).** A client who suffers from migraines may prefer to be treated in a dimly lit room because people with migraines are generally sensitive to light. The massage therapist may also choose to cover the client's eyes to give more relief from the light.

93. **The correct answer is (B).** The acute stage of healing commences immediately after an injury, while the subacute stage begins several days later and can last for several weeks. The maturation and chronic stages follow the subacute stage.

94. **The correct answer is (D).** When someone slouches, the line of gravity passes through the cervical spine and lumbar spine, behind the hip joint and knee joint, and in front of the ankle joint.

95. **The correct answer is (D).** Sway back posture occurs when the pelvis is tilted forward and there is an excessive arch in the lower back area as a result. Flattened back occurs when the pelvis is tilted backward. Extending the head forward is a type of neck posture error that can cause neck and upper back strain and pain.

96. **The correct answer is (C).** The humerus is a long bone located in the upper arm. The tibia, patella, and femur are all bones in the leg and the knee.

97. **The correct answer is (C).** Spinal nerves are classified as cervical, thoracic, lumbar, and sacral based on where they exit the spinal cord. Choice (B) lists cranial nerves, the terms in choice (A) are related to the brain, and choice (D) lists the three types of peripheral nerves (motor, sensory, and autonomic).

98. **The correct answer is (B).** The diaphragm is a muscle at the bottom of the lungs that helps with inhalation and exhalation by expanding and contracting. When a person breathes in air, the trachea filters air, gas exchange takes place in the alveoli, and red blood cells transport oxygen throughout the body.

99. **The correct answer is (C).** GnRH, or gonadotropin releasing hormone, is released by the pituitary and leads to increases in FSH and LH, hormones that play a vital role in male and female puberty. Increases in the levels of GnRH precede increases in the levels of testosterone and other androgens in males and estrogen in females.

100. **The correct answer is (C).** Joint play is a stretching technique used by massage therapists to allow clients' joints to achieve their full range of motion without causing pain. Choice (A) describes a technique known as joint mobilization, and choice (B) describes a massage technique known as healing touch.

101. **The correct answer is (B).** In a third-class lever the effort (exerted by the bicep) is located between the fulcrum (elbow) and the resistance (the weight). Nodding the head involves a first-class lever, while choices (C) and (D) involve second-class levers.

102. **The correct answer is (D).** Flexibility is mainly determined by the level of movement that is possible within the joints. Tendons are relatively inflexible, bones are not flexible, and muscles do not play so important of a role in overall flexibility as joints.

103. **The correct answer is (C).** Scoliosis is a lateral curvature of the spine. Scoliosis is usually congenital and results in abnormal posture or gait caused by the spinal curvature.

104. **The correct answer is (C).** Multiple sclerosis (MS) involves the degeneration of myelin sheaths in the nervous system, leading to a number of altered brain functions. Massage therapy may be used for stress reduction and mobility maintenance for clients with MS.

105. **The correct answer is (D).** Clients who are suffering from an infectious illness such as influenza and severe colds should not be treated with massage. People with disorders such as sciatica, arthritis, and neuralgia could most likely benefit from massage.

106. **The correct answer is (C).** Increased metabolism is one of the many physiological benefits of massage. Some of the other benefits include increased function of the lymphatic system, improved healing, and improved digestive processes.

107. **The correct answer is (C).** Massage helps the respiratory system by improving and promoting deep breathing. Massage can also benefit the respiratory system by increasing regulating respiration throughout the body.

108. **The correct answer is (B).** Any palpatory input used as part of your overall assessment is based on what you can observe by touching and/or physically manipulating the client's body.

109. **The correct answer is (A).** In addition to the information you receive directly from the client, the subjective portion of the SOAP system may also contain information shared by the client's other health-care providers.

110. **The correct answer is (B).** The Cong Fou describes how the ancient Chinese people used massage, along with medicinal plants and exercises, to treat illnesses and promote good health.

111. **The correct answer is (A).** The federal government gives various organizations the authority to award massage therapy schools with accreditation for the purpose of facilitating the distribution of federal aid grants for students.

112. **The correct answer is (D).** Misrepresenting your educational achievements to your clients would be considered a direct breach of the NCBTMB Code of Ethics, which requires you to represent yourself and your qualifications (including your educational achievements) honestly.

113. **The correct answer is (B).** When you wash soiled linens, you should always dry them in a heated dryer because the heat kills any remaining germs.

114. **The correct answer is (B).** Whenever you are working on a client, you should always remember to keep your elbows close to your body, rather than away from your body.

115. **The correct answer is (D).** Supination and pronation are the terms that describe the joint movement when the palms are turned upward and downward, respectively. Eversion describes the movement where the feet are turned to face outward, while inversion describes the movement where the feet are turned inward.

116. **The correct answer is (D).** Unlike sterilization, which is capable of destroying all forms of pathogens, disinfection does not destroy bacterial spores.

117. **The correct answer is (A).** When you are doing the taxes for your practice, it is important to remember that all of your business expenses can be claimed as tax deductions. Claiming your business expenses on your taxes can save you a considerable amount of money.

118. **The correct answer is (B).** This is a passive stretch since the athlete is not just relying on the strength of his muscle to complete the stretch but is using another part of the body to execute and hold the stretch (his hand). A stretch that relies solely on the muscle is active. Choices (A) and (D) are the two main types of exercise.

119. **The correct answer is (B).** Any sounds you hear as you manipulate the client's body can be classified as auditory input. Unusual or abnormal sounds are often an indication of a potential problem.

120. **The correct answer is (B).** Energetic input is derived from an intangible "vibe" received from the client and is not considered diagnostic for most practitioners. In most cases, only energy practitioners use energetic input as a diagnostic tool.

121. **The correct answer is (D).** When a client suffers from sciatica, it is important not to massage directly over the root of the nerve, as this could make the pain worse. Massaging the muscles around the root can help reduce pain and tension in the general area.

122. **The correct answer is (B).** Basal cell carcinoma is the most common form of skin cancer in humans. This form is characterized by a bump that may bleed and never heal.

123. **The correct answer is (D).** The trachea or wind pipe extends down into the chest cavity and then branches into two tubes called bronchi (one for each lung). The larynx and the pharynx are located in the neck region, and the alveolar sacs are tiny structures in the lungs where gas exchange occurs.

124. **The correct answer is (C).** Resistance exercises employ an opposing force (weights, bands, etc.) that will improve the size and strength of the skeletal muscles being targeted over time. Resistance exercises are not *primarily* designed to lengthen the muscles, make them more flexible, or reduce muscle pain.

125. **The correct answer is (C).** Kneading, or petrissage, stimulates blood flow in the deep veins and arteries. Stroking affects the capillaries, compression improves blood flow in the muscle, and friction affects the more superficial veins.

ANSWER SHEET PRACTICE TEST 3: NATIONAL CERTIFICATION EXAMINATION FOR THERAPEUTIC MASSAGE AND BODYWORK (NCETMB)

1. Ⓐ Ⓑ Ⓒ Ⓓ   33. Ⓐ Ⓑ Ⓒ Ⓓ   65. Ⓐ Ⓑ Ⓒ Ⓓ   97. Ⓐ Ⓑ Ⓒ Ⓓ   129. Ⓐ Ⓑ Ⓒ Ⓓ
2. Ⓐ Ⓑ Ⓒ Ⓓ   34. Ⓐ Ⓑ Ⓒ Ⓓ   66. Ⓐ Ⓑ Ⓒ Ⓓ   98. Ⓐ Ⓑ Ⓒ Ⓓ   130. Ⓐ Ⓑ Ⓒ Ⓓ
3. Ⓐ Ⓑ Ⓒ Ⓓ   35. Ⓐ Ⓑ Ⓒ Ⓓ   67. Ⓐ Ⓑ Ⓒ Ⓓ   99. Ⓐ Ⓑ Ⓒ Ⓓ   131. Ⓐ Ⓑ Ⓒ Ⓓ
4. Ⓐ Ⓑ Ⓒ Ⓓ   36. Ⓐ Ⓑ Ⓒ Ⓓ   68. Ⓐ Ⓑ Ⓒ Ⓓ   100. Ⓐ Ⓑ Ⓒ Ⓓ   132. Ⓐ Ⓑ Ⓒ Ⓓ
5. Ⓐ Ⓑ Ⓒ Ⓓ   37. Ⓐ Ⓑ Ⓒ Ⓓ   69. Ⓐ Ⓑ Ⓒ Ⓓ   101. Ⓐ Ⓑ Ⓒ Ⓓ   133. Ⓐ Ⓑ Ⓒ Ⓓ
6. Ⓐ Ⓑ Ⓒ Ⓓ   38. Ⓐ Ⓑ Ⓒ Ⓓ   70. Ⓐ Ⓑ Ⓒ Ⓓ   102. Ⓐ Ⓑ Ⓒ Ⓓ   134. Ⓐ Ⓑ Ⓒ Ⓓ
7. Ⓐ Ⓑ Ⓒ Ⓓ   39. Ⓐ Ⓑ Ⓒ Ⓓ   71. Ⓐ Ⓑ Ⓒ Ⓓ   103. Ⓐ Ⓑ Ⓒ Ⓓ   135. Ⓐ Ⓑ Ⓒ Ⓓ
8. Ⓐ Ⓑ Ⓒ Ⓓ   40. Ⓐ Ⓑ Ⓒ Ⓓ   72. Ⓐ Ⓑ Ⓒ Ⓓ   104. Ⓐ Ⓑ Ⓒ Ⓓ   136. Ⓐ Ⓑ Ⓒ Ⓓ
9. Ⓐ Ⓑ Ⓒ Ⓓ   41. Ⓐ Ⓑ Ⓒ Ⓓ   73. Ⓐ Ⓑ Ⓒ Ⓓ   105. Ⓐ Ⓑ Ⓒ Ⓓ   137. Ⓐ Ⓑ Ⓒ Ⓓ
10. Ⓐ Ⓑ Ⓒ Ⓓ   42. Ⓐ Ⓑ Ⓒ Ⓓ   74. Ⓐ Ⓑ Ⓒ Ⓓ   106. Ⓐ Ⓑ Ⓒ Ⓓ   138. Ⓐ Ⓑ Ⓒ Ⓓ
11. Ⓐ Ⓑ Ⓒ Ⓓ   43. Ⓐ Ⓑ Ⓒ Ⓓ   75. Ⓐ Ⓑ Ⓒ Ⓓ   107. Ⓐ Ⓑ Ⓒ Ⓓ   139. Ⓐ Ⓑ Ⓒ Ⓓ
12. Ⓐ Ⓑ Ⓒ Ⓓ   44. Ⓐ Ⓑ Ⓒ Ⓓ   76. Ⓐ Ⓑ Ⓒ Ⓓ   108. Ⓐ Ⓑ Ⓒ Ⓓ   140. Ⓐ Ⓑ Ⓒ Ⓓ
13. Ⓐ Ⓑ Ⓒ Ⓓ   45. Ⓐ Ⓑ Ⓒ Ⓓ   77. Ⓐ Ⓑ Ⓒ Ⓓ   109. Ⓐ Ⓑ Ⓒ Ⓓ   141. Ⓐ Ⓑ Ⓒ Ⓓ
14. Ⓐ Ⓑ Ⓒ Ⓓ   46. Ⓐ Ⓑ Ⓒ Ⓓ   78. Ⓐ Ⓑ Ⓒ Ⓓ   110. Ⓐ Ⓑ Ⓒ Ⓓ   142. Ⓐ Ⓑ Ⓒ Ⓓ
15. Ⓐ Ⓑ Ⓒ Ⓓ   47. Ⓐ Ⓑ Ⓒ Ⓓ   79. Ⓐ Ⓑ Ⓒ Ⓓ   111. Ⓐ Ⓑ Ⓒ Ⓓ   143. Ⓐ Ⓑ Ⓒ Ⓓ
16. Ⓐ Ⓑ Ⓒ Ⓓ   48. Ⓐ Ⓑ Ⓒ Ⓓ   80. Ⓐ Ⓑ Ⓒ Ⓓ   112. Ⓐ Ⓑ Ⓒ Ⓓ   144. Ⓐ Ⓑ Ⓒ Ⓓ
17. Ⓐ Ⓑ Ⓒ Ⓓ   49. Ⓐ Ⓑ Ⓒ Ⓓ   81. Ⓐ Ⓑ Ⓒ Ⓓ   113. Ⓐ Ⓑ Ⓒ Ⓓ   145. Ⓐ Ⓑ Ⓒ Ⓓ
18. Ⓐ Ⓑ Ⓒ Ⓓ   50. Ⓐ Ⓑ Ⓒ Ⓓ   82. Ⓐ Ⓑ Ⓒ Ⓓ   114. Ⓐ Ⓑ Ⓒ Ⓓ   146. Ⓐ Ⓑ Ⓒ Ⓓ
19. Ⓐ Ⓑ Ⓒ Ⓓ   51. Ⓐ Ⓑ Ⓒ Ⓓ   83. Ⓐ Ⓑ Ⓒ Ⓓ   115. Ⓐ Ⓑ Ⓒ Ⓓ   147. Ⓐ Ⓑ Ⓒ Ⓓ
20. Ⓐ Ⓑ Ⓒ Ⓓ   52. Ⓐ Ⓑ Ⓒ Ⓓ   84. Ⓐ Ⓑ Ⓒ Ⓓ   116. Ⓐ Ⓑ Ⓒ Ⓓ   148. Ⓐ Ⓑ Ⓒ Ⓓ
21. Ⓐ Ⓑ Ⓒ Ⓓ   53. Ⓐ Ⓑ Ⓒ Ⓓ   85. Ⓐ Ⓑ Ⓒ Ⓓ   117. Ⓐ Ⓑ Ⓒ Ⓓ   149. Ⓐ Ⓑ Ⓒ Ⓓ
22. Ⓐ Ⓑ Ⓒ Ⓓ   54. Ⓐ Ⓑ Ⓒ Ⓓ   86. Ⓐ Ⓑ Ⓒ Ⓓ   118. Ⓐ Ⓑ Ⓒ Ⓓ   150. Ⓐ Ⓑ Ⓒ Ⓓ
23. Ⓐ Ⓑ Ⓒ Ⓓ   55. Ⓐ Ⓑ Ⓒ Ⓓ   87. Ⓐ Ⓑ Ⓒ Ⓓ   119. Ⓐ Ⓑ Ⓒ Ⓓ   151. Ⓐ Ⓑ Ⓒ Ⓓ
24. Ⓐ Ⓑ Ⓒ Ⓓ   56. Ⓐ Ⓑ Ⓒ Ⓓ   88. Ⓐ Ⓑ Ⓒ Ⓓ   120. Ⓐ Ⓑ Ⓒ Ⓓ   152. Ⓐ Ⓑ Ⓒ Ⓓ
25. Ⓐ Ⓑ Ⓒ Ⓓ   57. Ⓐ Ⓑ Ⓒ Ⓓ   89. Ⓐ Ⓑ Ⓒ Ⓓ   121. Ⓐ Ⓑ Ⓒ Ⓓ   153. Ⓐ Ⓑ Ⓒ Ⓓ
26. Ⓐ Ⓑ Ⓒ Ⓓ   58. Ⓐ Ⓑ Ⓒ Ⓓ   90. Ⓐ Ⓑ Ⓒ Ⓓ   122. Ⓐ Ⓑ Ⓒ Ⓓ   154. Ⓐ Ⓑ Ⓒ Ⓓ
27. Ⓐ Ⓑ Ⓒ Ⓓ   59. Ⓐ Ⓑ Ⓒ Ⓓ   91. Ⓐ Ⓑ Ⓒ Ⓓ   123. Ⓐ Ⓑ Ⓒ Ⓓ   155. Ⓐ Ⓑ Ⓒ Ⓓ
28. Ⓐ Ⓑ Ⓒ Ⓓ   60. Ⓐ Ⓑ Ⓒ Ⓓ   92. Ⓐ Ⓑ Ⓒ Ⓓ   124. Ⓐ Ⓑ Ⓒ Ⓓ   156. Ⓐ Ⓑ Ⓒ Ⓓ
29. Ⓐ Ⓑ Ⓒ Ⓓ   61. Ⓐ Ⓑ Ⓒ Ⓓ   93. Ⓐ Ⓑ Ⓒ Ⓓ   125. Ⓐ Ⓑ Ⓒ Ⓓ   157. Ⓐ Ⓑ Ⓒ Ⓓ
30. Ⓐ Ⓑ Ⓒ Ⓓ   62. Ⓐ Ⓑ Ⓒ Ⓓ   94. Ⓐ Ⓑ Ⓒ Ⓓ   126. Ⓐ Ⓑ Ⓒ Ⓓ   158. Ⓐ Ⓑ Ⓒ Ⓓ
31. Ⓐ Ⓑ Ⓒ Ⓓ   63. Ⓐ Ⓑ Ⓒ Ⓓ   95. Ⓐ Ⓑ Ⓒ Ⓓ   127. Ⓐ Ⓑ Ⓒ Ⓓ   159. Ⓐ Ⓑ Ⓒ Ⓓ
32. Ⓐ Ⓑ Ⓒ Ⓓ   64. Ⓐ Ⓑ Ⓒ Ⓓ   96. Ⓐ Ⓑ Ⓒ Ⓓ   128. Ⓐ Ⓑ Ⓒ Ⓓ   160. Ⓐ Ⓑ Ⓒ Ⓓ

National Certification Examination for Therapeutic Massage and Bodywork (NCETMB)

Directions: Choose the option that best answers the questions.

1. To avoid hand and wrist strain while performing massage movements, the massage therapist should locate himself or herself
   (A) to the left of massage movements.
   (B) in front of massage movements.
   (C) on top of massage movements.
   (D) behind massage movements.

2. Which of the following is a general characteristic of organ systems?
   (A) They include at least one organ.
   (B) They transport nutrients to cells.
   (C) They consist of at least two organs.
   (D) They protect body structures.

3. During a massage session, an index knobber is mainly used to
   (A) apply firm pressure.
   (B) locate trigger points.
   (C) soothe the skin.
   (D) stimulate the nerves.

4. Which of the following is NOT one of the major organ systems in the human body?
   (A) Lymphatic
   (B) Homeostatic
   (C) Endocrine
   (D) Nervous

5. Which of the following is NOT a standard precaution to take when administering a therapeutic massage?
   (A) Make sure nails are cut short.
   (B) Make sure the room is warm enough.
   (C) Make sure hands are clean.
   (D) Make sure the client has just eaten.

6. What is one function of the hormones secreted by the pituitary gland?
   (A) Regulating calcium levels
   (B) Controlling body metabolism
   (C) Encouraging bone growth
   (D) Supporting immune functions

7. If the massage therapist wants to observe a client's posture, the BEST position for the client to be in is
   (A) standing erect.
   (B) sitting down.
   (C) lying supine.
   (D) bent over.

8. What is the name of the hormone related to digestion that stimulates the production of stomach acid?
   (A) Peptide YY
   (B) CCK
   (C) Gastrin
   (D) Secretin

9. Shiatsu massage involves the use of acupressure along certain points of the body in order to do what?
   (A) Stimulate the pineal gland
   (B) Relieve inflammation
   (C) Release blocked energy
   (D) Assess muscle condition

10. For your new practice, you plan to customize client intake forms so that you can ask specific questions of your new clientele. All of the following would be considered appropriate questions to ask of potential massage clients EXCEPT
    (A) "Why are you seeking my services?"
    (B) "What kind of work are you currently engaged in?"
    (C) "How long have you been married?"
    (D) "What kind of work have you done in the past?"

11. You find yourself becoming strongly attracted to one of your clients. What should you do?
    (A) Continue both the professional and romantic relationships.
    (B) Continue the professional relationship but seek guidance before proceeding.
    (C) End the professional relationship and continue the romantic relationship.
    (D) End the professional relationship and seek guidance before proceeding.

12. If CPR ever becomes necessary, what is the correct rate for chest compressions?
    (A) 25 compressions/minute
    (B) 50 compressions/minute
    (C) 75 compressions/minute
    (D) 100 compressions/minute

13. In what way can massage help the functioning of the body's lymphatic system?
    (A) It can improve blood circulation throughout the body.
    (B) It can improve the flow of lymph throughout the body.
    (C) It can help promote healing after a sports injury.
    (D) It can help increase the volume of lymph in the body.

14. Which of the following clients is likely experiencing problems with kinesthetic awareness?
    (A) The client tenses up every time you touch a certain spot.
    (B) The client claims to be relaxed but resists your movement of his limbs.
    (C) The client feels a great deal of muscle pain due to a sports injury.
    (D) The client whose postural imbalance causes the spine to curve to the right.

15. All of the following organs are part of the urinary system EXCEPT the
    (A) urethra.
    (B) bladder.
    (C) ureters.
    (D) epididymis.

16. During your initial assessment, you attempt to take a client's pulse rate and temperature. The client resists, because she believes these measures to be unnecessary. Which of the following describes the BEST way to proceed?
    (A) Tell the client she must allow you to take these measures or leave.
    (B) Explain that abnormally high temperatures may render massage treatment inadvisable.
    (C) Describe the physiological effects of massage on a person with an elevated temperature.
    (D) Terminate the interview and the session.

17. The Health Insurance Portability and Accountability Act is primarily concerned with
    (A) protecting health-care practitioners.
    (B) privacy of client/patient medical information.
    (C) making health-care available to the wider population.
    (D) solidifying relationships between insurers and providers.

18. Which of the following organs helps expel waste from the body?
    (A) Stomach
    (B) Esophagus
    (C) Gallbladder
    (D) Bladder

19. Practicing massage therapy as an independent contractor means you will
    (A) have taxes and social security costs deducted by your employer.
    (B) be responsible for paying unemployment and sales taxes.
    (C) work out of someone else's office on agreed-upon terms for a negotiated fee.
    (D) receive health benefits and paid time off.

20. Prior to beginning treatment, you asked your client to indicate his pain level on a scale of 1–10. The client indicates his pain hovers near a 6. After the treatment session, you ask the client to rate his pain a second time. The client indicates the pain has been reduced to about a 4. Where in your SOAP charts will you indicate this second rating?
    (A) Subjective
    (B) Objective
    (C) Assessment
    (D) Planning

21. Which of these is the primary organ to which the circulatory system carries waste products?
    (A) Kidneys
    (B) Bladder
    (C) Appendix
    (D) Colon

22. Which of the following body systems is MOST affected by the flow of lymph through the body?
    (A) Muscular system
    (B) Digestive system
    (C) Urinary system
    (D) Immune system

23. Which of the following exercises would be MOST effective if the massage therapist wanted to enhance a client's kinesthetic awareness?
    (A) Ask the client to describe the difference between tense and relaxed muscles.
    (B) Ask the client to classify whether various muscles are contracted or relaxed.
    (C) Ask the client to rapidly contract and relax various muscles.
    (D) Ask the client to contract a muscle and note the sensation.

24. The BEST definition of a postural imbalance is
    (A) the body is out of alignment with the various planes.
    (B) the back curves inward and the stomach protrudes.
    (C) the body appears slightly hunched over and stooped.
    (D) the back appears bent to the left or right.

25. In the digestive system, the duodenum is part of the
    (A) sphincter.
    (B) small intestine.
    (C) stomach.
    (D) gallbladder.

26. The massage therapist is assessing a college student. The therapist finds that the muscles in the client's right shoulder are extremely tense. Which of the following ergonomic factors is MOST likely causing this problem?
    (A) The student is hunching over a computer.
    (B) The student is using a keyboard incorrectly.
    (C) The student is carrying a heavy knapsack on one shoulder.
    (D) The student is sitting in chairs with flat backs.

27. A client frequently experiences tension and knots in the erector spinae. Between sessions, what tool might the client use as part of his or her self-care to release these knots?
    (A) Soup can
    (B) Cold pack
    (C) Warming oil
    (D) Tennis ball

28. Which of the following is true about diverticulitis and diverticulosis?
    (A) Both diverticular diseases are common in children.
    (B) Both diverticular diseases form inflamed pouches in tissue.
    (C) Both diverticular diseases occur in the colon.
    (D) Both diverticular diseases are problems of the urinary system.

29. Which two fingers should the massage therapist use to assess cardiac pulse rate?
    (A) Thumb and index
    (B) Index and middle
    (C) Thumb and middle
    (D) Middle and ring

30. During assessment, the therapist discovers that a client's spine is more curved than it should be, which is likely due to years of poor posture while sitting. To address this problem, the therapist will have to alter the client's
    (A) nervous impulses.
    (B) bone structure.
    (C) work environment.
    (D) muscle memory.

31. Which of the following is the BEST definition of proprioception?
    (A) It is the internal sense of how the body is oriented in space.
    (B) It is the sense of body orientation based on external stimuli.
    (C) It is the sense used to take in information from the environment.
    (D) It is the internal sense used to ensure the body is in balance.

32. Which of the following is considered a suitable initial stroke for the start of a massage session?
    (A) Static touch
    (B) Petrissage
    (C) Kneading
    (D) Friction

33. The inferior nasal concha extends
    (A) horizontally along the lateral wall of the nasal cavity.
    (B) vertically along the lateral wall of the nasal cavity.
    (C) horizontally along the floor of the nasal cavity.
    (D) vertically along the floor of the nasal cavity.

34. If the massage therapist uses the top cover method for draping, what is the FIRST step to take once the client is positioned on the massage table?
    (A) Ask the client to remove his or her wrap.
    (B) Place the cover over the buttocks and upper legs.
    (C) Place the cover over the client so only the head is exposed.
    (D) Ask the client to remove his or her clothing.

35. A client with a postural imbalance will typically present with all of the following EXCEPT
    (A) muscular pain.
    (B) strong muscles.
    (C) muscular contraction.
    (D) trigger points.

36. A mechanical vibrator is being used to treat a client. If the main goal of the session is to release the tension in the soft tissues, the massage therapist should
    (A) use the vibrator for a short period of time.
    (B) apply heavy pressure when using the vibrator.
    (C) use the vibrator for a long period of time.
    (D) apply light pressure when using the vibrator.

37. The olecranon process is located at the upper and
    (A) front of the ulna.
    (B) back of the ulna.
    (C) front of the radius.
    (D) back of the radius.

38. All of the following are long bones EXCEPT the
    (A) femur.
    (B) humerus.
    (C) fibula.
    (D) scapula.

39. Which of the following BEST describes major trigger points in muscles?
    (A) Areas of the muscle that help improve the flow of energy in the body
    (B) Areas of the muscle that are prone to holding waste
    (C) Areas of the muscle that are connected to ligaments and joints
    (D) Areas of the muscle that are too tender to be massaged or touched

40. To gauge pressure during a massage, the therapist should
    (A) start by applying firm pressure.
    (B) ask for feedback from the client.
    (C) watch for signs of muscle injury.
    (D) only increase pressure upon request.

41. While assessing a client, the therapist palpates the bony landmark known as the iliac crest. Which of the following is a characteristic of this bony landmark?
    (A) It is at the end of a long bone.
    (B) It is smooth and rounded.
    (C) It has a pronounced ridge.
    (D) It has a rounded head.

42. The main goal of the structural and functional integration therapy known as the Trager method is to do all of the following EXCEPT
    (A) limit freedom of movement.
    (B) retrain the muscles.
    (C) promote greater body awareness.
    (D) alter body movement.

43. The chakra located at the top of the head is known as the
    (A) seventh chakra.
    (B) third eye chakra.
    (C) sacral chakra.
    (D) root chakra.

44. All of the following are true about the latissimus dorsi muscle EXCEPT
    (A) its proximal attachment is located near the lower ribs.
    (B) its role is partially to abduct the shoulder.
    (C) its dorsal attachment is parallel to the pectoralis major attachment.
    (D) its role is partially to assist in depressing the radius.

45. Which physiological process related to pain occurs immediately after tissue damage?
    (A) Transduction
    (B) Transmission
    (C) Modulation
    (D) Perception

46. The massage therapist is palpating a client's muscles during assessment. Which of the following observations would MOST likely mean that a particular muscle contains one or more trigger points?
    (A) The muscle has overly loose areas.
    (B) The muscle feels cool when pressed.
    (C) The muscle is hot to the touch.
    (D) The muscle contains a taut band.

47. Which of the following muscles connects to four lateral toes with tendons and supports the medial and longitudinal arches?
    (A) Flexor hallucis brevis
    (B) Flexor digitorum longus
    (C) Flexor digitorum brevis
    (D) Flexor hallucis longus

48. Which type of joint has very limited movement and is characterized by cartilage occurring between bones?
    (A) Amphiarthrosis
    (B) Diarthrosis
    (C) Synarthrosis
    (D) Synchondrosis

49. Which part of the lymphatic system filters the lymph before returning the lymph to the bloodstream?
    (A) Lymph capillaries
    (B) Lymph nodes
    (C) Lymph trunks
    (D) Lymph vessels

50. Which of the following is an accurate definition of Bell's palsy?
    (A) Paralysis of facial muscles
    (B) Degenerative disease of the nervous system
    (C) Decalcification and gradual weakening of bones
    (D) The inward curvature of the spine

51. The massage therapist notices a client's head is positioned so that it is in front of the line of gravity. What other effect associated with gravity is the practitioner also likely to observe?
    (A) The anterior neck muscles may be strained.
    (B) The upper trapezius muscles may be weak.
    (C) The posterior neck muscles may be strained.
    (D) The lower trapezius muscles may be tight.

52. During assessment, the massage therapist identifies numerous problems with a client's posture. Which of the following therapies should the therapist use to address the issues?
    (A) Chiropractic alignment
    (B) Acupuncture
    (C) Ultrasound
    (D) Therapeutic massage

53. All of the following are true about the long and short plantar ligaments EXCEPT they
    (A) connect to the calcaneus and the cuboid.
    (B) limit the movement of the talocrural joint.
    (C) transmit rotary force to the calcaneus.
    (D) help support the foot arch.

54. Which of the following holding patterns might indicate a client suffered a sprain to his right ankle at some point in the past?
    (A) The client places more weight on the left side of the body.
    (B) The client places more weight on the right side of the body.
    (C) The client places more weight on the lower parts of the legs.
    (D) The client places more weight on the upper parts of the legs.

55. When the massage therapist manipulates a client's soft tissues in such a way that one tissue layer rubs against another, it is known as
    (A) percussion.
    (B) vibration.
    (C) gliding.
    (D) friction.

56. A client complains of chronic pain in the neck area. The massage therapist suspects this pain may be due to prolonged periods of hyperextension while working. Which of the following is the BEST recommendation the massage therapist can give the client regarding his or her computer screen at work?
    (A) Make sure the screen is below eye level.
    (B) Make sure the screen is at eye level.
    (C) Make sure the screen is large enough.
    (D) Make sure the screen is close enough.

57. Which of the following is a definition of a localized edema?
    (A) A deterioration of muscle cells in joints
    (B) A skin rash characterized by excessive dryness
    (C) An excessive buildup of fluid in body tissues
    (D) An accumulation of mucus causing respiratory problems

58. A trained massage therapist regularly uses heat hydrotherapy in her practice. She should NOT use heat hydrotherapy on any client who has
    (A) acute inflammation.
    (B) kidney problems.
    (C) Reynaud's disease.
    (D) hypothyroidism.

59. Which of the spinal curvature conditions is characterized by an inward curve?
    (A) Kyphosis
    (B) Lordosis
    (C) Scoliosis
    (D) Osteoporosis

60. All of the following are true of the diaper draping method EXCEPT
    (A) it is suitable for cool environments.
    (B) a single towel is used for male clients.
    (C) it is used in conjunction with a table covering.
    (D) it provides concealment for the genitals.

61. After a client has a full-body hot hydrotherapy session, how long should the massage therapist allow the client to rest?
    (A) 5 minutes
    (B) 10 minutes
    (C) 15 minutes
    (D) 30 minutes

62. Which of these is true about eccrine sweat glands?
    (A) They are located in only a few places on the body.
    (B) The secretions they produce contain lipids.
    (C) They are capable of producing only small amounts of secretions.
    (D) The ducts open onto the skin's surface.

63. During assessment, the massage therapist may observe a variety of body imbalances. Which of the following MOST accurately describes the relationship of gravity to body imbalances?
    (A) Gravity tends to pull the body backward.
    (B) Gravity tends to pull the body to one side.
    (C) Gravity tends to pull the body forward.
    (D) Gravity tends to pull the body downward.

64. What is the first step of the post-isometric relaxation technique?
   (A) Lengthening the muscle
   (B) Exerting an isometric contraction
   (C) Relaxing the muscle
   (D) Massaging the muscle

65. When a person has a healthy standing posture, the chin is
   (A) tucked in slightly.
   (B) protruding slightly.
   (C) tilted noticeably upward.
   (D) tilted noticeably downward.

66. A person bends his knee and lifts his foot off the ground. This is an example of
   (A) flexion.
   (B) extension.
   (C) abduction.
   (D) adduction.

67. Which of the following spinal sections is located at the lowest point in the human spine?
   (A) Cervical
   (B) Thoracic
   (C) Lumbar
   (D) Sacral

68. An individual is having trouble with hand adduction. What muscle is MOST likely causing this problem?
   (A) Flexor carpi ulnaris
   (B) Extensor carpi radialis brevis
   (C) Flexor digitorum longus
   (D) Extensor digitorum longus

69. Mucous and serous membranes are examples of what kind of membranes?
   (A) Epithelial
   (B) Connective tissue
   (C) Cutaneous
   (D) Synovial

70. A client is currently experiencing some congestion. Which of the following essential oils commonly used during aromatherapy massage might help alleviate the client's congestion?
   (A) Eucalyptus
   (B) Chamomile
   (C) Lavender
   (D) Geranium

71. What is the primary function of the superior vena cava of the heart?
   (A) It receives blood from the inferior vena cava.
   (B) It pumps blood into the right ventricle.
   (C) It delivers blood to the right atrium.
   (D) It receives blood from the left atrium.

72. You are examining a small number of cells under a microscope. You want to know whether the cells are skeletal muscle cells. What is the BEST way to determine this?
   (A) Determine whether the cells are attached by a series of branches.
   (B) Examine the shape of the cells to see if they look like flattened discs.
   (C) Look to see if there are individual cells with more than one nucleus.
   (D) Establish whether the cells are surrounded by protective cell walls.

73. The massage therapist is conducting a posterior postural assessment. During this assessment, the therapist will look to see whether the spine runs along which of the following lines?
   (A) Coronal
   (B) Frontal
   (C) Midsagittal
   (D) Axial

74. While conducting a postural assessment, the massage therapist notes a client's hips have a forward displacement, the upper back has a convex curve, and the neck is slightly extended. What type of posture is consistent with these observations?
   (A) Sway-back posture
   (B) Ideal posture
   (C) Flat-back posture
   (D) Lordotic posture

75. Nervous tissue is composed of neurons and
   (A) neuroglia.
   (B) neuropeptides.
   (C) neurotransmitters.
   (D) neurohypophyseals.

76. The first and MOST important step you must take if you decide to operate your own practice would be to prepare a
    (A) marketing plan.
    (B) budget.
    (C) business plan.
    (D) mission statement.

77. During a client's assessment, the therapist conducts passive range-of-motion (ROM) exercises. The client experiences pain before the therapist completes the movement, but the therapist does not feel any resistance or muscular spasm. Which of the following conditions does the client MOST likely have?
    (A) Bursitis
    (B) Sprain
    (C) Tendonitis
    (D) Cramp

78. A potentially harmful substance sits just outside of a cell. Which cellular structure can prevent this substance from entering the cell?
    (A) Nucleic acid
    (B) Golgi apparatus
    (C) Endoplasmic reticulum
    (D) Plasma membrane

79. A massage therapist treating a client with asthma should exercise caution because
    (A) massage may spread infection to other body areas.
    (B) there is a possible risk of skin breakage or blistering.
    (C) the therapist's hands could be contaminated and become infected.
    (D) steroids used as asthma treatment may deteriorate organs and bones.

80. The two extraordinary meridians are known as
    (A) yin vessel and yang vessel.
    (B) central vessel and governing vessel.
    (C) heart governor and conception vessel.
    (D) circulatory vessel and central vessel.

81. A palpation assessment can help a massage therapist distinguish between healthy muscles and unhealthy ones. Which of the following muscle characteristics would indicate an unhealthy muscle?
    (A) The muscle expands when palpated.
    (B) The muscle feels warm when palpated.
    (C) The muscle resists movement when palpated.
    (D) The muscle has a firm but flexible feel when palpated.

82. During a massage session, the therapist asks the client to perform a variety of stretches. Each stretch is held for only two seconds, but is repeated a number of times. What stretching technique is the massage therapist using?
    (A) Reciprocal inhibition
    (B) Neuromuscular facilitation
    (C) Active isolated stretching
    (D) Muscle energy technique

83. If a massage therapist wishes to use an essential citrus oil with a calming effect, the BEST option is
    (A) grapefruit oil.
    (B) mandarin oil.
    (C) lemon oil.
    (D) orange oil.

84. What is the function of the dendrites in neurons?
    (A) They carry information away from the cell body.
    (B) They form synapses with nearby neurons.
    (C) They carry information to the cell body.
    (D) They provide protection against infection.

85. Which of the following types of pathologies was formerly absolutely contraindicated for massage?
    (A) Diabetes
    (B) Cancer
    (C) Nephritis
    (D) Parkinson's disease

86. Which of the following is the point of origin for the internal oblique muscles?
    (A) Iliac crest
    (B) Subclavius
    (C) Scapula
    (D) Upper ribs

87. Which of the following molecules stores energy produced during catabolic reactions?
    (A) ATP
    (B) CTC
    (C) AGT
    (D) CTG

88. Which of the following is controlled by a positive feedback loop?
    (A) Blood glucose
    (B) Blood pressure
    (C) Blood clotting
    (D) Blood pH

89. What is one action of the trapezius muscle?
    (A) It compresses the abdomen.
    (B) It rotates the scapula.
    (C) It elevates the shoulders.
    (D) It flexes the trunk.

90. A client presents with Achilles tendonitis. In this situation, which of the following is true?
    (A) Massage is absolutely contraindicated.
    (B) Massage is contraindicated only at the ankle.
    (C) Massage is an acceptable treatment for this condition.
    (D) Massage can be performed only after an extended ice bath.

91. Which of the following muscles of the human body has a fusiform shape?
    (A) Extensor digitorum longus
    (B) Rectus femoris
    (C) Psoas major
    (D) Lumbricals

92. When a massage therapist is performing passive joint movements, which of the following guidelines should be followed?
    (A) Movement should be in the opposite direction of the joint being targeted.
    (B) Movement should reflect both normal and abnormal movement of the joint.
    (C) Movement should be continued only until a slight resistance in the joint is felt.
    (D) Movement should encourage the limb to move to the fullest extent possible.

93. Muscles are often found in agonist/antagonist muscle pairs. Which of the following muscles is the antagonist for the abdominals?
    (A) Posterior deltoids
    (B) Spinal erectors
    (C) Latissimus dorsi
    (D) Forearm flexors

94. The dorsal cavity includes which of the following two cavities?
    (A) Abdominal and pelvic
    (B) Cranial and vertebral
    (C) Vertebral and abdominal
    (D) Pelvic and cranial

95. Which of the following is a common symptom of sciatica?
    (A) Pain in the head and face
    (B) Pain in the lower back and leg
    (C) Pain in the arm and shoulder
    (D) Pain in the lower leg and foot

96. To maintain a sanitary environment, which of the following materials would be the BEST choice to drape and cover a massage table?
    (A) Vinyl
    (B) Cotton
    (C) Linen
    (D) Nylon

97. A massage therapist is using range-of-motion (ROM) exercises to help a client recover from a recent wrist injury. Which of the following would be an example of a passive ROM exercise?
    (A) The therapist asks the client to move his or her hand in a circle without assistance from the therapist.
    (B) The therapist asks the client to lift a small weight without assistance from the therapist.
    (C) The therapist moves the client's hand from side to side without assistance from the client.
    (D) The therapist supports the client's hand while the client moves the hand from side to side.

98. In order for a person to feel pain in response to a stimulus, nociceptors must transmit signals
    (A) from the brain.
    (B) from the muscles.
    (C) via the spinal cord.
    (D) via the nerves.

99. What is one precaution a massage therapist should take when cleaning up bodily fluids?
    (A) Wear a mask.
    (B) Put on gloves.
    (C) Wash hands before.
    (D) Wear a biohazard suit.

100. An athlete is warming up. She lies on her back and pulls her right leg into her chest as far as she can. Which of the following would make this stretch an active-assisted stretch?
(A) A teammate pulls on the leg while the athlete holds it to her chest.
(B) The athlete removes her hands from her right leg.
(C) The athlete extends her leg to fully straighten it.
(D) A teammate pushes on the leg to bring it even closer to the chest.

101. In which of the following body parts can cartilaginous joints be found?
(A) Hip
(B) Ankle
(C) Skull
(D) Vertebrae

102. Gait assessment is a type of visual assessment in which a massage therapist observes how a client walks. Which of the following is NOT observed during a gait assessment?
(A) The number of steps the client takes
(B) The evenness of the shoulder movements
(C) The position of the head over the spine
(D) The height of the arms when swung

103. Facial restriction is a condition associated with unhealthy fascia. How is this condition best described?
(A) Lengthened and thin areas of fascia
(B) Ripped and torn areas of fascia
(C) Shortened, thickened areas of fascia
(D) Gelatinous and elastic areas of fascia

104. A massage therapist locates a trigger point in a client's back. When the therapist applies pressure, the client feels pain in the left leg. This is known as
(A) referred pain.
(B) reflexive pain.
(C) retrieved pain.
(D) represented pain.

105. Which of the following is considered an inflammatory condition?
(A) Arteriosclerosis
(B) Pitting edema
(C) Rheumatoid arthritis
(D) Athlete's foot

106. During the telophase of mitosis, which of the following occurs?
(A) Four daughter cells are formed.
(B) The chromosome strands separate.
(C) Two daughter cells are formed.
(D) The chromosome strands condense.

107. When assessing range of motion, a massage therapist must assess both contractile and inert tissues. An example of an inert tissue is
(A) tendons.
(B) muscle tissue.
(C) ligaments.
(D) muscle attachments.

108. All connective tissues include what as part of their structure?
(A) Collagen
(B) Extracellular matrix
(C) Plasma
(D) Elastic fibers

109. Which of the following is NOT a pathology of the reproductive system?
(A) Salpingitis
(B) Bursitis
(C) Endometriosis
(D) Prostatitis

110. Which of the following describes the main function of synovial membranes?
(A) They sense pain.
(B) They cover the organs.
(C) They help the joints move.
(D) They line the digestive tract.

111. The sagittal axis is formed by the intersection of which of the following two planes?
(A) Frontal and transverse
(B) Sagittal and frontal
(C) Sagittal and transverse
(D) Coronal and frontal

112. The massage therapist is conducting an assessment of a client who works in an office. The therapist notices that the client has a tendency to slump. What is one ergonomic factor that could be causing this?
(A) The client's chair has a flat back.
(B) The client's chair has a curved back.
(C) The client's phone is out of reach.
(D) The client's phone is too close.

113. Which axis passes through the body from left to right?
    (A) Frontal
    (B) Sagittal
    (C) Vertical
    (D) Inferior

114. Which of the following organs of the male reproductive system produces sperm cells?
    (A) Vas deferens
    (B) Glans
    (C) Seminal vesicles
    (D) Testes

115. Which of the following assessment techniques would be MOST effective in terms of testing an individual's proprioception?
    (A) Ask the individual to throw a ball at a target.
    (B) Ask the individual to bend backward as far as possible.
    (C) Ask the individual to push against a board with her legs.
    (D) Ask the individual to close her eyes and touch her nose.

116. Massage can have positive effects on the body's circulatory system. What is the BEST way for a massage therapist to enhance the circulatory benefits of massage?
    (A) Apply movements that create friction between tissue layers.
    (B) Apply movements that encourage blood flow toward the heart.
    (C) Apply movements that involve gentle superficial touch only.
    (D) Apply movements that stimulate blood flow away from the heart.

117. An example of an anabolic reaction is the conversion of
    (A) polysaccharides to monosaccharides.
    (B) amino acids to proteins.
    (C) nucleic acids to nucleotides.
    (D) cortisol to glucagon.

118. All of the following would be included in a standard emergency action plan for a massage therapy practice EXCEPT
    (A) methods to report fires.
    (B) emergency escape routes.
    (C) methods to handle dissatisfied clients.
    (D) emergency shutdown procedures.

119. Which of the following is a possible consequence of massaging a client with blood clots?
    (A) Massage could dislodge and move a clot, leading to possible heart attack.
    (B) Massage may cause direct damage to the artery tissue.
    (C) Massage may damage the client's immune system.
    (D) Massage may alter the client's heart circulation rate.

120. Body temperature is regulated by a negative feedback loop. When body temperature increases, what occurs?
    (A) Blood vessels constrict.
    (B) Blood vessels dilate.
    (C) Shivering starts.
    (D) Shivering stops.

121. The abdominopelvic cavity is generally divided into quadrants. Which of the following organs is found in the right lower quadrant?
    (A) Duodenum
    (B) Spleen
    (C) Stomach
    (D) Cecum

122. Which of the following is true of a parasagittal plane?
    (A) It is parallel to a median or midsagittal plane.
    (B) It divides the body into regions of equal size.
    (C) It is a horizontal line through the midsection.
    (D) It divides the body into front and back regions.

123. Which of the following is a cause of gout?
    (A) Growth of misshapen blood cells
    (B) Buildup of uric acid in blood
    (C) Malignant tumor inside of bone
    (D) Excess absorption of water by intestine

124. A client with a knee injury is unable to move the knee through its full range of motion. To restore mobility, the BEST type of joint movement technique for the therapist to use would be
(A) passive.
(B) active.
(C) active-assistive.
(D) active-resistive.

125. Which of the following is true of superficial gliding?
(A) It has a mechanical effect on the muscles.
(B) It can help stimulate the flow of blood.
(C) It is usually done before other movements.
(D) It can be used to stimulate the body's nerves.

126. Which of the following is the correct definition of ankylosing spondylitis?
(A) A type of arthritis caused by poor muscle adaptation
(B) A type of rheumatic arthritis affecting the spine
(C) A type of arthritis caused by buildup of air in the joints
(D) A type of rheumatic arthritis that can degrade bone structure

127. If a client presents with athlete's foot, the massage therapist should
(A) treat with topical steroids.
(B) rub the infected area with tree oil.
(C) use static touch only on the client.
(D) avoid the infected area.

128. When conducting a range-of-motion assessment, a massage therapist makes observations about different types of movements. Which of the following correctly lists the order, from first to last, in which these movements should be performed?
(A) Active, resisted, passive
(B) Passive, active, resisted
(C) Active, passive, resisted
(D) Passive, resisted, active

129. Which of the following most accurately describes torticollis?
(A) Infectious disease of the lungs
(B) Deformation of soft tissue around the palate
(C) Asymmetry of neck muscles leading to wry neck
(D) Improper positioning of spine leading to abnormal gait

130. Which of the following is NOT a typical cause of back pain?
(A) Misaligned vertebrae
(B) Degeneration of joints
(C) Psychological stress
(D) Low blood sugar levels

131. The massage therapist is assessing a client who presents with several postural problems. What is one gravitational effect the therapist can expect to see in this client?
(A) Spinal fusion
(B) Spinal compression
(C) Spinal slackness
(D) Spinal herniation

132. Which of the following is an accurate description of Osgood-Schlatter disease?
(A) Buildup of fluid around the anterior muscles of the leg
(B) Gradual weakening of joints and bones of the foot
(C) Inflammation of the joints in the fingers and hands
(D) Inflammation of the intersection between ligaments and the tibia

133. A massage therapist should conduct a visual assessment of soft tissues once the client is on the table. Which of the following would NOT be considered during a visual assessment of the soft tissues?
(A) Bilateral symmetry
(B) Skin coloration
(C) Wounds
(D) Temperature

134. If massage is being used for stress relief, the therapist can enhance its stress-relieving benefits by making suggestions to the client. To be effective, these suggestions should be made
(A) before any contact with the client is made.
(B) following a period of static touching or holding.
(C) after the final movements of the massage.
(D) once the massage is complete and the client is dressed.

135. While assessing a new client, the therapist notes the client consistently positions her body in a way that shelters her left forearm. The MOST probable explanation for this condition is that the client
    (A) experiences chronic muscle pain at that location.
    (B) injured the arm at some point in the past.
    (C) finds this position physically comfortable.
    (D) is reacting to the stress of the new situation.

136. The massage therapist is speaking with a potential client who is also an athlete. The client recently injured his back muscles and is experiencing a great deal of pain. The client is expressing skepticism about the benefits of massage in his case. Which of the following massage benefits should the therapist focus on?
    (A) Massage treatment can help reduce stress.
    (B) Massage treatment can boost the immune system.
    (C) Massage treatment can promote tissues healing.
    (D) Massage treatment can facilitate relaxation.

137. A massage therapist is using the muscle energy technique (MET) to help a client with shortened leg muscles. How long should the client contract the leg muscles against the anti-force or stationary surface applied by the therapist?
    (A) 5 seconds
    (B) 10 seconds
    (C) 15 seconds
    (D) 20 seconds

138. What is the term for topical analgesics that produce a warming or cooling sensation by chemically stimulating thermal receptors in the skin?
    (A) Counterirritants
    (B) Salicylates
    (C) Capsaicin
    (D) Statins

139. The massage therapist can help clients relax by encouraging deep breathing. To promote relaxation, the therapist should advise the client to
    (A) breathe in through the mouth.
    (B) expand the abdominal area last.
    (C) breathe in through the nose.
    (D) expand the chest area first.

140. Effective massage therapists strive to follow several principles of holistic practice. Which of the following is NOT a principle of holistic practice?
    (A) The main goal of holistic practice is identifying and treating symptoms.
    (B) The holistic practitioner should strive to set a positive example for clients.
    (C) The body has the capacity to heal itself from within with the proper support.
    (D) The focus should be on preventing rather than correcting problems.

141. When considering the use of heavy strokes, remember these strokes should
    (A) not be performed on clients with circulatory issues.
    (B) be applied in the direction of venous blood supply.
    (C) not be used on clients who are severely obese.
    (D) be applied only in a downward direction.

142. The massage therapist suggests that a client do some stretching at home as part of his self-care. What is the BEST way to ensure that the client knows how to stretch properly?
    (A) Provide pamphlets explaining stretch techniques.
    (B) Ask the client to demonstrate the stretches.
    (C) Inform the client about the end feel of the stretches.
    (D) Take a few moments to show the client the stretches.

143. The massage therapist wants to use a topical analgesic to reduce inflammation and provide relief from pain. Which of the following would be the BEST product for the massage therapist to use?
    (A) Eucalyptamint
    (B) Atomic Balm
    (C) Aspercreme
    (D) Prossage Heat

144. Massage therapy is a holistic approach. That means practitioners view all body systems and tissues as
    (A) interconnected.
    (B) distinct.
    (C) balanced.
    (D) destabilized.

145. Which of the following is true of the horse stance commonly used by massage therapists?
    (A) The feet are held together.
    (B) The shoulders are rolled forward.
    (C) The knees are flexed slightly.
    (D) The back is bent slightly.

146. Agreeing to give a client a free massage if he will clean the carpets at your practice is an example of
    (A) scope of practice.
    (B) dual roles.
    (C) HIPAA violation.
    (D) transference.

147. While in the treatment area, a client trips and sustains what you suspect is a closed fracture. Which of the following should you do while waiting for the paramedics to arrive?
    (A) Offer food and drink.
    (B) Apply ice to the area.
    (C) Massage the area.
    (D) Try to straighten the bone.

148. You are having lunch with a therapist from another practice. During your conversation, he asks you personal questions about one of your clients. How should you respond?
    (A) Decline to answer and politely steer the conversation in a different direction.
    (B) Answer him honestly, since he is also a professional massage therapist.
    (C) Answer some questions to satisfy his curiosity, but avoid revealing too much.
    (D) Ask him for information about his clients in return for information about yours.

149. You are interviewing a new client who is interested in pursuing massage to relieve pain she experiences due to back and neck injuries sustained in a car accident. Based on your assessment, you determine that although massage treatment may afford some relief, there is also a significant risk that it may also lead to further injury. How should you proceed?
    (A) Provide the massage if the client is willing to give her consent.
    (B) Decline to provide treatment because of the risk of injury.
    (C) Refer the client to a more experienced massage therapist.
    (D) Perform the massage and charge a higher fee due to the extra risk.

150. If you are accused of professional negligence, liability insurance generally covers the cost of any covered judgment against you, up to the
    (A) limits specified in your policy.
    (B) amount the insurance company can afford.
    (C) maximum amount allowed by law.
    (D) full amount of the judgment minus your deductible.

151. The NCBTMB Code of Ethics requires massage therapy practitioners to do all of the following EXCEPT
    (A) provide draping and treatment in a way that ensures the safety, comfort, and privacy of the client.
    (B) exercise the right to refuse to treat any person or part of the body for just and reasonable cause.
    (C) charge fees that are reasonable and consistent with the current national standards of the industry.
    (D) conduct business and professional activities with honesty and integrity, and respect the inherent worth of all individuals.

152. After assessing a new client, you wish to let him know how you would like to proceed. Based on your scope of practice, you could suggest all of the following EXCEPT
    (A) a deep tissue massage technique.
    (B) relaxation or breathing exercises.
    (C) the use of hot stone therapy.
    (D) alterations to the client's diet.

153. How should a self-employed massage therapist expect to handle income taxes?
    (A) Ask clients to withhold 25 percent of fees.
    (B) Report own income tax information to the government.
    (C) Arrange for employers to withhold and forward income tax.
    (D) Self-employed contractors do not need to pay income tax.

154. As you work on a client, she begins to casually ask questions about your personal life. How should you respond?
   (A) Keep the conversation focused on the massage.
   (B) Answer questions truthfully to make her feel more comfortable.
   (C) Ask her to remain quiet during the session and return to your work.
   (D) Ignore the questions and continue with the massage.

155. A new client presents with fibrous, hypersensitive adhesions along an old surgery scar. Where in your SOAP notes would you record this information?
   (A) Subjective
   (B) Objective
   (C) Assessment
   (D) Planning

156. Revealing a client's personal information is acceptable
   (A) if you are covered by liability insurance.
   (B) when you cannot get in touch with the client.
   (C) only if it is being provided to a medical professional.
   (D) with the client's consent.

157. The primary risk involved with taking on dual roles with a client is the possibility of
   (A) violating HIPAA and related laws.
   (B) upsetting the power differential in the relationship.
   (C) breaching the professional scope of practice.
   (D) opening yourself up to potential legal risk.

158. Which of the following is true of business insurance?
   (A) It is usually obtained through professional massage organizations.
   (B) It provides coverage for losses caused by fire or theft.
   (C) Its purchase should be based on your reliance on continuing income.
   (D) It can be purchased in an occurrence form.

159. The human body includes how many primary meridians?
   (A) 10
   (B) 12
   (C) 16
   (D) 20

160. In Ayurvedic practice, the Kapha dosha is aggravated by
   (A) excessive heat or sun exposure.
   (B) travel and irregular meals.
   (C) excessive activity.
   (D) oversleeping or overeating.

ANSWER KEY AND EXPLANATIONS

1. D	33. A	65. A	97. C	129. C
2. C	34. C	66. A	98. C	130. D
3. A	35. B	67. D	99. B	131. B
4. B	36. D	68. A	100. D	132. D
5. D	37. B	69. A	101. D	133. D
6. C	38. D	70. A	102. D	134. C
7. A	39. B	71. C	103. C	135. B
8. C	40. B	72. C	104. A	136. C
9. C	41. C	73. C	105. C	137. A
10. C	42. A	74. A	106. C	138. A
11. D	43. A	75. A	107. C	139. C
12. D	44. D	76. C	108. B	140. A
13. B	45. A	77. A	109. B	141. B
14. B	46. D	78. D	110. C	142. B
15. D	47. C	79. D	111. C	143. C
16. B	48. D	80. B	112. A	144. A
17. B	49. B	81. C	113. A	145. C
18. D	50. A	82. C	114. D	146. B
19. C	51. C	83. B	115. D	147. B
20. C	52. D	84. C	116. B	148. A
21. A	53. B	85. B	117. B	149. B
22. D	54. A	86. A	118. C	150. A
23. D	55. D	87. A	119. A	151. C
24. A	56. B	88. C	120. B	152. D
25. B	57. C	89. B	121. D	153. B
26. C	58. A	90. C	122. A	154. A
27. D	59. B	91. C	123. B	155. B
28. C	60. A	92. D	124. C	156. D
29. B	61. D	93. B	125. C	157. B
30. D	62. D	94. B	126. B	158. B
31. A	63. D	95. B	127. D	159. B
32. A	64. A	96. A	128. C	160. D

1. **The correct answer is (D).** One way to avoid injury when performing massage is to ensure that the wrists are not forced to bend at an excessive angle, which can happen if you are positioned on top of massage movements. Good body mechanics dictate that you should remain behind massage movements.

2. **The correct answer is (C).** An organ system is made up of two or more organs that carry out specialized functions in the body. All organ systems are made up of more than one organ.

3. **The correct answer is (A).** An index knobber is used to apply compression to muscle tissue. When utilized properly, this tool delivers deep, firm pressure to the target muscle.

4. **The correct answer is (B).** Maintaining homeostasis is one of the functions of the endocrine system, but there is no homeostatic system in the body. The lymphatic system consists of lymph nodes, the thymus, and the spleen, and the nervous system is made up of the brain, spinal cord, and nerves.

5. **The correct answer is (D).** Standard precautions include cutting nails short to avoid injuring the client's skin, keeping the climate temperate, and making sure the hands have been washed. Making sure the client has just eaten is not a standard precaution (in fact, massage should not be performed directly after a meal).

6. **The correct answer is (C).** One of the hormones secreted by the pituitary gland is growth hormone, which plays a vital role in the growth of bones and muscles. Hormones secreted by the thyroid help control metabolism and calcium levels.

7. **The correct answer is (A).** While assessing posture, the massage therapist should note whether parts of the body are higher or lower on one side of the body or the other, as well as whether any parts of the body are twisted or rotated. To complete this assessment, the client should stand erect and be observed from all four sides.

8. **The correct answer is (C).** Stomach acid, which aids in the digestion of certain foods, is produced in response to the digestive hormone known as *gastrin*. Peptide YY reduces hunger after eating, CCK helps encourage the production of pancreatic juice enzymes, and secretin stimulates the pancreas, but not the stomach, to release a digestive juice.

9. **The correct answer is (C).** Shiatsu involves the use of acupressure with the fingers. Acupressure is applied along specific points in the body in order to release blocked energy.

10. **The correct answer is (C).** The length of the client's marriage is personal information that does not impact treatment. All of the other questions would provide information that might help you to assess issues the client is experiencing and design an appropriate treatment plan.

11. **The correct answer is (D).** Carrying on a romantic or sexual relationship with a client is a serious ethical breach. With that in mind, if you find yourself desiring to enter such a relationship with a client, you should immediately end the professional relationship and seek guidance from a supervisor or another experienced professional before proceeding.

12. **The correct answer is (D).** Chest compressions involve pushing down on the center of the chest, and should be done in conjunction with mouth-to-mouth resuscitation. Compressions should be given at a rate of 100 per minute, or more than one compression per second.

13. **The correct answer is (B).** Lymph massage can help clear blockages within the lymphatic system so lymph can travel more freely throughout the body, but this type of massage will not increase the amount of lymph in the body. Lymph is a bodily fluid that is distinct from blood and is not part of the muscular system.

14. **The correct answer is (B).** Individuals with poor kinesthetic awareness often can't tell whether their own muscles are in a relaxed or contracted state. In this example, the client is tensing the muscles to resist movement without even being aware of doing so.

15. **The correct answer is (D).** The urethra, ureters, bladders, and kidneys are all part of the urinary system. The epididymis, however, is part of the male reproductive system.

16. **The correct answer is (B).** The best approach in this situation is to educate the client on the

reasons why such measures are appropriate prior to treatment. Describing the physiological effects may present entirely too much information for the client; there is no reason to terminate the session unless the client refuses to allow you to conduct an appropriate assessment.

17. **The correct answer is (B).** The Health Insurance Portability and Accountability Act (HIPAA) is primarily concerned with the privacy of a person's medical and health-care records.

18. **The correct answer is (D).** The bladder is an organ that stores urine until it is excreted through the urethra. The stomach, esophagus, and intestines all play a role in digestion and are part of the digestive system. The urethra is part of the urinary system.

19. **The correct answer is (C).** Those massage therapists who choose to practice as independent contractors may work out of someone else's office on agreed-upon terms for pre-determined fees.

20. **The correct answer is (C).** Information about functional improvement from treatment should be recorded in the Assessment portion of your SOAP notes. Here you will note any changes (mild, moderate, significant) in posture, range of motion, or reported symptoms.

21. **The correct answer is (A).** The circulatory system carries waste products through the blood to different organs in the body that rid the body of waste. The primary organs that filter waste from the blood are the kidneys.

22. **The correct answer is (D).** The flow of the lymph through the body has an important effect on the immune system as the lymphatic system helps remove waste, toxins, and other harmful materials. The removal of such substances helps the immune system fight off illnesses.

23. **The correct answer is (D).** A client with poor kinesthetic awareness often contracts or tenses muscles without being aware of it. One way to develop better awareness is to ask the client to contract or relax a muscle, ensure the client is doing it correctly, and then ask the client to consciously observe how it feels.

24. **The correct answer is (A).** A postural imbalance occurs any time the body is out of alignment with the coronal, midsagittal, and horizontal planes. This can affect the body in a variety of ways and may cause the changes mentioned in choices (B), (C), and (D).

25. **The correct answer is (B).** The duodenum is the first part of the small intestine. The duodenum is located in the digestive system between the stomach and the middle part of the small intestine, which is called the jejunum.

26. **The correct answer is (C).** The most likely explanation for the tension is that the student is regularly carrying a knapsack on that shoulder. One suggestion the therapist could make to help address this pain would be to alternate the shoulder used.

27. **The correct answer is (D).** A tennis ball can be an integral part of self-care for those with chronic tension in the erector spinae or the rhomboids. Instruct the client to roll the ball along the back by moving up and down against a wall, or to lie on the floor to apply additional pressure to severe knots.

28. **The correct answer is (C).** Both diverticular diseases—diverticulitis and diverticulosis—occur in the colon. These diseases occur when pouches form in the tissue of the colon. Although both diseases are characterized by these pouches, only diverticulitis is characterized by the inflammation of the pouches. These diseases are both more common in adults than in children.

29. **The correct answer is (B).** The massage therapist should use the index and middle fingers to assess pulse rate. The therapist should pay particular attention to differences in pulse strength when the left and right sides are compared. The radial, carotid, and temporal arteries are often palpated when a client's cardiac pulse is being assessed.

30. **The correct answer is (D).** When an individual develops chronic holding patterns (such as bending over or slouching while at a desk), the muscles eventually "remember" these positions. The holding patterns begin to feel natural. Massage can help release these patterns and alter muscle memory so more positive patterns can be developed.

31. **The correct answer is (A).** Proprioception is a human sense that is controlled by the whole

nervous system, and it relates to the perception of how the body and its limbs are positioned in space. It is not based on external stimuli from the outside environment.

32. **The correct answer is (A).** Of the options provided, the best initial stroke for a new session is static touch, to get acquainted with the client's body and allow the client to get acclimated to your touch.

33. **The correct answer is (A).** The inferior nasal concha extends horizontally along the lateral wall of the nasal cavity. This piece of spongy bone articulates with the maxilla, the palatine, the ethmoid, and the lacrimal.

34. **The correct answer is (C).** When the top cover method is used, the sheet is large enough to cover all body parts excepting the head. Positioning this sheet is the first task the massage therapist should complete after the client is positioned on the table. If the client is wearing a wrap, it is usually removed after the cover is placed over the body.

35. **The correct answer is (B).** When a postural imbalance exists, the muscles of the body try to correct it. This typically results in abnormal muscle contraction, muscle weakening and lengthening, and trigger points, all of which can cause pain.

36. **The correct answer is (D).** Mechanical vibrators can help soothe muscles and release tension when very light pressure is applied. Applying heavier pressure can stimulate tissues, while using mechanical vibrators for an extended period of time tends to numb them.

37. **The correct answer is (B).** The olecranon process, which is also called the olecranon, is a curved eminence located at the upper and back part of the ulna.

38. **The correct answer is (D).** The scapula is flat bone rather than a long bone. Long bones—such as the femur, the humerus, and the fibula—are longer than they are wide. Flat bones are bones that are not rounded.

39. **The correct answer is (B).** Major trigger points, which are also called muscle knots, are areas of the muscle that twitch and clump together. These areas generally do not allow waste products to be properly released.

40. **The correct answer is (B).** Asking for feedback is one of the most effective ways to gauge pressure during massage, as some people have more sensitive tissue than others. The client can let the therapist know when the touch is too firm or too light.

41. **The correct answer is (C).** The iliac crest is part of the pelvic bone. It has a pronounced border. Bony landmarks such as the head of the humerus and femur are found at the end of long bones and have rounded heads, while condyles are smooth and rounded.

42. **The correct answer is (A).** The Trager method involves gentle shaking and rocking and is designed to encourage freedom of movement through the release of tension in the body, as well as promote all other options indicated.

43. **The correct answer is (A).** The chakra at the top of the head is known as the seventh chakra, or the crown chakra.

44. **The correct answer is (D).** The latissimus dorsi muscle helps depress the humerus, not the radius. Other primary actions of this muscle are to extend and rotate the shoulder.

45. **The correct answer is (A).** Transduction occurs when an unpleasant stimulus is converted into electrical energy. Transmission, modulation, and perception are the three steps of the pain process that occur after transduction.

46. **The correct answer is (D).** Taut bands are hardened areas that often span the entire length of a muscle. They can result from injuries, strains, or excessive stress over time. They are often indicators of trigger points.

47. **The correct answer is (C).** The flexor digitorum brevis is a muscle in the foot that is connected to four lateral toes with four tendons and supports the medial and longitudinal arches. This muscle also flexes the four lateral toes.

48. **The correct answer is (D).** Synchondrosis joints allow for very limited movement. These joints, which are part of the articular system, are characterized by cartilage occurring between bones.

49. **The correct answer is (B).** In the lymphatic system, the lymph nodes act as filters. After being

filtered by the nodes, the lymph is returned to the bloodstream.

50. **The correct answer is (A).** Bell's palsy is the paralysis of facial muscles. Bell's palsy can be treated by massage as this therapy can help relax some of the damaged muscles.

51. **The correct answer is (C).** When the head is in front of the line of gravity, this is known as a *forward head posture*. In this position, the force of gravity places great strain on the body. Associated problems include increased strain on posterior neck muscles, tighter upper trapezius muscles, and weaker lower trapezius muscles.

52. **The correct answer is (D).** Massage therapists are trained to use massage therapy as a tool for providing physical relief to clients. All other listed modalities require specialized knowledge and training. Remember, massage therapists must always stay within the defined scope of practice.

53. **The correct answer is (B).** The long and short plantar ligaments are in the foot and limit the movement of the midtarsal joint, not the talocrural joint. The plantar ligaments are in the foot, but the talocrural joint is located in the ankle. This ankle joint helps connect the leg to the foot.

54. **The correct answer is (A).** A protective holding pattern that might occur in response to a sprained ankle is to shift more weight to the uninjured side (in this case, the left). Such holding patterns can become problematic when they persist after the injury has healed.

55. **The correct answer is (D).** Friction is a basic massage movement in which layers of tissue are moved in ways that allow them to rub against each other. Percussion involves striking the client's body. Vibration involves applying a continuous shaking motion to the client's body. Gliding is sliding the hand over parts of the body.

56. **The correct answer is (B).** Placing a screen at eye level is important because it ensures individuals will not have to constantly look up or down to see it. The neck will remain in a natural position, and problems associated with both prolonged periods of hyperextension and flexion can be avoided or mitigated.

57. **The correct answer is (C).** Localized edema is an excessive buildup of fluid in body tissues. Generalized edema is usually caused by inflammation or muscle injuries and can be localized to a specific area of body.

58. **The correct answer is (A).** Heat should not be used to treat conditions associated with acute inflammation, such as bursitis, arthritis, and tendonitis. Cold should not be used if clients have kidney problems, hypothyroidism, or Reynaud's disease (or for those who have previously suffered from frostbite).

59. **The correct answer is (B).** Lordosis occurs when a person's spine curves too far inward. This condition is also called sway back.

60. **The correct answer is (A).** Used in conjunction with a table covering, the diaper draping method is effective for concealing the genitals and promoting privacy. This method involves the use of a single towel for men and two towels for women. However, this method is only suitable for very warm environments.

61. **The correct answer is (D).** A half hour is the minimum amount of time a client should rest after a hydrotherapy session. This allows the body to return to its normal state. Temperature and pulse rate return to normal during the rest period.

62. **The correct answer is (D).** The ducts of eccrine sweat glands open on the skin's surface. Apocrine glands, not eccrine glands, produce only small amounts of secretions, and their secretions may contain lipids. Furthermore, eccrine sweat glands are located over almost all of the body's skin, but apocrine glands are located on only a few spots on the body.

63. **The correct answer is (D).** When the body is balanced, it is in harmony with the field of gravity so that this force does not affect the body in a negative way. If the body is not in alignment with the field of gravity, the body can be pulled in a downward direction. The person is forced to "fight" gravity instead of coexisting with it.

64. **The correct answer is (A).** The post-isometric relaxation technique involves three steps: (1) lengthening the target muscle, (2) exerting a gentle

isometric contraction and holding it for several seconds, and (3) relaxing the muscle.

65. **The correct answer is (A).** When a person has a healthy standing posture, the head is straight and the chin is slightly tucked. In addition, the shoulders are held back, the chest is forward, and the balls of the feet support most of the body's weight.

66. **The correct answer is (A).** Flexion is a movement that decreases the angle between two body parts. Extension increases the angle between two body parts. Abduction and adduction refer to moving a body part away from or toward the midline, respectively.

67. **The correct answer is (D).** Of the options listed, the sacral section is lowest on the human spine. Below the sacral is the coccyx, or tailbone. The sections of spine, in order from highest to lowest, are cervical, thoracic, lumbar, sacral, and coccygeal.

68. **The correct answer is (A).** The flexor carpi ulnaris is a forearm muscle involved in hand flexion and adduction. The extensor carpi radialis brevis is involved with wrist movement, and the flexor digitorum longus and extensor digitorum longus are found near the foot.

69. **The correct answer is (A).** Mucous and serous membranes are composed of epithelial tissue and help provide lubrication. Connective tissue membranes (which include synovial membranes) are made up of connective tissue; *cutaneous membrane* is another term for the body's skin.

70. **The correct answer is (A).** Essential oils known to have decongesting properties include eucalyptus, pine, and tea tree. Chamomile, lavender, and geranium are types of essential oils known to have calming effects.

71. **The correct answer is (C).** The large vein of the heart, known as the *superior vena cava*, delivers deoxygenated blood from the head and arm areas to the right atrium. Choices (A) and (B) are functions of the right atrium and choice (D) is the function of the left ventricle of the heart.

72. **The correct answer is (C).** Skeletal muscle cells are multinucleated, so you could identify skeletal muscle if individual cells appeared with more than one nucleus. Series of branches attaching cells are found in cardiac muscle cells, red blood cells are shaped like flattened discs, and cell walls are found in plant cells.

73. **The correct answer is (C).** The midsagittal line divides the body into left and right halves of equal size. The spine should follow this line. The coronal, or frontal, plane divides the body into posterior and anterior sections, while the axial plane divides the body into upper and lower portions.

74. **The correct answer is (A).** Sway-back posture is characterized by forward displacement of the hips, an outwardly curving upper back, a slightly extended neck, hyperextended knees, and a somewhat flattened lower back. A flat-back posture is characterized by a decreased or absent curvature in the lower back. A lordotic posture is characterized by an increased curve in the lower back.

75. **The correct answer is (A).** Nervous tissue is made up of neurons that transmit impulses and supportive neuroglia cells. Neurotransmitters are chemicals that help carry signals from neurons to other cells. Neuropeptides and neurohypophyseals are both types of neurotransmitters.

76. **The correct answer is (C).** If you decide that you want to own and operate a practice, the first and most important step to take is the preparation of a business plan. Your business plan should contain your mission statement, budget, and marketing plan, among other information.

77. **The correct answer is (A).** Bursitis results in inflammation of the fluid-filled structures found near many joints. It is commonly associated with the knee and hip and can cause discomfort when the affected joint is moved. Choices (B), (C), and (D) are conditions associated with ligaments, tendons, and muscles, respectively.

78. **The correct answer is (D).** The plasma membrane is a semi-permeable barrier that can control what is permitted to enter or leave cells. The Golgi apparatus is involved with protein and lipid storage and distribution. The endoplasmic reticulum is involved with protein synthesis and enzyme storage. Nucleic acid is not a cellular structure.

79. **The correct answer is (D).** Steroids used as treatment to reduce inflammation in those suffering

from asthma may cause a deterioration of internal organs and bones. Caution should be used when applying massage therapy.

80. **The correct answer is (B).** The two extraordinary meridians are the central vessel and the governing vessel.

81. **The correct answer is (C).** A massage therapist can use touch to differentiate healthy muscles from those that are unhealthy or tense. Unhealthy muscles may feel knotty, resist movement or feel unyielding, or cause pain during palpation.

82. **The correct answer is (C).** Active isolated stretching involves holding a stretch for a few seconds and repeating several times. This stretching technique lengthens both the muscles and the fascia.

83. **The correct answer is (B).** Mandarin essential oil is the most calming of the citrus-based oils, and may even be used before bed. Grapefruit, lemon, and orange essential oils all have energizing effects.

84. **The correct answer is (C).** Dendrites are a nerve process in neurons that transmit signals to the cell bodies of neurons. Axons carry information away from the cell body and end at synapses. Protection is provided by the neuroglia in nervous tissue.

85. **The correct answer is (B).** Cancer used to be an absolute contraindication due to fear that massage could spread cancer. Currently, massage therapy is used for almost all types of cancer with consultation with the client's oncologist.

86. **The correct answer is (A).** The point of origin of the internal oblique muscles of the abdomen is the iliac crest. The subclavius is the insertion point for the lower surface of the clavicle. The upper ribs are the point of origin for the serratus anterior muscle. The scapula connects the humerus with the clavicle.

87. **The correct answer is (A).** Adenosine triphosphate (ATP) stores the energy released during catabolism, and this energy is used to complete anabolic reactions. CTC, AGT, and CTG are DNA codons (sets of three nucleotides) vital to the synthesis of amino acids.

88. **The correct answer is (C).** When damage to a blood vessel occurs, thrombin is released, and this stimulates the release of even more thrombin so

clotting can occur quickly. Choices (A), (B), and (D) are all regulated by negative feedback loops.

89. **The correct answer is (B).** The action of the trapezius muscle (which has a point of origin at the occipital bone and vertebrae and a point of insertion at the clavicle and scapula) is to rotate the scapula. The internal and external obliques compress the abdomen, the sternocleidomastoid elevates the shoulders, and the rectus abdominis compresses and flexes the trunk.

90. **The correct answer is (C).** Massage treatment is indicated in this situation. The ankle area should be treated using sports massage techniques.

91. **The correct answer is (C).** Fusiform muscles such as the psoas major and the biceps brachii have a spindle shape and are narrower at their points of insertion and origin than at the center. Choices (A), (B), and (D) are all examples of pennate muscles, which have high concentrations of muscle fibers, are strong, and become tired quickly.

92. **The correct answer is (D).** During passive joint movements, the movements should be directed toward the joint being targeted. The movement should be consistent with the joint's normal movement and the limb should be moved as far as possible. Passive movements performed until a slight resistance is felt are used during the assessment stage.

93. **The correct answer is (B).** Agonist/antagonist muscle pairs such as the abdominals and spinal erectors are responsible for moving a limb and returning it to its original position. The anterior deltoids and posterior deltoids, pectorals and latissimus dorsi, and forearm flexors and extensors are other examples of agonist/antagonist muscle pairs.

94. **The correct answer is (B).** The dorsal body cavity consists of two subdivisions: the cranial cavity (which includes the brain) and the vertebral cavity (which includes the spinal cord). The abdominal and pelvic cavities are subdivisions of the ventral body cavity.

95. **The correct answer is (B).** Sciatica is characterized by pain in the lower back and leg. Sciatica is caused by inflammation of the sciatic nerve, which controls sensation in the lower extremities.

96. **The correct answer is (A).** In this situation vinyl is the best choice since it can easily be wiped down and sanitized between each client.

97. **The correct answer is (C).** Passive ROM exercises are performed by the therapist and do not require any client effort. Choices (A) and (D) are examples of active ROM exercises (choice (D) would be classified as active assistive), and choice (B) is an example of a resistive ROM exercise.

98. **The correct answer is (C).** When tissue is damaged or is in danger of being damaged, nociceptors detect this and send a signal along the spinal cord. Once the signal reaches and is processed by the brain, the person experiences the pain sensation.

99. **The correct answer is (B).** Massage therapists will periodically have to deal with bodily fluids in their practice, which are potential biohazards. Putting on gloves and washing hands afterwards are two precautions the massage therapist should take, but masks and biohazard suits typically are not necessary.

100. **The correct answer is (D).** An active-assisted stretch is performed with the help of a partner. The partner applies an additional force to enhance a stretch after the individual has performed a stretch to his or her maximum ability.

101. **The correct answer is (D).** Cartilaginous joints such as the vertebrae are capable of slight movement and are characterized by bones joined together by cartilage. The joints in the skull are called fibrous joints, and the joints of the hip and ankle are synovial.

102. **The correct answer is (D).** Choices (A), (B), and (C) are all observed during a visual gait assessment. With respect to the arms, while the therapist will look at whether the client swings each arm equally while walking, he or she will generally not measure how high the arms swing.

103. **The correct answer is (C).** Poor posture, repetitive motion, injuries, and other factors can result in thickened areas of fascia, otherwise known as facial restriction.

104. **The correct answer is (A).** The correct term for this phenomenon is *referred pain*. The pain arises in the trigger point, but the individual feels the sensation of pain in another area of the body.

105. **The correct answer is (C).** Rheumatoid arthritis is an autoimmune disease that causes an inflammatory condition in which immune cells attack healthy cells, causing them to deteriorate and produce pain.

106. **The correct answer is (C).** Telophase is the final stage of mitosis. It is the point at which two genetically identical daughter cells are formed. Four daughter cells are formed during meiosis; the chromosome strands separate during anaphase. The last choice is incorrect since chromosome strands are already in condensed form.

107. **The correct answer is (C).** As the name suggests, contractile tissues are involved in muscle contractions, and include the structures listed in choices (A), (B), and (D). Inert tissues do not contract and include ligaments, cartilage, blood vessels, and bone.

108. **The correct answer is (B).** All connective tissues are composed of cells and an extracellular matrix in which these cells are embedded. Collagen is found in only certain types of connective tissues, elastic fibers are a type of loose connective tissue, and plasma is the extracellular matrix of blood.

109. **The correct answer is (B).** Bursitis is an inflammation of the bursae, or fluid-filled sacs found in the separations between tendons and skin or bone. Salpingitis is an infection of the fallopian tubes that leads to inflammation, endometriosis is the abnormal growth of uterine-like cells on the ovaries or other structures, and prostatitis is characterized by inflammation of the prostate gland.

110. **The correct answer is (C).** Synovial membranes are made of soft tissue. They secrete the synovial fluid that allows the joints to move more easily. The skin (cutaneous membrane) senses pain, serous membranes cover certain organs, and mucous membranes line the digestive tract.

111. **The correct answer is (C).** The sagittal and transverse planes form the sagittal axis, which is a horizontal line from the front to the back of the body. The frontal and transverse planes form the frontal axis, the sagittal and frontal planes form

the vertical axis, and coronal and frontal are two terms for the same plane.

112. **The correct answer is (A).** The spine has natural curves, and chairs with flat backs and flat seats do not adequately support this natural curvature. Without proper support, individuals have a tendency to slump.

113. **The correct answer is (A).** The frontal axis is a horizontal axis with a left-to-right direction. It is formed by intersecting frontal and transverse planes. The sagittal axis has a front-to-back direction and the vertical axis has an up-and-down (vertical) direction. "Inferior" is not a type of body axis.

114. **The correct answer is (D).** The testes, or testicles, produce and store sperm and testosterone. The glans is the tip of the penis, the vas deferens transports semen, and the seminal vesicles produce fluids found in semen.

115. **The correct answer is (D).** Proprioception is the internal sense of one's own body. Asking an individual to close her eyes and touch her nose can demonstrate the individual's level of awareness of the body and how it is positioned in space. Choices (A) and (C) involve the use of external stimuli and therefore are not the best choices. Choice (B) is a test of flexibility, not proprioception.

116. **The correct answer is (B).** All massage movements should encourage the flow of blood towards the heart to maximize circulatory benefits of treatment. Circulation can be enhanced by both gentle gliding strokes and techniques such as kneading.

117. **The correct answer is (B).** Anabolic reactions create more complex substances (such as proteins) from simpler substances (such as amino acids). Choices (A) and (C) are examples of catabolic reactions, and cortisol and glucagon are catabolic hormones.

118. **The correct answer is (C).** Emergency action plans must be completed by all types of organizations. They outline the procedures that should be followed during unseen and potentially catastrophic events, but the plan would not apply to upset clients unless they became violent.

119. **The correct answer is (A).** Massage could dislodge and move a clot, leading to a possible heart attack. Precautions are necessary when dealing with a blood clot, and sometimes it is appropriate to cancel any massage treatments.

120. **The correct answer is (B).** Body temperature is regulated by a negative feedback loop, so the body works to reduce a higher-than-normal temperature by dilating the blood vessels to release heat or initiate sweating. Choices (A) and (D) are both responses to a lower-than-normal body temperatures. A person generally does not shiver when body temperature increases.

121. **The correct answer is (D).** Structures found in the right lower quadrant of the abdominopelvic cavity include the cecum and appendix. The left upper quadrant contains the stomach, spleen, and duodenum.

122. **The correct answer is (A).** A parasagittal plane, like a median (or midsagittal) plane, divides the body into left and right regions, but the main difference is that these regions are different sizes. Choice (C) describes a transverse plane, while choice (D) describes a frontal or coronal plane.

123. **The correct answer is (B).** Gout is caused by the improper oxidation of uric acid that leads to excess uric acid around joints of the big toe, ankle, and fingers.

124. **The correct answer is (C).** Active-assistive joint movements involve effort from both the client and the therapist. The client first performs independently, and then the therapist assists the client in completing the movement. This is the preferred technique when attempting to restore joint mobility after an injury.

125. **The correct answer is (C).** Superficial gliding involves the application of only very light pressure. It is usually completed first so that the therapist can assess the client and the client can get accustomed to the therapist's touch. The other answer choices are not generally true of superficial gliding.

126. **The correct answer is (B).** Ankylosing spondylitis, which may affect breathing, is a type of rheumatic arthritis that affects the spine.

127. **The correct answer is (D).** Athlete's foot is a type of fungal infection. Massaging the foot is contraindicated, as doing so can spread the infection. However, the massage therapist can work on other areas of the client's body.

128. **The correct answer is (C).** Active movements, in which the client moves his or her limbs without any assistance from the therapist, are done first. Passive movements, in which the therapist performs the movement and makes note of client reactions and end feel are completed next, while resisted movements are performed last.

129. **The correct answer is (C).** Torticollis is characterized by an asymmetry of head muscles, leading to twisting of the neck. Massage is indicated and can relieve muscle contractions.

130. **The correct answer is (D).** Low blood sugar is not generally a primary cause of back pain; however, misaligned vertebrae, degenerated disks, and psychological stress are all common causes of back pain.

131. **The correct answer is (B).** When the spine is not in balance with the field of gravity, gravity exerts a downward force on the spine that can cause the vertebrae to become compacted and compressed over time. Spinal fusion occurs as a result of some diseases, while spinal herniation is a specific type of spinal disc injury.

132. **The correct answer is (D).** Osgood-Schlatter disease is characterized by the inflammation of intersection between ligaments and the tibia. Massage therapy can be used to relax muscles around the tibial tuberosity.

133. **The correct answer is (D).** A massage therapist should conduct a visual examination of bilateral symmetry of soft tissues, skin coloration, and wounds or blemishes. Temperature is also important to assess since a higher than normal temperature can be a sign of inflammation and a lower than normal temperature could indicate muscles are not getting the required blood flow. However, temperature would not be determined visually.

134. **The correct answer is (C).** Massage is a deeply relaxing experience for most individuals, and in this relaxed state they are often receptive to suggestions. To ensure that suggestions are as effective as possible, make them at the end of the massage, before the client emerges from his or her state of heightened relaxation.

135. **The correct answer is (B).** This type of holding pattern is known as a *trauma reflex*, and it may persist for years after an injury to a specific area of the body. Individuals with this type of holding pattern tend to double over the injury site as a protective measure.

136. **The correct answer is (C).** The benefit most likely to appeal to this individual is the promotion of tissue healing. Although massage treatment can alleviate stress, support the immune system, and facilitate relaxation, they would be secondary concerns to the client at this point.

137. **The correct answer is (A).** MET is used to lengthen and strengthen muscles, and also to improve range of motion. The therapist will apply an anti-force and ask the client to contract the muscle against this force for five seconds. The contraction will then be repeated several times.

138. **The correct answer is (A).** Counterirritants such as Icy Hot and Tiger Balm are routinely used to provide relief from pain and irritation. Salicylates include products such as BenGay; capsaicin-based products include Zostrix.

139. **The correct answer is (C).** To encourage relaxation, advise the client to breathe in through the nose and then expand the abdomen before the chest. The client should hold the breath for a short period of time before exhaling.

140. **The correct answer is (A).** A holistic approach looks not only to treat ailments but also promote the well-being of the mind and body. A holistic practice focuses more on identifying and addressing underlying causes of pain as opposed to merely treating individual symptoms.

141. **The correct answer is (B).** Heavy stroking can be a part of a massage therapy session for a variety of clients, including those in special populations. The main precaution to remember is that heavy strokes should not be applied in the opposite direction of the venous blood supply.

142. The correct answer is (B). The best way to make sure the client is stretching correctly and safely is to have him or her demonstrate technique to you. You can observe and offer pointers if necessary. Pamphlets, information about end feel, and demonstration are also useful educational tools.

143. The correct answer is (C). A salicylate product such as Aspercreme helps reduce inflammation and pain. The other choices are counterirritants, which create a cooling or warming sensation by chemically irritating the skin.

144. The correct answer is (A). A holistic approach involves looking at the body as a whole and recognizing the interrelationships that exist among organs and tissues.

145. The correct answer is (C). Massage therapists often utilize the horse stance while performing petrissage on the back or leg area. The feet are spaced apart and aligned with the edge of the massage table, the shoulders are held back, the back is held straight, and the knees are flexed slightly to make it easier to apply firm pressure.

146. The correct answer is (B). If you exchange services with a client, you are engaging in dual roles with that client.

147. The correct answer is (B). Immediate first aid for a suspected bone fracture includes the application of ice along with attempts to keep the injured individual calm with a normal breathing pattern.

148. The correct answer is (A). Divulging any personal information about a client to anyone without his or her consent is highly unethical and might also be against the law. If a colleague asks you for personal information about a client, you should diplomatically steer the conversation in a different direction.

149. The correct answer is (B). Because of the risk of further injuries, you should decline to perform a massage when treatment is contraindicated. The NCBTMB Code of Ethics requires therapists to provide treatment only if there is a reasonable expectation that it will be advantageous and to exercise the right to refuse treatment for just and reasonable cause.

150. The correct answer is (A). In the event that a judgment is levied against you for a claim covered by your policy, your liability insurance should cover the full cost of the judgment, up to the policy limits specified in your policy.

151. The correct answer is (C). The NCBTMB Code of Ethics is not concerned with the pricing of services.

152. The correct answer is (D). Suggesting that a client make alterations to his or her diet would be outside the scope of practice. Even if you believe the client would benefit by such a change, such suggestions should come only from the client's physician, nutritionist, or other qualified individual.

153. The correct answer is (B). As a self-employed person, you will be required to withhold and report your own income tax.

154. The correct answer is (A). While you should not reveal any personal information to clients, you should be sure to deliver this message tactfully.

155. The correct answer is (B). The objective portion of your SOAP notes should deal with tangible, observed data from your assessment.

156. The correct answer is (D). Client information cannot be released to anyone without the client's consent. Such an action would constitute an ethical violation and an HIPAA violation, which could result in serious consequences.

157. The correct answer is (B). The primary cause of concern when you take on dual roles with a client is the possibility of upsetting the power differential in the client/therapist relationship.

158. The correct answer is (B). Business insurance provides coverage for losses incurred as the result of fire, theft, or other similar incidents.

159. The correct answer is (B). The body includes 12 primary meridians running in pairs.

160. The correct answer is (D). The three doshas are the Kapha, the Pitta, and the Vata. The Pitta is aggravated by excessive heat or sun exposure (among other things). The Vata is aggravated by irregular routines, irregular meals, travel, and excessive activity (among other things).

APPENDIXES

APPENDIX A
NCBTMB Code of Ethics and Standards of Practice

211

APPENDIX B
NCBTMB National Examination for State Licensing (NESL) Option

219

APPENDIX C
Helpful Resources

221

APPENDIX D
Complementary/Alternative Medicine

225

NCBTMB Code of Ethics and Standards of Practice

NCBTMB CODE OF ETHICS

NCBTMB certificants and applicants for certification shall act in a manner that justifies public trust and confidence, enhances the reputation of the profession, and safeguards the interest of individual clients. Certificants and applicants for certification will:

I. Have a sincere commitment to provide the highest quality of care to those who seek their professional services.

II. Represent their qualifications honestly, including education and professional affiliations, and provide only those services that they are qualified to perform.

III. Accurately inform clients, other health-care practitioners, and the public of the scope and limitations of their discipline.

IV. Acknowledge the limitations of and contraindications for massage and bodywork and refer clients to appropriate health professionals.

V. Provide treatment only where there is a reasonable expectation that it will be advantageous to the client.

VI. Consistently maintain and improve professional knowledge and competence, striving for professional excellence through regular assessment of personal and professional strengths and weaknesses and through continued education training.

VII. Conduct their business and professional activities with honesty and integrity, and respect the inherent worth of all persons.

VIII. Refuse to unjustly discriminate against clients and/or health professionals.

IX. Safeguard the confidentiality of all client information, unless disclosure is requested by the client in writing, is medically necessary, is required by law, or necessary for the protection of the public.

X. Respect the client's right to treatment with informed and voluntary consent. The certified practitioner will obtain and record the informed consent of the client, or client's advocate, before providing treatment. This consent may be written or verbal.

XI. Respect the client's right to refuse, modify, or terminate treatment regardless of prior consent given.

XII. Provide draping and treatment in a way that ensures the safety, comfort, and privacy of the client.

XIII. Exercise the right to refuse to treat any person or part of the body for just and reasonable cause.

XIV. Refrain, under all circumstances, from initiating or engaging in any sexual conduct, sexual activities, or sexualizing behavior involving a client, even if the client attempts to sexualize the relationship unless a preexisting relationship exists between an applicant or a practitioner and the client prior to the applicant or practitioner applying to be certified by NCBTMB.

XV. Avoid any interest, activity, or influence which might be in conflict with the practitioner's obligation to act in the best interests of the client or the profession.

XVI. Respect the client's boundaries with regard to privacy, disclosure, exposure, emotional expression, beliefs, and the client's reasonable expectations of professional behavior. Practitioners will respect the client's autonomy.

XVII. Refuse any gifts or benefits that are intended to influence a referral, decision, or treatment, or that are purely for personal gain and not for the good of the client.

XVIII. Follow the NCBTMB Standards of Practice, this Code of Ethics, and all policies, procedures, guidelines, regulations, codes, and requirements promulgated by the National Certification Board for Therapeutic Massage and Bodywork.

NCBTMB STANDARDS OF PRACTICE

Copyright © 2007 National Certification Board for Therapeutic Massage and Bodywork (Revised 10/09)

Background

The purpose of the National Certification Board for Therapeutic Massage and Bodywork (NCBTMB) is to foster high standards of ethical and professional practice in the delivery of services through a recognized credible certification program that assures the competency of practitioners of therapeutic massage and bodywork.

These Standards of Practice ensure that certificants and applicants for certification are aware of, and committed to, upholding high standards of practice for the profession. The Standards of Practice are also meant to assist members of the general public, including consumers, other health-care professionals, and state and municipal regulatory agencies or boards with understanding the duties and responsibilities of NCBTMB certificants and applicants for certification.

The NCBTMB developed and adopted the Standards of Practice to provide certificants and applicants for certification with a clear statement of the expectations of professional conduct and level of practice afforded the public in, among other things, the following areas: Professionalism, Legal and Ethical Requirements, Confidentiality,

Business Practices, Roles and Boundaries, and Prevention of Sexual Misconduct. These Standards of Practice were approved and ratified by the NCBTMB Board of Directors, representatives of the certificant population, and key stakeholders of the NCBTMB.

Preamble

These Standards of Practice for the profession of therapeutic massage and bodywork are the guiding principles by which certificants and applicants for certification conduct their day-to-day responsibilities within their scope of practice. These principles help to assure that all professional behaviors are conducted in the most ethical, compassionate, and responsible manner. Through these Standards of Practice, NCBTMB seeks to establish and uphold high standards, traditions, and principles of the practices that constitute the profession of therapeutic massage and bodywork. The Standards are enforceable guidelines for professional conduct, and therefore, are stated in observable and measurable terms intended as minimum levels of practice to which certificants and applicants for certification are held accountable. Upon submission of the application for the National Certification Examinations, each applicant for certification must agree to uphold and abide by the NCBTMB Code of Ethics, Standards of Practice, and applicable policies. Certificants, or applicants for certifications, failure to comply with the Code of Ethics and the Standards of Practice as provided herein constitutes professional misconduct and may result in sanctions, or other appropriate disciplinary actions, including the suspension or revocation of certification.

NCBTMB certificants and applicants for certification are obligated to report unethical behavior and violations of the Code of Ethics and/or the Standards of Practice they reasonably and in good faith believe have been performed by other NCBTMB certificants and applicants for certification to NCBTMB.

These Standards of Practice reflect NCBTMB's clear commitment that certificants and applicants for certification provide an optimal level of service and strive for excellence in their practice. This includes remaining in good standing with NCBTMB, committing to continued personal and professional growth through continuing education, and understanding and accepting that personal and professional actions reflect on the integrity of the therapeutic massage and bodywork profession and NCBTMB. Certificants and applicants for certification are responsible for showing and maintaining professional compliance with the Standards of Practice.

NCBTMB requires certificants and applicants for certification to conduct themselves in a highly professional and dignified manner. NCBTMB will not consider and/or adjudicate complaints against certificants and applicants for certification that are based solely on consumer-related issues or are based on competitive marketplace issues.

As the therapeutic massage and bodywork profession evolves, so, too, will the Standards of Practice. The Standards of Practice are, therefore, a live and dynamic document and subject to revision in keeping with the changing demands and expectations of the therapeutic massage and bodywork profession.

Standard I: Professionalism

The certificant or applicant for certification must provide optimal levels of professional therapeutic massage and bodywork services and demonstrate excellence in practice by promoting healing and well-being through responsible, compassionate, and respectful touch. In his/her professional role, the certificant or applicant for certification shall

a. adhere to the NCBTMB Code of Ethics, Standards of Practice, policies, and procedures.

b. comply with the peer review process conducted by the NCBTMB Ethics and Standards Committee regarding any alleged violations of the NCBTMB Code of Ethics and Standards of Practice.

c. treat each client with respect, dignity, and worth.

d. use professional verbal, nonverbal, and written communications.

e. provide an environment that is safe and comfortable for the client and which, at a minimum, meets all legal requirements for health and safety.

f. use standard precautions to ensure professional hygienic practices and maintain a level of personal hygiene appropriate for practitioners in the therapeutic setting.

g. wear clothing that is clean, modest, and professional.

h. obtain voluntary and informed consent from the client prior to initiating the session.

i. if applicable, conduct an accurate needs assessment, develop a plan of care with the client, and update the plan as needed.

j. use appropriate draping to protect the client's physical and emotional privacy.

k. be knowledgeable of his/her scope of practice and practice only within these limitations.

l. refer to other professionals when in the best interest of the client and practitioner.

m. seek other professional advice when needed.

n. respect the traditions and practices of other professionals and foster collegial relationships.

o. not falsely impugn the reputation of any colleague.

p. use the initials NCTMB only to designate his/her professional ability and competency to practice therapeutic massage and bodywork, or the initials NCTM only to designate his/her professional ability and competency to practice therapeutic massage.

q. remain in good standing with NCBTMB.

r. understand that the NCBTMB certificate may be displayed prominently in the certificant's principal place of practice.

s. use the NCBTMB logo and certification number on business cards, brochures, advertisements, and stationery only in a manner that is within established NCBTMB guidelines.

t. not duplicate the NCBTMB certificate for purposes other than verification of the practitioner's credentials.

u. immediately return the certificate to NCBTMB if certification is revoked.

v. inform NCBTMB of any changes or additions to information included in his/her application for NCBTMB certification or recertification.

Standard II: Legal and Ethical Requirements

The certificant or applicant for certification must comply with all the legal requirements in applicable jurisdictions regulating the profession of therapeutic massage and bodywork. In his/her professional role, the certificant or applicant for certification shall

a. obey all applicable local, state, and federal laws.

b. refrain from any behavior that results in illegal, discriminatory, or unethical actions.

c. accept responsibility for his/her own actions.

d. report to the proper authorities any alleged violations of the law by other certificants or applicants for certification.

e. maintain accurate and truthful records.

f. report to NCBTMB any criminal conviction of, or plea of guilty, nolo contendere, or no contest to, a crime in any jurisdiction (other than a minor traffic offense) by himself/herself and by other certificants or applicants for certification.

g. report to NCBTMB any pending litigation and resulting resolution related to the certificant or applicant for certification's professional practice and the professional practice of other certificants or applicants for certification.

h. report to NCBTMB any pending complaints in any state or local government or quasi-government board or agency against his/her professional conduct or competence, or that of another certificant, and the resulting resolution of such complaint.

i. respect existing publishing rights and copyright laws, including, but not limited to, those that apply to NCBTMB's copyright-protected examinations.

Standard III: Confidentiality

The certificant or applicant for certification shall respect the confidentiality of client information and safeguard all records. In his/her professional role, the certificant or applicant for certification shall

a. protect the confidentiality of the client's identity in conversations, all advertisements, and any and all other matters unless disclosure of identifiable information is requested by the client in writing, is medically necessary, is required by law or for purposes of public protection.

b. protect the interests of clients who are minors or clients who are unable to give voluntary and informed consent by securing permission from an appropriate third party or guardian.

c. solicit only information that is relevant to the professional client/therapist relationship.

d. share pertinent information about the client with third parties when required by law or for purposes of public protection.

e. maintain the client files for a minimum period of four years.

f. store and dispose of client files in a secure manner.

Standard IV: Business Practices

The certificant or applicant for certification shall practice with honesty, integrity, and lawfulness in the business of therapeutic massage and bodywork. In his/her professional role, the certificant or applicant for certification shall

a. provide a physical setting that is safe and meets all applicable legal requirements for health and safety.

b. maintain adequate and customary liability insurance.

c. maintain adequate progress notes for each client session, if applicable.

d. accurately and truthfully inform the public of services provided.

e. honestly represent all professional qualifications and affiliations.

f. promote his/her business with integrity and avoid potential and actual conflicts of interest.

g. advertise in a manner that is honest, dignified, accurate and representative of services that can be delivered and remains consistent with the NCBTMB Code of Ethics and Standards of Practice.

h. advertise in a manner that is not misleading to the public and shall not use sensational, sexual, or provocative language and/or pictures to promote business.

i. comply with all laws regarding sexual harassment.

j. not exploit the trust and dependency of others, including clients and employees/coworkers.

k. display/discuss a schedule of fees in advance of the session that is clearly understood by the client or potential client.

l. make financial arrangements in advance that are clearly understood by and safeguard the best interests of the client or consumer.

m. follow acceptable accounting practices.

n. file all applicable municipal, state, and federal taxes.

o. maintain accurate financial records, contracts, and legal obligations, appointment records, tax reports, and receipts for at least four years.

Standard V: Roles and Boundaries

The certificant or applicant for certification shall adhere to ethical boundaries and perform the professional roles designed to protect both the client and the practitioner, and safeguard the therapeutic value of the relationship. In his/her professional role, the certificant or applicant for certification shall

a.   recognize his/her personal limitations and practice only within these limitations.

b.   recognize his/her influential position with the client and not exploit the relationship for personal or other gain.

c.   recognize and limit the impact of transference and counter-transference between the client and the certificant.

d.   avoid dual or multidimensional relationships that could impair professional judgment or result in exploitation of the client or employees and/or coworkers.

e.   not engage in any sexual activity with a client.

f.   acknowledge and respect the client's freedom of choice in the therapeutic session.

g.   respect the client's right to refuse the therapeutic session or any part of the therapeutic session.

h.   refrain from practicing under the influence of alcohol, drugs, or any illegal substances (with the exception of a prescribed dosage of prescription medication which does not impair the certificant).

i.   have the right to refuse and/or terminate the service to a client who is abusive or under the influence of alcohol, drugs, or any illegal substance.

Standard VI: Prevention of Sexual Misconduct

The certificant or applicant for certification shall refrain from any behavior that sexualizes, or appears to sexualize, the client/therapist relationship. The certificant or applicant for certification recognizes the intimacy of the therapeutic relationship may activate practitioner and/or client needs and/or desires that weaken objectivity and may lead to sexualizing the therapeutic relationship. In his/her professional role, the certificant or applicant for certification shall

a.   refrain from participating in a sexual relationship or sexual conduct with the client, whether consensual or otherwise, from the beginning of the client/therapist relationship and for a minimum of 6 months after the termination of the client/therapist relationship unless a preexisting relationship exists between a certificant or applicant for certification and client prior to the certificant or applicant for certification applying to be certified by NCBTMB.

b.   in the event that the client initiates sexual behavior, clarify the purpose of the therapeutic session, and, if such conduct does not cease, terminate or refuse the session.

c.   recognize that sexual activity with clients, students, employees, supervisors, or trainees is prohibited even if consensual.

d.   not touch the genitalia.

e.   only perform therapeutic treatments beyond the normal narrowing of the ear canal and normal narrowing of the nasal passages as indicated in the plan of care and only after receiving informed voluntary written consent.

f.   only perform therapeutic treatments in the oropharynx as indicated in the plan of care and only after receiving informed voluntary consent.

g. only perform therapeutic treatments into the anal canal as indicated in the plan of care and only after receiving informed voluntary written consent.

h. only provide therapeutic breast massage as indicated in the plan of care and only after receiving informed voluntary written consent from the client.

NCBTMB National Examination for State Licensing (NESL) Option

WHAT IS THE NESL OPTION?

The National Examination for State Licensing (NESL) is an option offered by the National Certification Board for Therapeutic Massage and Bodywork (NCBTMB). The NESL option is available to those individuals who plan to practice massage therapy and/or bodywork in locations that recognize the validity of the NCBTMB certification exams, but do not require licensing applicants to become certified by NCBTMB.

The primary difference with the NESL option is that the individual is allowed to take either the National Certification Examination for Therapeutic Massage and Bodywork (NCETMB) or the National Certification Examination for Therapeutic Massage (NCETM) examination at *any time* during the student's training. (In other words, you do not need to have graduated from your massage therapy training program before taking the exam of your choice.) In addition, you will NOT actually be certified by NCBTMB even after passing the examination of your choice.

Successfully passing the examination does, however, allow the student to become immediately eligible for licensing, as long as he or she has met all other educational/experience requirements set by the licensing body in question.

WHO SHOULD TAKE ADVANTAGE OF THE NESL OPTION?

The NESL option is designed for those who live in states/locations where NCBTMB certification is recognized, but not required for a license to practice massage therapy/bodywork. It is important to recognize that if you choose the NESL option, you may be licensed to practice, but you will not actually be considered certified by NCBTMB.

Before attempting this option, the student should be sure he or she is reasonably prepared to pass the examination. In addition, it is important to confirm that your state/location accepts the NESL option as valid. You can confirm this by calling the NCBTMB at 800-296-0664 or by e-mailing your questions to schooloutreach@ncbtmb.org.

HOW DOES NESL CONVERSION WORK?

If you choose to pursue the NESL option, under certain circumstances, you can later request this option be converted to full certification. In other words, even if you tested using the NESL option, once you have met all other requirements for NCETMB or NCETM certification, you can request that your NESL status be converted to either NCETMB or NCETM certification.

You can make this request by completing and mailing the *NESL Option Certification Conversion Application*. This form can be downloaded from the NCBTMB Web site (www.ncbtmb.org). To qualify for a full conversion, you need to meet the following qualifications:

- You must have successfully passed either the NCETMB or the NCETM.

- Your NESL conversion application must be completed in full, and the appropriate fee included. (The fee is lower if your request is postmarked within 6 months of the testing date. The fee is higher if your request is postmarked later than 6 months from your testing date.)

- Your request for conversion must be postmarked within 24 months of your test date. If it is later than 24 months, you will need to retest.

- You must submit a sealed, official school transcript proving that you completed the required level of education.

- You must include a clear and fully legible photocopy of your current government-issued photo identification, such as your driver's license, passport, or military ID.

- You must answer all questions about your background and agree to a background check, just like any other certification applicant.

Helpful Resources

A number of massage therapy and bodywork resources are available to guide you as you launch your new career path. The resources listed below represent the largest, most reputable professional organizations related to therapeutic massage. As you review each organization's Web site, bookmark it so you can find it easily in the future.

AMERICAN MASSAGE THERAPY ASSOCIATION (AMTA)

The American Massage Therapy Association (AMTA) is a nonprofit professional association open to practicing massage therapists, students, and massage schools. The AMTA provides many benefits to its members, including a continuous promotion of the profession with both health-care practitioners and the public at large; the facilitation and push for fair and standard regulations and licensing for massage practitioners across all states; the opportunity to network at both local and national levels; and access to a variety of continuing education opportunities. AMTA is also an excellent source of liability insurance for the profession.

The AMTA has more than 56,000 members. AMTA's resources include:

- **Primary Web site:** www.amtamassage.org/index.html

- **State regulations:** www.amtamassage.org/regulation/stateRegulations.html

- **States with massage practice laws:** www.amtamassage.org/about/lawstate.html

ASSOCIATED BODYWORK AND MASSAGE PROFESSIONALS (ABMP)

Associated Bodywork and Massage Professionals (ABMP) is a national organization that exists to facilitate the professional advancement of individuals in the bodywork and massage professions. The ABMP provides its members with a number of benefits, including career assistance; business resources and materials; affordable, comprehensive professional liability insurance; and continuing education (CE) workshops and programs. The ABMP also advocates for a fair regulatory environment for the profession and keeps its members apprised of major issues and educational developments within the profession.

The ABMP is open to both current practitioners and students. The ABMP was founded in 1987 and is the largest massage membership organization in the United States, with more than 70,000 members. ABMP's resources include:

- **Primary Web site:** www.abmp.com/home/

- **Liability insurance for massage therapists:** www.abmp.com/insurance/

- *Massage & Bodywork* **magazine:** http://massagebodywork.idigitaledition.com

COMMISSION ON MASSAGE THERAPY ACCREDITATION (COMTA)

The mission of the Commission on Massage Therapy Accreditation (COMTA) is to accredit educational institutions and programs that provide instruction in massage therapy and bodywork. COMTA accreditation indicates that the school or program has undergone rigorous review by COMTA staff and been approved as a provider of high-quality education. COMTA's purpose is to "establish and maintain the quality and integrity of the profession."

COMTA was recognized by the U.S. Department of Education in 2002 as a specialized accrediting agency, which acknowledges COMTA's expertise in ensuring the quality of therapeutic massage education provided by the organizations it accredits.

This recognition allows COMTA-accredited programs to access federal student aid funds. COMTA's resources include:

- **Primary Web site:** www.comta.org
- **All about accreditation:** www.comta.org/students.php
- **COMTA-accredited schools listing:** www.comta.org/directory.php

FEDERATION OF STATE MASSAGE THERAPY BOARDS (FSMTB)

The Federation of State Massage Therapy Boards (FSMTB) is an organization founded in 2005 to "formally bring the [massage and bodywork] regulatory community together." FSMTB's membership is comprised of massage therapy regulatory boards from various states along with other organizations with a vested interest in the profession.

FSMTB's goals are to facilitate the acceptance of a single, reliable licensing examination and to standardize licensing requirements for massage therapists and bodyworkers across the country. FSMTB's stated mission is to "…support our member boards in their work to ensure that the practice of massage therapy is provided to the public in a safe and effective manner."

FSMTB developed and administers the Massage and Bodywork Licensing Exam (MBLEx). FSMTB's resources include:

- **Primary Web site:** www.fsmtb.org
- **Massage and Bodywork Licensing Exam (MBLEx):** www.fsmtb.org/licensing.html
- **States accepting MBLEx for licensure:** www.fsmtb.org/html/licensing/mblex.html

NATIONAL CENTER FOR COMPLEMENTARY AND ALTERNATIVE MEDICINE (NCAAM)

The National Center for Complementary and Alternative Medicine (NCCAM) is the federal government's leading agency for scientific research and information on health-care practices that are generally considered outside the bounds of conventional Western medicine. The NCCAM is a division of the National Institutes of Health (NIH). NCCAM's resources include:

- **Primary Web site:** http://nccam.nih.gov

- **Complementary and alternative medicine defined:** http://nccam.nih.gov/health/whatiscam

- **All about massage therapy:** http://nccam.nih.gov/health/massage

- **A-to-Z topic list:** http://nccam.nih.gov/health/atoz.htm

NATIONAL CERTIFICATION BOARD FOR THERAPEUTIC MASSAGE AND BODYWORK (NCBTMB)

The National Certification Board for Therapeutic Massage and Bodywork (NCBTMB) is a nonprofit organization founded in 1992. NCBTMB's mission is to "define and advance the highest standards in the massage therapy and bodywork profession." NCBTMB works to establish national certification as a recognized credentialing standard and to promote the massage and bodywork professions to the public as well as to public policy makers.

NCBTMB developed and administers the National Certification Examination for Therapeutic Massage (NCETM) and National Certification Examination for Therapeutic Massage and Bodywork (NCETMB) examinations. NCBTMB's resources include:

- **Primary Web site:** www.ncbtmb.org

- **State licensing requirements:** www.ncbtmb.org/legislators.php

- **NCBTMB-assigned schools:** http://ncbtmb.org/cgi-bin/SchoolSearch.cgi

Complementary/Alternative Medicine

The term *complementary medicine* (sometimes called alternative medicine) refers to practices outside the bounds of traditional Western medicine (i.e., pharmaceutical solutions). Complementary medicine includes a broad and varied spectrum of healing practices. The term *complementary* is meant to be descriptive of the way such practices can be used in conjunction with Western therapies to provide holistic health-care solutions to clients/patients.

The list provided here is not meant to be comprehensive. Rather, it is designed to introduce you to some of the more common complementary practices in use today. As you review this list, remember that all complementary medicine practices require some level of training before they can be put into use. Some of these modalities are quite advanced and require deep study (acupuncture, for example, is doctoral-level work). Less complex practices can be introduced to new practitioners following a short course of study. Some of the more specific modalities require practitioners to be certified by the sponsoring organization before they can be put to use.

- Acupuncture is the practice of inserting fine needles into the skin to stimulate specific anatomical sites on the human body. The anatomical sites are referred to as acupoints or acupuncture points. Stimulating these points is said to balance energy in the body. Acupuncture is used as both preventive medicine and as treatment for a variety of health issues such as chronic pain. Acupuncture is an advanced practice requiring doctoral-level study.

- Aromatherapy is a holistic treatment in which essential oils such as rose, lavender, and peppermint are combined with carrier oils, lotions, and/or creams to create unique blends. These aromatic blends can be inhaled or diffused into the environment. Aromatherapy is said to alleviate moods, relieve pain, reduce tension/anxiety, and promote relaxation.

- Energy therapy is a broad grouping of practices involving the manipulation of the body's energy fields. Polarity therapy and Reiki are two examples of well-known energy therapies.

- Hydrotherapy involves the use of water in treatment. Water can be utilized in its various forms (liquid, steam, ice) to treat bodily discomfort and effect positive change. Some examples of hydrotherapy include hot/cold baths, saunas, and wraps.

- Hypnotherapy or hypnosis is a therapeutic approach used to treat a variety of health conditions, such as headaches, uncontrolled pain, and irritable bowel syndrome. Hypnotherapy is also sometimes used to assist patients in stopping addictive behaviors such as smoking.

- Meditation is the mindfulness-based practice of focusing awareness on the breath, bodily sensations, or some other focal point. Meditation can be used to balance one's mental, emotional, and physical states.

- Movement therapy is a collective term for a wide variety of practices that involve moving the human body in specific ways. Some practitioners use movement approaches such as dance, yoga, tai chi, and Pilates in their therapeutic work. Others become trained in specialized modalities such as continuum movement therapy, authentic movement therapy, Body-Mind Centering®, Alexander Technique, Aston-Patterning Bodywork®, the Trager® Approach, or the Feldenkrais Method®.

- Visualization or guided imagery therapy involves focusing on images that represent who or what one would like to be and have in life. Visualization requires the practitioner to create specific, detailed images and really believe these represent one's true potential. Visualization therapy is frequently used to promote relaxation, lower stress, reduce cravings, and promote maximal performance.

SPECIAL ADVERTISING SECTION

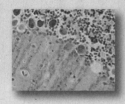

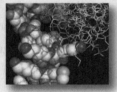
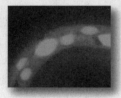
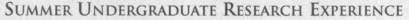

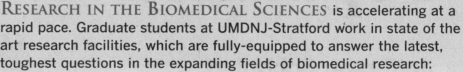

Learn from a National Leader in
Population Health

Jefferson School of Population Health

- Master of Public Health (MPH); CEPH accredited
- PhD in Population Health Sciences

Online programs

- Master of Science in Health Policy (MS-HP)
- Master of Science in Healthcare Quality and Safety (MS-HQS)
- Master of Science in Chronic Care Management (MS-CCM)
- Certificates in Public Health, Health Policy, Healthcare Quality and Safety, Chronic Care Management

Population health – putting health and health care together

215-503-0174

www.jefferson.edu/population_health/ads.cfm

Jefferson
School of Population Health

THOMAS JEFFERSON UNIVERSITY

AMIT SOOD | sports business major

BE A BILLIKEN

Find out how the breadth and depth of the fully accredited undergraduate and graduate programs at Saint Louis University's **JOHN COOK SCHOOL OF BUSINESS** will give you the knowledge and tools necessary for success in today's global and highly technical business world.

— + Visit **BeABilliken.com** for more information on our undergraduate business programs and to see what life is like as a Billiken.

To learn about our graduate business programs, attend an open house or visit **gradbiz.slu.edu.** + ——

SAINT LOUIS UNIVERSITY

CONCENTRATIONS IN THE JOHN COOK SCHOOL OF BUSINESS

Accounting

Economics

Entrepreneurship

Finance

Information Technology Management

International Business

Leadership and Change Management

Marketing

Sports Business

GRADUATE PROGRAMS IN THE JOHN COOK SCHOOL OF BUSINESS

One-Year MBA

Part-Time MBA

Master of Supply Chain Management

Master of Accounting

Executive Master of International Business

Post-MBA Certificate

GLOBAL EXPERIENCE *Ethical Leadership* EXPERIENTIAL LEARNING

PREPARE FOR ETHICAL LEADERSHIP

IN ST. MARY'S BILL GREEHEY SCHOOL OF BUSINESS

Recognized for world-class faculty, access to top industry leaders, and connections with elite internships, the Bill Greehey School of Business shapes graduates who are committed to leading ethically.

Learn more about St. Mary's values-based education online.
www.stmarytx.edu/business

THE BILL GREEHEY SCHOOL OF BUSINESS IS AACSB ACCREDITED

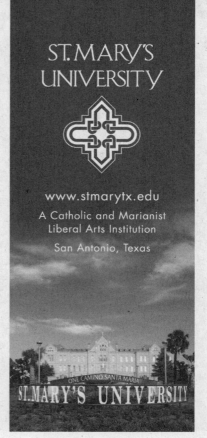

ST. MARY'S UNIVERSITY

www.stmarytx.edu
A Catholic and Marianist
Liberal Arts Institution
San Antonio, Texas

ONE CAMINO SANTA MARIA
ST. MARY'S UNIVERSITY

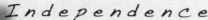

NOTES

NOTES

NOTES